Praise for previous editions:

"*The State of the World Atlas* is something else – an occasion of wit and an act of subversion...These are the bad dreams of the modern world, given color and shape and submitted to a grid that can be grasped instantaneously."
New York Times

"Unique and uniquely beautiful...a discerning eye for data and a flair for the most sophisticated techniques of stylized graphic design; the atlas succeeds in displaying the geopolitical subtleties of global affairs in a series of dazzling color plates...tells us more about the world today than a dozen statistical abstracts or scholarly tomes."
Los Angeles Times

"Coupled with an unusual non-distorting map projection and a series of brilliant cartographic devices, this gives a positively dazzling set of maps. It deserves to be widely used."
New Society

"A super book that will not only sit on your shelf begging to be used, but will also be a good read. To call this book an atlas is like calling Calvados, applejack – it may be roughly accurate but it conveys nothing of the richness and flavour of the thing. Its inventive brilliance deserves enormous rewards."
New Scientist

"Outspoken cataloguing of global oppressions and inequities, painstakingly sourced."
Independent on Sunday

"Packed with fascinating facts and figures on everything from the international drugs industry to climate change."
Evening Standard

"A political reference book which manages to translate hard, boring statistics into often shocking visual statements... required reading."
NME

Also available now:

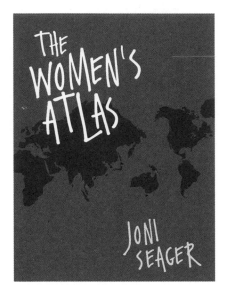

"Here is the innovative atlas no thoughtful person, male
or female, should be without."
Washington Post

"A life-saver and page-turner... This will add to everyone's
knowledge and power. Nobody should be without this book."
Gloria Steinem

"The most important book that will be published this year."
Catherine Mayer, Women's Equality Party

"This one-of-a-kind book brings women's lives out of the shadows.
Every page lights up injustices and makes clear the work that
remains to be done."
Leymah Gbowee, Nobel Laureate and Liberian peace activist

"Not only offers a global view of the lives of women, it also shows their
desires to effect revolutionary change."
Vigdís Finnbogadóttir, President of Iceland 1980–1996

THE
STATE
OF THE
WORLD
ATLAS

DAN SMITH

This tenth edition first published in 2020 by
Myriad Editions
www.myriadeditions.com

Myriad Editions
An imprint of New Internationalist Publications
The Old Music Hall, 106–108 Cowley Rd, Oxford OX4 1JE

First printing
1 3 5 7 9 10 8 6 4 2

A catalogue record for this book is available from the British Library

ISBN: 978-1-912408-87-0 (paperback)
ISBN is: 978-1-912408-88-7 (ebook)

Publishing direction: Candida Lacey
Creative direction: Corinne Pearlman
Editing and coordination: Jannet King
Design and graphics: Clare Shepherd
Cartography and original graphics: Isabelle Lewis
Based on an original design by Caroline Beavon

Printed by Jelgavas Tipografija in Latvia

Contents

Introduction

The first step in trying to understand the state of the world is to recognize the simple yet not-so-simple fact that the world is always changing.

Big or small, sudden or slowly building, soon over or with a lasting impact, alterations in the situation and condition of the world and its people are constant.

A lot of that change is progress of one sort or another. Some of what we sometimes call progress is of little worth or merit – useless technological baubles that are modish for a while. And some of it when seen in larger context is downright dangerous – a contribution to global heating or the crisis of air pollution. But in even larger context, human progress is real. More people live longer, healthier lives than ever. Fewer live in extreme poverty than 20 or 30 years ago. The store of human knowledge continues to enlarge. Human rights are respected now in a way that was not dreamed of 200 years ago. And in the first two decades of the 21st century, warfare has taken far fewer human lives than it did in the first two decades of the 20th.

Amid multiple world problems – and perhaps especially writing in 2020 as we wonder what the full effects of the Covid-19 pandemic will be – the point is worth stressing. Human progress has been real over the last century and a half, despite world wars, despite colonialism, despite environmental crises. It has been real and because of that we know that further progress is possible.

It is important to hang onto that because it is also true that a lot of the change we experience is not progress at all. If progress is a journey, it is not about rolling along a smooth path or gliding through space. It is more like lurching in and out of massive potholes in the road or, if you prefer the space metaphor, from one big astral collision to another, juddering all the while under the impact of an unending, randomized shower of meteorites. One thing that matters in trying to understand the state of the world and gauge its progress or regress at any time is to distinguish between the big collisions and the meteorites.

The past 30 years – the passage of time normally associated with one human generation – has seen four big moments of change, approximately once a decade. The first came in the years 1989 to 1991, as the Cold War between East and West, between the USSR and its allies on the one side, and the USA and its much richer and larger alliance on the other, came to an end. Not only did the confrontation between the USSR and USA terminate but so also the USSR itself. As the 1990s began, the world order changed, along with the possibilities for what the United Nations could do. Agreements were reached to dismantle tens of thousands of nuclear weapons, military spending started to fall, and the number of countries with a functioning democracy grew throughout the decade. It was not by any means painless. The transition to democracy is often fraught with danger and the first half of the 1990s saw an increase in the number of armed conflicts.

The second big change came in 2001 in the shape of the terrorist attacks of 9/11 in New York and Washington, DC. The peace dividend of the 1990s started to look less peaceful, the long war in Afghanistan that had begun with the Soviet invasion in December 1979 took on a new form as the USA and its allies intervened, and at the same time headed towards war on and then in Iraq.

The third change was the financial crash of 2008 to 2009, which became a general economic crisis in 2009 and 2010. The depth of the crash was different in different countries; economic output recovered but in many of the richer countries in the world, the sense of economic well-being that marked most of the previous two decades has gone for good.

And the fourth big change has come with the Covid-19 pandemic in 2020 – not just the pandemic itself but the economic impact associated with it. At the time of completing this atlas in mid-2020, it is not possible to know what the full impact will be. Though we live in an age that wants instant everything, it remains true that historical significance can only be gauged once the event is well in the past. And even then it is an art rather than a

science to understand what it all meant. Nonetheless, the economic impact of the Covid-19 lockdowns – the crash in production, consumption, trade and travel – even though in some aspects recovery may also be equally dramatic, seems likely to be profound and long-lasting.

∎

These events have had a dramatic and lasting impact (or will do in the case of the current pandemic) not simply because of their sheer weight as big events, but also because they interact with other, slower-moving combinations of events. These are the unfolding trends that form the backdrop to the immediate drama. Here we encounter issues such as climate change and today's many-sided environmental crisis. Here is rising inequality in most countries over the past 40-plus years, demographic developments including both population growth – and, more important than the global numbers, where it is concentrated – and urbanization. We see economic growth and seemingly unending technological innovation. And relations between people change, with something closer to gender equality in many countries, with greater acceptance of the rights of LGBTQ+ people, with assumptions about freedoms and responsibilities altering, and with contestation about the rights of different races and ethnic and religious groups within a country.

This atlas offers snapshots of all this. Not one snapshot of the state of the world but, rather, a series of snapshots of diverse aspects of the state of the world as it changes. It captures the big moments and the background trends. It does not and cannot – and does not want to try to – say everything about every, or indeed any, topic. The information here is not the whole story. The treatment of the issue is as an introduction, pointing out a door that, if opened, could be the way towards getting fuller knowledge.

.

In 2015, the United Nations agreed a potentially era-defining programme – Agenda 2030, with its 17 Sustainable Development Goals (SDGs). If achieved, they could mark the next phase in human progress. Thinking about this agenda in terms of the journey of human progress, I see it as the process of navigating a safe route, increasing the ability to avoid the big collisions, and staying on course despite all the impediments. Under the headline goals there are 169 targets to achieve by 2030. This is human progress as it

The Sustainable Development Goals of the United Nations Agenda 2030

1. End poverty in all its forms everywhere
2. End hunger, achieve food security and improved nutrition and promote sustainable agriculture
3. Ensure healthy lives and promote well-being for all
4. Ensure inclusive and equitable quality education and promote lifelong learning opportunities for all
5. Achieve gender equality and empower all women and girls
6. Ensure availability and sustainable management of water and sanitation for all
7. Ensure access to affordable, reliable, sustainable and modern energy for all
8. Promote sustained, inclusive and sustainable economic growth, full and productive employment and decent work for all
9. Build resilient infrastructure, promote inclusive and sustainable industrialization and foster innovation
10. Reduce inequality within and among countries
11. Make cities and human settlements inclusive, safe, resilient and sustainable
12. Ensure sustainable consumption and production patterns
13. Take urgent action to combat climate change and its impacts
14. Conserve and sustainably use the oceans, seas and marine resources for sustainable development
15. Protect, restore and promote sustainable use of terrestrial ecosystems, sustainably manage forests, combat desertification, and halt and reverse land degradation and halt biodiversity loss
16. Promote peaceful and inclusive societies for sustainable development, provide access to justice for all and build effective, accountable and inclusive institutions at all levels
17. Strengthen the means of implementation and revitalize the Global Partnership for Sustainable Development

could be, towards a better world that is not just imaginable but practicable. In this atlas, I group the issues covered by the SDGs under the heading of five big challenges that face humanity, challenges we must rise to if we are to thrive.

Having looked at who we are – some of the basics of demography, diversity, and dwelling place – the five challenges that confront humanity form the substance of this atlas. They are the production and distribution of wealth and poverty; human rights and the respect with which ordinary people are treated by those in power; the question of war and peace; the health of the people; and the health of the planet.

These are distinct but linked challenges. The effects of the Covid-19 pandemic are not the same for all. Not surprisingly, wealth, privilege and power offer more effective protection to some than is available to all. The same is true of the effects of climate change and many other aspects of environmental deterioration. Throughout the industrial age, rich factory owners managed to live well away from the part of the city their factories polluted. There is no health or environmental issue that is purely about physiological health or how things are in nature. The source of the problem, how it is defined, the allocation of resources to address it are all shaped by how society is governed. Social inequalities and lack of respect for human rights often mean there is no way to express grievances except through anger, to which power responds through repression. That explosive mixture can quickly generate political instability and open armed conflict. The socially destabilising effects of climate change and environmental crisis only add to those pressures.

" Cooperation is the new realism "

Recent years have seen a distinct decline in how well these challenges are addressed. This is the tenth edition of this atlas. For the ninth in 2013, summing it up, I had a relatively positive assessment on rights and respect, partly because democracy was growing, as well as on war and peace, and on health. But any progress on wealth and poverty was marred by growing inequalities and damage to the natural environment. So on three of the five challenges, the record, while not perfect, was not bad; on the other two, the record was clearly deficient. Since then, while the statistics of democracy remain good, its quality is weaker in many countries. Worse, geopolitics have turned toxic, the number of armed conflicts has increased, and the scale of military preparations now is back to Cold War levels. And on the health front, there is the pandemic.

So there is more bad news than a few years ago. But the tools for improvement are available. The UN's Agenda 2030 and the SDGs themselves demonstrate that. We can see it in the snapshots in this atlas when we look at peace operations, at advances in healthcare, at the possibilities for reshaping economic functioning so the natural environment is better respected. Further, in some places, the tools are in use. We can see them in initiatives to build peace and support neighbours in highly diverse local communities; in small-scale environmental protection projects and some initiatives that are pretty large scale; in choices some people are making to live lives and to run businesses in ways that are more in tune with the rhythms of nature.

One characteristic of world politics today is a visibly declining appetite for international cooperation among the biggest players and many of the smaller ones. That is the severest single difficulty to overcome so the work of improvement and progress can resume in good order. None of the challenges and problems depicted in this atlas can be successfully addressed by any state acting alone. Not even the biggest, the richest, or the most populous. Going it alone is a fantasy; cooperation is the new realism.

If we face the bad news, perhaps we will see that it is not so bad. There are so many other things happening. And that should be a spur to action, to take the decisions that are needed to stem the rise of inequality, ensure our rights are respected, expand the world's zone of peace again, keep improving public health and prepare better against the next pandemic, and put our relationship with nature onto a healthier footing. And above all, to start working together to those ends.

•

Finally, my thanks to those who make this book possible but don't get on the title page. In the Myriad team, Jannet King has once again been the editor for this tenth edition in the series, assiduous and sharp yet kindly. The cartography and visuals are the work of Clare Shepherd and of Isabelle Lewis, within the design framework established by Corinne Pearlman. All this happens under the inspiring and supportive leadership of Candida Lacey. The research assistance,

which means all the hard work, was done by Jakob Faller.

It was a semi-surreal experience to complete the work on this edition in the midst of the first wave of the Covid-19 pandemic, even if doing it in the lockdown-lite of Sweden rather than the full-on isolation of many other countries. What helped keep me sane in that was family – Åsa, Felix and Bob close at hand, and further away in two homes in one city, Jake, Jess, Josie and Jed, and Rebecca, Marcus and Zac. My thanks and love to you all whether you knew how much you were helping or not.

Dan Smith
Stockholm
June 2020

Who we are

What is the name of our age? It continues to be the age of more, most, and never before.

There are more people, living in more countries, and more of us living in cities, than at any time. And along with that come things never before experienced, so much so that the idea of "the new normal" has become the defining cliché of our time.

New – the consequences of climate change.
New – the loss of biodiversity and land quality.
New – the acidification of the oceans.
New – the crisis of air pollution.
New – plastic garbage covering the ocean.
New – our dependence on cyberspace, and with it vulnerability to its failure.
New – the cycle of pandemics from SARS to MERS to Covid-19.
New – the combination of all of the above.

It is only just over 200 years ago – less than a blink of an eye in the timescale of the planet, and not much more in the timescale of human beings – that the world's population passed the 1 billion mark. Today, there are just under 8 billion of us. Despite signs of deceleration in the rate of growth, world population is still projected to increase by another 2 billion people to around 10 billion by 2050. By then, towns and cities are expected to hold just over two-thirds of humanity.

There has never been demographic change on such a huge scale. The movement from the countryside to the cities in the industrial revolution two centuries ago has nothing on this. Nor has migration from Europe to the American New World between the mid-19th century and the early 20th century – just 30 million people. Compared to that, the increase in the global population so far this century is almost 100 million every year, and urban population growth is even faster.

Because there are more of us, we inevitably consume more of everything. But technological advance means that we also consume massively more per person. Our population, eight times that of 200 years ago, produces over 50 times the economic output, and uses more than 60 times as much water and 75 times as much energy.

The figures testify to the creativity unleashed through the Industrial Revolution. They should also encourage us to ask: For how long can we continue?

States of the world

CANADA

USA

MEXICO

GUATEMALA
EL SALVADOR
COSTA RICA
PANAMA

BELIZE
HONDURAS
NICARAGUA

CAYMAN IS. (UK)
CUBA
JAMAICA
HAITI

BERMUDA (UK)

BAHAMAS
TURKS & CAICOS IS. (UK)
PUERTO RICO
DOMINICAN (USA)
REP.
HAITI
VIRGIN IS. (USA)
ST KITTS & NEVIS
MONTSERRAT (UK)
ARUBA (Neths)
CURAÇAO (Neths)
BONAIRE (Neths)
ANGUILLA (UK)
VIRGIN IS. (UK)
ST MARTIN (Fr)
SINT MAARTEN (Neths)
ST BARTHÉLEMY (Fr)
ANTIGUA & BARBUDA
GUADELOUPE (Fr)
DOMINICA
MARTINIQUE (Fr)
ST LUCIA
GRENADA
BARBADOS
ST VINCENT & GRENADINES
TRINIDAD & TOBAGO

VENEZUELA
COLOMBIA
ECUADOR
PERU

GUYANA
SURINAME
FRENCH GUIANA (Fr)

BRAZIL

BOLIVIA
PARAGUAY
CHILE
ARGENTINA
URUGUAY

FALKLANDS IS. (UK)

S GEORGIA & S SANDWICH IS. (UK)

ST PIERRE & MIQUELON (Fr)

GREENLAND (Den)

SVALBARD (Nor.)

ICELAND
FAROE IS. (Den)
NORWAY
SWEDEN
FINLA
UK
IS. OF MAN (UK)
IRELAND
CHANNEL IS. (UK)
DENMARK
NETH.
BEL.
LUX.
GERMANY
POLAN
CZ.REP.
SLOV
AUS.
SW
SL.
FRANCE
ITALY
CR. B-H
MONT.
N. MAC.
ALB.
PORTUGAL
SPAIN
GIBRALTAR (UK)
GRE
TUNISIA
MALTA
MOROCCO
WESTERN
SAHARA (Mor.)
ALGERIA
LIBYA
CAPE
VERDE
SENEGAL
GAMBIA
GUINEA-BISSAU
SIERRA LEONE
LIBERIA
MAURITANIA
MALI
NIGER
CHAD
GUINEA
BURKINA
FASO
CÔTE
D'IVOIRE
GHANA
TOGO
BENIN
NIGERIA
EQUATORIAL
GUINEA
SÃO TOME
& PRINCIPE
GABON
CONGO
CAMEROON
C.A.R.
ANGOLA
NAMIBIA
ST HELENA, ASCENSION & TRISTAN
(UK)

Sovereignty

Effective independence gained
by existing states

- before 11 November 1918
- 11 November 1918 – 23 October 1945
- 24 October 1945 – 8 November 1989
- 9 November 1989 – 30 September 2019
- not a sovereign state (affiliation)

GUAM (USA)
NORTHERN MARIANA IS. (USA)
MICRONESIA, FED. ST. OF
MARSHALL ISLANDS
PALAU
NAURU
KIRIBATI
TUVALU
TOKELAU
AMERICAN SAMOA (USA)
SAMOA
WALLIS & FUTUNA IS. (Fr)
VANUATU
FIJI
COOK IS. (NZ)
NIUE (NZ)
TONGA
NEW CALEDONIA (Fr)
NORFOLK IS. (Aus)
FRENCH POLYNESIA (Fr)
PITCAIRN IS. (UK)

State formation

Number of states gaining effective independence
in each decade including states that no longer exist
as of September 2019

▬▬▬ before 11 November 1918
▬▬▬ 11 November 1918 – 23 October 1945
▬▬▬ 24 October 1945 – 8 November 1989
▬▬▬ 9 November 1989 – 30 September 2019

Some of our sense of who we are comes from where we were born and grew up – our countries, most of which are quite recent creations. In 1945, the United Nations was founded by just 51 states, some of which were not fully independent at the time (and the defeated states in World War II were initially excluded). Today, the UN has 193 member states.

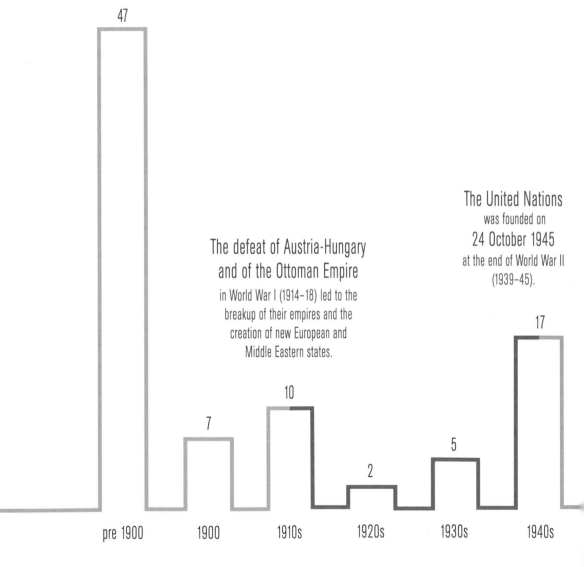

47

The defeat of Austria-Hungary
and of the Ottoman Empire

in World War I (1914–18) led to the
breakup of their empires and the
creation of new European and
Middle Eastern states.

The United Nations
was founded on
24 October 1945
at the end of World War II
(1939–45).

17

10

7

5

2

pre 1900   1900   1910s   1920s   1930s   1940s

Over the past century, states have won, lost, and regained independence, divided and (re-) unified, often but not always against a background of war and bloodshed.

Some have become formally independent before achieving real independence; with others, it has been the other way round.

On other pages, this atlas shows many ways – economic, environmental, political – in which independent states do not have full sovereignty in the modern world – yet the evidence is clear that sovereignty is a highly desirable political commodity. The age of forming new states is not yet over.

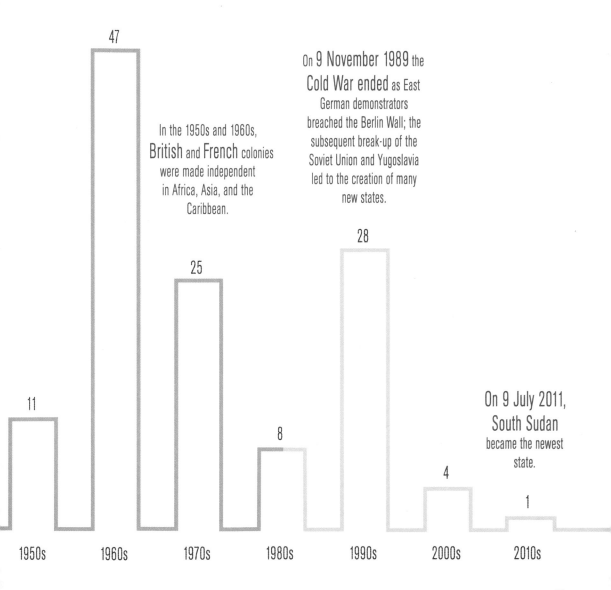

47

In the 1950s and 1960s, **British** and **French** colonies were made independent in Africa, Asia, and the Caribbean.

On **9 November 1989** the **Cold War ended** as East German demonstrators breached the Berlin Wall; the subsequent break-up of the Soviet Union and Yugoslavia led to the creation of many new states.

28

25

11

8

On **9 July 2011**, **South Sudan** became the newest state.

4

1

1950s   1960s   1970s   1980s   1990s   2000s   2010s

Population

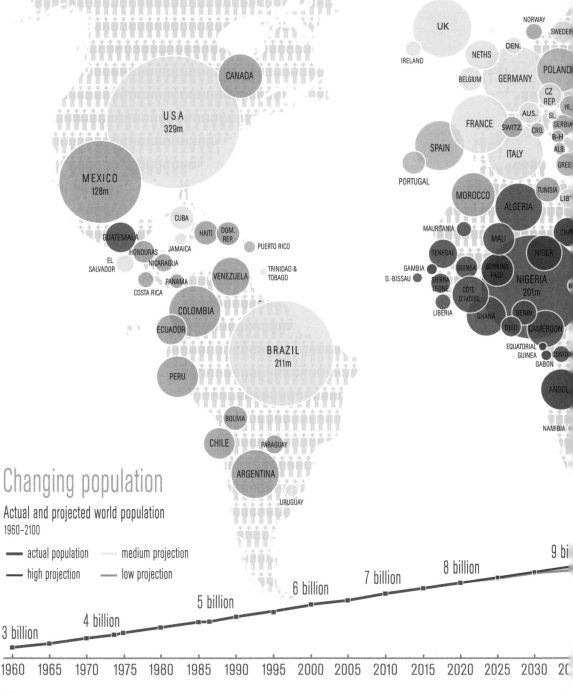

CANADA

USA
329m

MEXICO
128m

CUBA

HAITI   DOM. REP.

PUERTO RICO

GUATEMALA

HONDURAS   JAMAICA

EL SALVADOR   NICARAGUA

PANAMA   TRINIDAD & TOBAGO

COSTA RICA

VENEZUELA

COLOMBIA

ECUADOR

BRAZIL
211m

PERU

BOLIVIA

CHILE   PARAGUAY

ARGENTINA

URUGUAY

UK

NORWAY

SWEDEN

IRELAND

NETHS   DEN.

POLAND

BELGIUM   GERMANY

CZ REP.   HU

FRANCE   SWITZ.   AUS.   SL   SERBIA

CRO.   B-H

SPAIN   ITALY   ALB.

GREE

PORTUGAL

MOROCCO   TUNISIA   LIB'

ALGERIA

MAURITANIA   MALI   CHA

SENEGAL   NIGER

GAMBIA   GUINEA   BURKINA FASO   NIGERIA
201m

G.-BISSAU   SIERRA LEONE   CÔTE D'IVOIRE

LIBERIA   GHANA   BENIN   CAMEROON

TOGO

EQUATORIAL GUINEA   CONGO

GABON

ANGOL

NAMIBIA

Changing population

Actual and projected world population
1960–2100

— actual population   — medium projection
— high projection   — low projection

3 billion

4 billion

5 billion

6 billion

7 billion

8 billion

9 bi

1960 1965 1970 1975 1980 1985 1990 1995 2000 2005 2010 2015 2020 2025 2030 20

People in the world
Annual percentage change
2019

● 3.0% or more
● 2.0% – 2.9%
● 1.0% – 1.9%
● 0.0% – 0.9%
● -0.1% – -2.8%
○ 1 million people

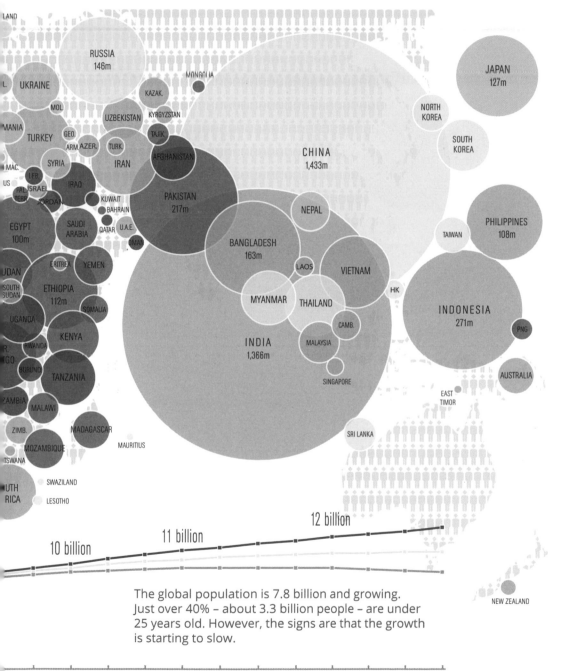

LAND

RUSSIA
146m

UKRAINE

MONGOLIA

JAPAN
127m

L.

MOL

KAZAK.

KYRGYZSTAN

NORTH
KOREA

MANIA

TURKEY

GEO.
ARM AZER.

UZBEKISTAN

TAJIK.

SOUTH
KOREA

MAC.

SYRIA

IRAN

TURK.

AFGHANISTAN

CHINA
1,433m

LFB

IRAQ

KUWAIT

PAKISTAN
217m

NEPAL

PHILIPPINES
108m

US
PAL ISRAEL
TERR
JORDAN

BAHRAIN

TAIWAN

EGYPT
100m

SAUDI
ARABIA

QATAR U.A.E.

OMAN

BANGLADESH
163m

LAOS

VIETNAM

UDAN

ERITREA

YEMEN

HK

SOUTH
SUDAN

ETHIOPIA
112m

SOMALIA

MYANMAR

THAILAND

INDONESIA
271m

UGANDA

CAMB.

PNG

RWANDA

KENYA

INDIA
1,366m

MALAYSIA

GO

BURUNDI

TANZANIA

SINGAPORE

AUSTRALIA

ZAMBIA

MALAWI

EAST
TIMOR

ZIMB.

MADAGASCAR

MOZAMBIQUE

MAURITIUS

SRI LANKA

TSWANA

UTH
RICA

SWAZILAND

LESOTHO

NEW ZEALAND

10 billion

11 billion

12 billion

The global population is 7.8 billion and growing.
Just over 40% – about 3.3 billion people – are under
25 years old. However, the signs are that the growth
is starting to slow.

| 2045 | 2050 | 2055 | 2060 | 2065 | 2070 | 2075 | 2080 | 2085 | 2090 | 2095 | 2100 |

Life expectancy

Living longer

Average years life expectancy at birth

1870–2016

Data points: 29.7, 32, 34.1, 48, 60, 65.2, 66.5, 70.1, 72

Y-axis: 0, 10, 20, 30, 40, 50, 60, 70, 80

X-axis: 1870, 1880, 1890, 1900, 1910, 1920, 1930, 1940, 1950, 1960, 1970, 1980, 1990, 2000, 2010, 2020

Life expectancy at birth

2016

● 53 – 59 years ● 70 – 79 years
● 60 – 69 years ● 80 – 84 years

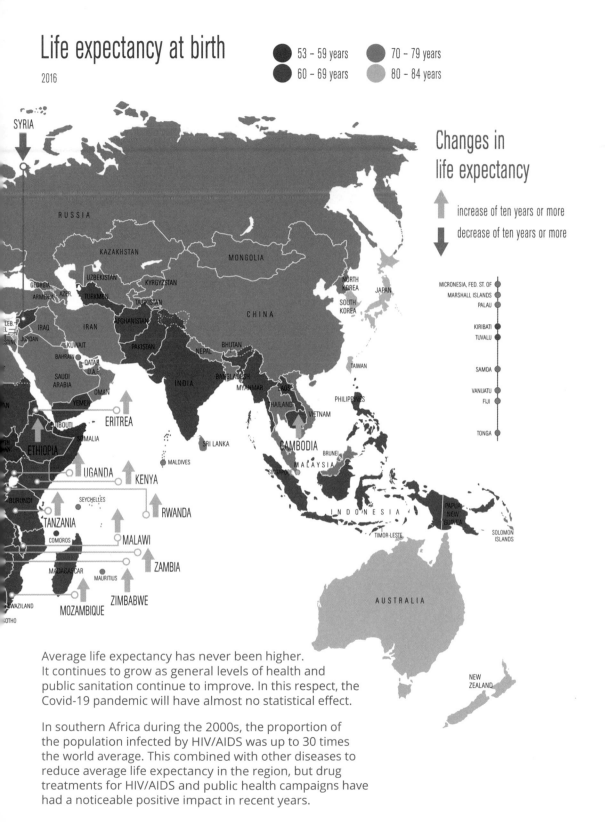

Changes in life expectancy

↑ increase of ten years or more
↓ decrease of ten years or more

Average life expectancy has never been higher. It continues to grow as general levels of health and public sanitation continue to improve. In this respect, the Covid-19 pandemic will have almost no statistical effect.

In southern Africa during the 2000s, the proportion of the population infected by HIV/AIDS was up to 30 times the world average. This combined with other diseases to reduce average life expectancy in the region, but drug treatments for HIV/AIDS and public health campaigns have had a noticeable positive impact in recent years.

Women and men

Women in the world

Female population as percentage of total population

2018

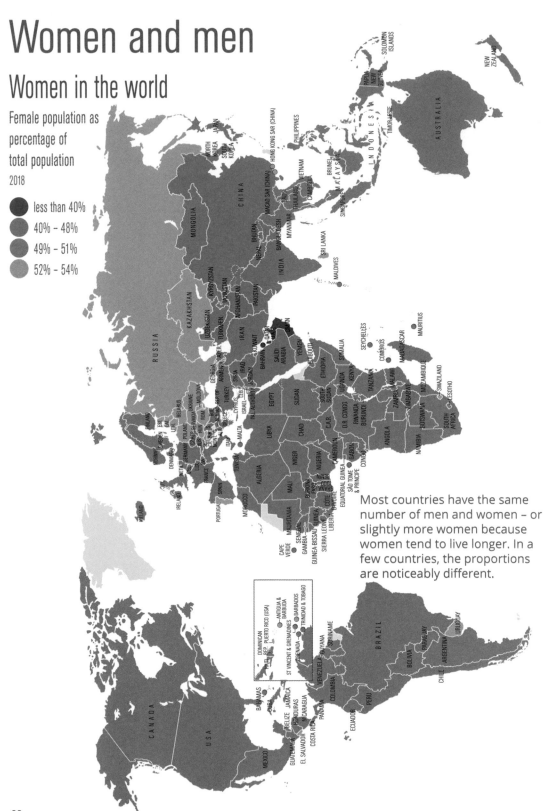

- less than 40%
- 40% – 48%
- 49% – 51%
- 52% – 54%

Most countries have the same number of men and women – or slightly more women because women tend to live longer. In a few countries, the proportions are noticeably different.

Baby boys and girls

The number of boys
born for every 100 girls
2017

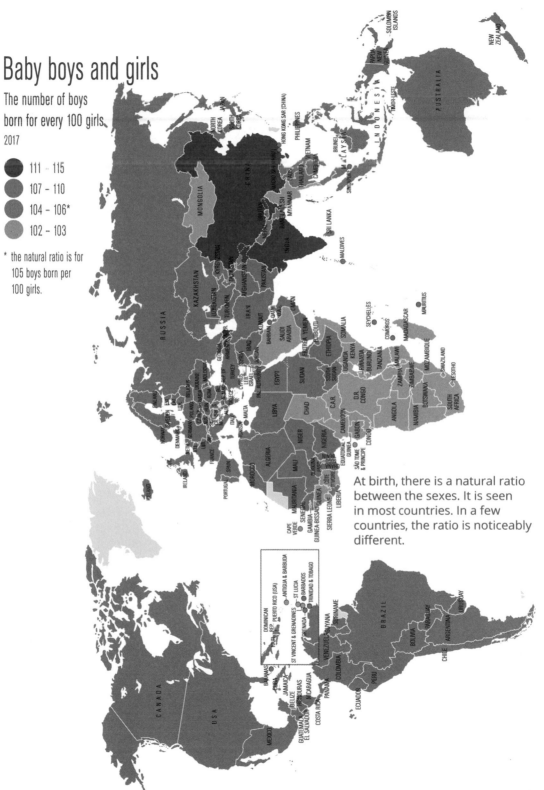

- 111 – 115
- 107 – 110
- 104 – 106*
- 102 – 103

* the natural ratio is for
105 boys born per
100 girls.

At birth, there is a natural ratio
between the sexes. It is seen
in most countries. In a few
countries, the ratio is noticeably
different.

23

Ethnicity and diversity

Minorities and indigenous peoples

As a percentage of the population*

2019 or latest available data
* definitions differ among countries

- less than 10%
- 10% – 29%
- 30% – 49%
- 50% or more (there is no majority group)
- data lacking or inadequate

Part of human diversity lies in our membership of large groups – nations, ethnic groups, races, tribes, clans. How these are defined varies from one culture to another. How important they are varies both from one person to the next and from time to time. Groups take on the most explicit importance for their members when they are or feel threatened – whether by day-to-day discrimination and ill treatment or by traumatic events as in war.

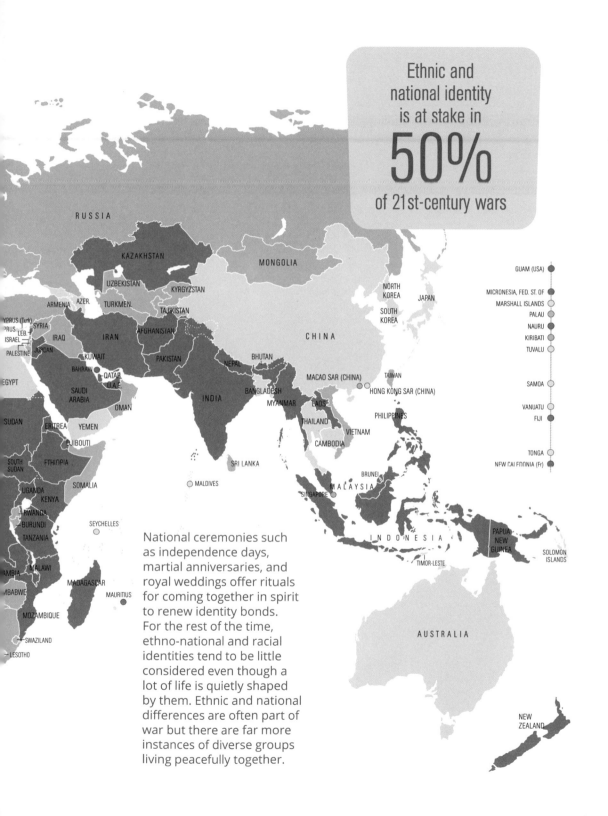

Ethnic and national identity is at stake in

50%

of 21st-century wars

GUAM (USA)

MICRONESIA, FED. ST. OF
MARSHALL ISLANDS
PALAU
NAURU
KIRIBATI
TUVALU

SAMOA

VANUATU
FIJI

TONGA
NEW CALEDONIA (Fr)

National ceremonies such as independence days, martial anniversaries, and royal weddings offer rituals for coming together in spirit to renew identity bonds. For the rest of the time, ethno-national and racial identities tend to be little considered even though a lot of life is quietly shaped by them. Ethnic and national differences are often part of war but there are far more instances of diverse groups living peacefully together.

Migrants

People living in country other than that in which they were born as a percentage of total population

2017

- 50% or more
- 30% – 49%
- 10% – 29%
- less than 10%

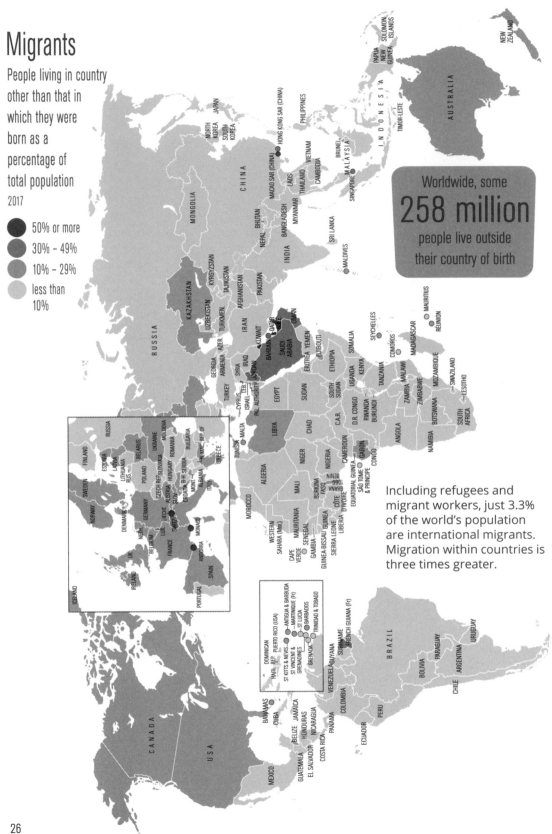

Worldwide, some
258 million
people live outside their country of birth

Including refugees and migrant workers, just 3.3% of the world's population are international migrants. Migration within countries is three times greater.

The language of government

The number of official
languages in use
nationally and/or
locally

2019 or latest available data

- 4 languages or more
- 3 languages
- 2 languages
- 1 language
- none designated

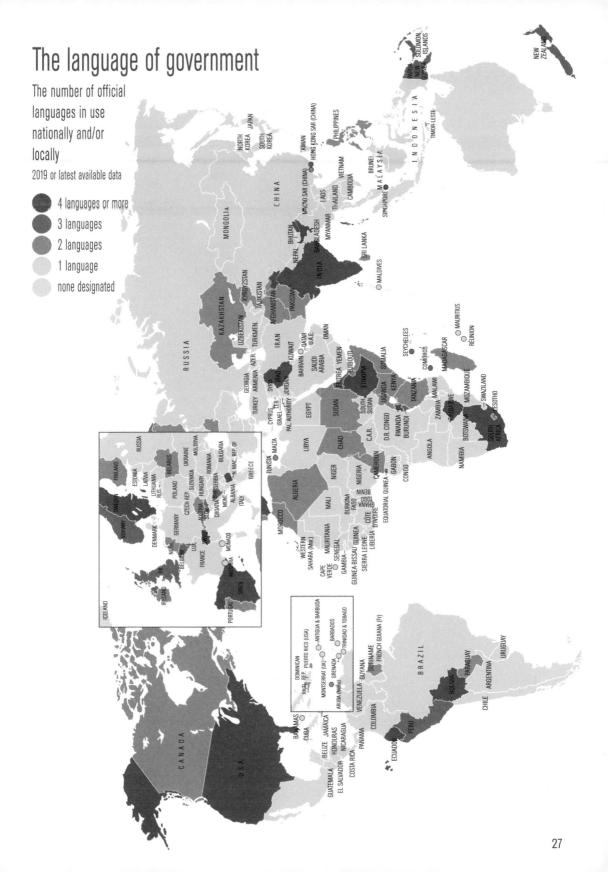

Religious beliefs

The vast majority of people profess a religious faith. Although professing a faith on a population census form and actually practising it are two very different things, faith is, for many, a basic marker of identity. Shared religious conviction can unite people where other things divide them, and even between different faiths there is significant ethical common ground and a shared openness to the spiritual and immaterial.

But religious identity coincides with other markers of identity – regional, national, ethnic, and cultural. When and where religious leaders cannot or will not restrain the way in which adherents to different faiths express their differences, conflicts can overheat and explode. Some of the world's most brutal violence is – and has been throughout history – inflicted in the name of religion. And some of the worst violence is over differences within the same religion: between Protestants and Catholic Christians, or between Sunni and Shi'a Muslims. Yet common to all major religions is the over-riding value of peace.

Map labels:

ICELAND, GREENLAND (Den), NORWAY, SWEDEN, FINLAND, ESTONIA, RUSSIA, LATVIA, LITHUANIA, DENMARK, RUS., BELARUS, IRELAND, UK, NETH., GERMANY, POLAND, BELGIUM, LUX., CZECH REP., SLOVAKIA, UKRAINE, FRANCE, LIECHT., AUSTRIA, HUNGARY, MOLDOVA, SWITZ., SLOVENIA, CROATIA, ROMANIA, PORTUGAL, ANDORRA, MONACO, ITALY, B-H, SERBIA, BULGARIA, SPAIN, MONT., KOSOVO, F.Y.R. MAC. REP. OF, GIBRALTAR, ALBANIA, TURKEY, GREECE

CANADA, USA 251m, MEXICO 124m, BERMUDA (UK), BAHAMAS, CUBA, CAYMAN IS (UK), BELIZE, JAMAICA, GUATEMALA, HONDURAS, EL SALVADOR, NICARAGUA, COSTA RICA, PANAMA

DOMINICAN REP., PUERTO RICO (USA), HAITI, ST KITTS & NEVIS, MONTSERRAT (UK), ARUBA (Neths), GRENADA, ANGUILLA (UK), ANTIGUA & BARBUDA, GUADELOUPE (Fr), DOMINICA, ST LUCIA, BARBADOS, ST VINCENT & GRENADINES, TRINIDAD & TOBAGO

VENEZUELA, GUYANA, COLOMBIA, SURINAME, FRENCH GUIANA (Fr), ECUADOR, PERU, BRAZIL 190m, BOLIVIA, PARAGUAY, CHILE, ARGENTINA, URUGUAY

MOROCCO, WESTERN SAHARA (Mor.), CAPE VERDE, MAURITANIA, MA, SENEGAL, GAMBIA, GUINEA-BISSAU, GUINEA, SIERRA LEONE, LIBERIA, CÔTE D'IVOIRE, BURK. FAS., TOGO

Believers

Most popular faiths
Latest available data

Buddhism
 Mahayana
Theravada

Christianity
 Catholicism
Protestantism
Orthodox
Independent

Islam
 Sunni
Shi'a
Ibadiyyah

Other religions
 Hinduism
Judaism
Indigenous
officially irreligious

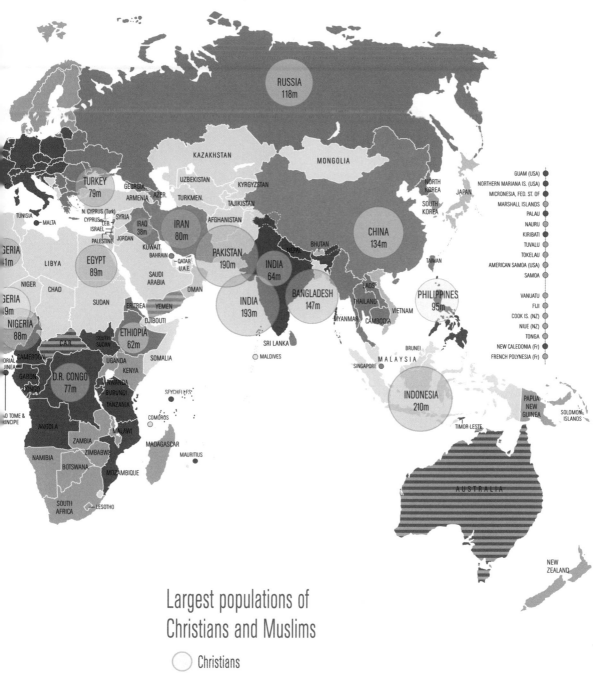

Largest populations of
Christians and Muslims

○ Christians

○ Muslims

World faiths

Estimated number of followers

Latest available data

Christianity
- Catholicism
- Protestantism
- Orthodox
- other

Islam
- Sunni
- Shi'a

Other religions
- Buddhism
- Hinduism
- Judaism
- Sikhism
- other religions

2.5 million people

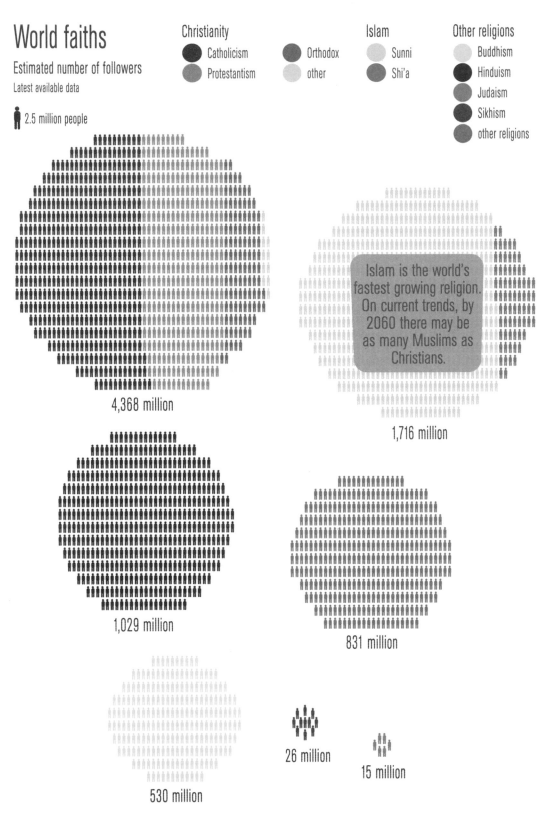

4,368 million

1,716 million

Islam is the world's fastest growing religion. On current trends, by 2060 there may be as many Muslims as Christians.

1,029 million

831 million

530 million

26 million

15 million

Non-believers

People who profess no religion
as a percentage of population

Latest available data

- 20% or more
- 10% – 19%
- fewer than 10%

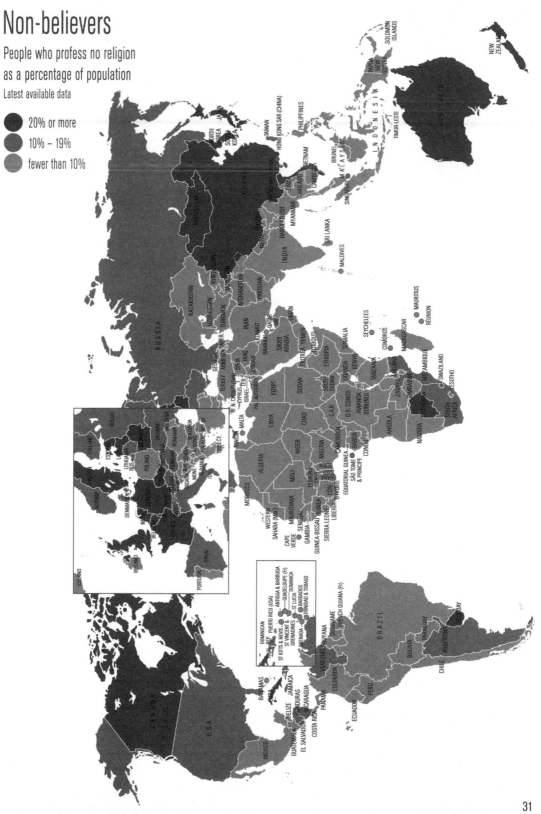

Literacy and education

1 in 7
adults is functionally illiterate

Mauritania   Mali
Senegal   Niger   Ch
         Gambia   Burkina
Guinea-Bissau   Faso   Nigeria
Sierra Leone   Guinea   Togo
         Liberia Côte   Ben
              d'Ivoire

Haiti

Literacy is simultaneously a functional need for modern societies, a basic tool for individual advancement, and a personal source of knowledge, access to the world, and satisfaction. Thanks to a major international effort, trends this century have been positive, although there remain places where more than half of adults are functionally illiterate, which means they are unable to read or write a short statement about their everyday life.

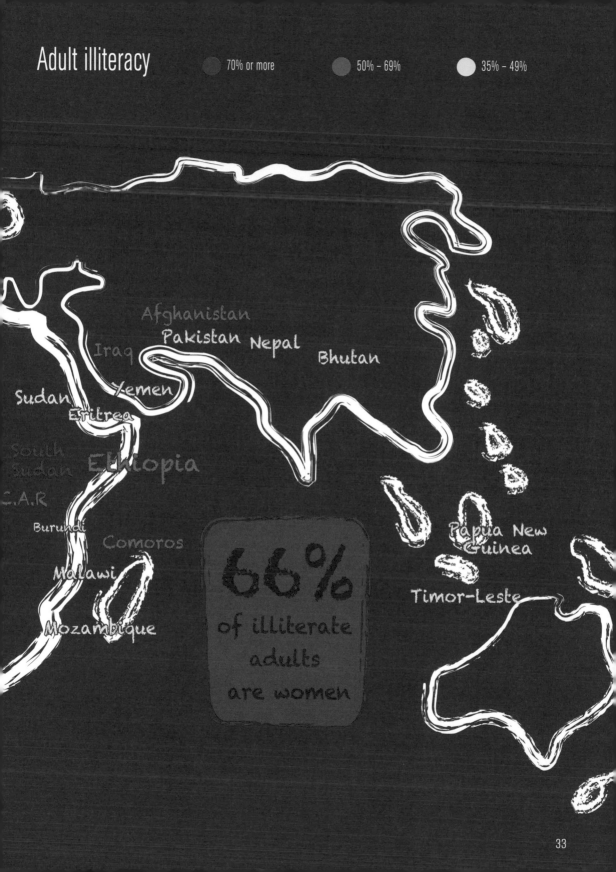

Adult illiteracy

70% or more   50% – 69%   35% – 49%

Afghanistan
Pakistan Nepal
Iraq   Bhutan
Yemen
Sudan
Eritrea
South
Sudan Ethiopia
C.A.R
Burundi
Comoros
Malawi
Mozambique

66%
of illiterate
adults
are women

Papua New
Guinea

Timor-Leste

Primary education

Percentage of children
of the correct age
enrolled in primary school

2017 or latest available data

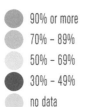

- 90% or more
- 70% – 89%
- 50% – 69%
- 30% – 49%
- no data

Where the foundations have
been laid, primary education
has shown real forward
movement, although in Africa
and some other areas, progress
in secondary and tertiary
education remains slow.

SOLOMON
ISLANDS

NEW
ZEALAND

PAPUA
NEW
GUINEA

AUSTRALIA

TIMOR-LESTE

I N D O N E S I A

BRUNEI

M A L A Y S I A

SINGAPORE

PHILIPPINES

VIETNAM

HONG KONG SAR (CHINA)

MACAU SAR (CHINA)

CAMBODIA

THAILAND

LAOS

MYANMAR

JAPAN

NORTH
KOREA

SOUTH
KOREA

BANGLADESH

BHUTAN

NEPAL

INDIA

SRI LANKA

MALDIVES

MONGOLIA

KYRGYZSTAN

TAJIKISTAN

KAZAKHSTAN

UZBEKISTAN

PAKISTAN

R U S S I A

GEORGIA

AZER.

ARMENIA

IRAN

OMAN

QATAR
U.A.E.

KUWAIT

BAHRAIN

SAUDI
ARABIA

YEMEN

DJIBOUTI

ERITREA

ETHIOPIA

SEYCHELLES

COMOROS

MAURITIUS

MADAGASCAR

MOZAMBIQUE

SWAZILAND

LESOTHO

SOUTH
AFRICA

BOTSWANA

NAMIBIA

ZIMBABWE

ZAMBIA

MALAWI

TANZANIA

BURUNDI

RWANDA

KENYA

UGANDA

SOMALIA

CONGO

ANGOLA

DEM. REP.
CONGO

CAR

SUDAN

EGYPT

CHAD

SÃO TOMÉ
& PRÍNCIPE

GABON

EQUATORIAL
GUINEA

CAMEROON

NIGERIA

NIGER

BENIN

TOGO

GHANA

BURKINA
FASO

MALI

CÔTE
D'IVOIRE

LIBERIA

SIERRA LEONE

GUINEA

GUINEA-BISSAU

GAMBIA

SENEGAL

CAPE
VERDE

MAURITANIA

MOROCCO

ALGERIA

LIBYA

TUNISIA

MALTA

SYRIA

JORDAN

ISRAEL

PALESTINE

LEBANON

CYPRUS

TURKEY

GREECE

ALBANIA

MACEDONIA

BULGARIA

ROMANIA

HUNGARY

SERBIA

MONT.

KOS.

CROATIA

ITALY

BOSNIA

SWITZ.

FRANCE

SPAIN

PORTUGAL

IRELAND

UK

ICELAND

NETH.

BELGIUM

LUX.

GERMANY

DENMARK

NORWAY

SWEDEN

FINLAND

ESTONIA

LATVIA

LITHUANIA

BELARUS

RUS.

POLAND

CZ.

SLOV.

AUSTRIA

SLO.

UKRAINE

MOLDOVA

RUSSIA

CANADA

USA

MEXICO

GUATEMALA

BELIZE

HONDURAS

EL SALVADOR

NICARAGUA

COSTA RICA

PANAMA

CUBA

BAHAMAS

JAMAICA

HAITI

DOMINICAN
REP.

BERMUDA (UK)

PUERTO RICO (USA)

ANTIGUA & BARBUDA

DOMINICA

ST LUCIA

BARBADOS

ST VINCENT & GRENADINES

GRENADA

TRINIDAD & TOBAGO

VENEZUELA

COLOMBIA

ECUADOR

PERU

GUYANA

SURINAME

B R A Z I L

BOLIVIA

PARAGUAY

CHILE

ARGENTINA

URUGUAY

Secondary education

Percentage of children of the correct age enrolled in secondary school

2017 or latest available data

- 90% or more
- 70% – 89%
- 50% – 69%
- 30% – 49%
- fewer than 30%

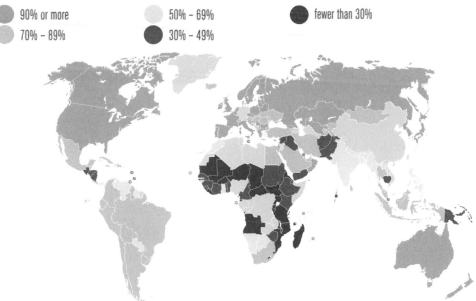

Tertiary education

Percentage of people of the correct age enrolled in tertiary education

2017 or latest available data

- 90% or more
- 70% – 89%
- 50% – 69%
- 30% – 49%
- fewer than 30%

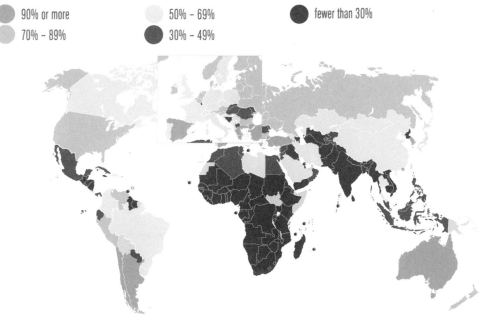

Urbanization

CANADA

USA

MEXICO

BAHAMAS

CUBA

BELIZE
GUATEMALA
EL SALVADOR
HONDURAS
NICARAGUA
COSTA RICA
PANAMA

JAMAICA
HAITI

DOMINICAN
REP.
PUERTO RICO

ST KITTS & NEVIS
GRENADA

ANTIGUA & BARBUDA
DOMINICA
ST LUCIA
BARBADOS
ST VINCENT & GRENADINES
TRINIDAD & TOBAGO

VENEZUELA
COLOMBIA

GUYANA
SURINAME

ECUADOR

PERU

BRAZIL

BOLIVIA

CHILE

PARAGUAY

URUGUAY
ARGENTINA

ICELAND

NORWAY

FINLAND

SWEDEN

ESTONIA
LATVIA
LITHUANIA

DENMARK

UK

IRELAND

NET.
BEL.
LUX.
FRANCE

GERMANY

POLAND

BELARUS

SWITZ.

CZ. REP.
AUS.
SL.

CROATIA

SL.
HUN.

B-H

ROM.

SERB.

BUL.

M.—
ALB.

PORTUGAL

SPAIN

ITALY

N. MAC.

GREECE

TUNISIA

MOROCCO

ALGERIA

LIB

M

CAPE
VERDE

MAURITANIA

MALI

NIGER

CH

SENEGAL

GAMBIA

GUINEA-BISSAU

GUINEA

SIERRA LEONE

CÔTE
D'IVOIRE

LIBERIA

BURKINA
FASO

GHANA
TOGO
BENIN

NIGERIA

CAMEROON

EQUATORIAL
GUINEA

GABON
CONGO

SAO TOME
& PRINCIPE

AN

NAM

SO
AF

Urban population

As a percentage of total population
2017

Legend:
- 90% or more
- 70% – 89%
- 50% – 69%
- 30% – 49%
- 10% – 29%
- no data
- metropolitan areas with 10 million or more inhabitants

RUSSIA

UKRAINE
MOLDOVA
GEORGIA
TURKEY
ARMENIA
AZER.
CYPRUS
SYRIA
LEB
ISRAEL
PAL.
JORDAN
IRAQ
IRAN
KUWAIT
BAHRAIN
QATAR
UAE
EGYPT
SAUDI ARABIA
OMAN

KAZAKHSTAN
UZBEKISTAN
TURKMEN.
KYRGYZSTAN
TAJIKISTAN
AFGHANISTAN
PAKISTAN
NEPAL
BHUTAN
INDIA
BANGLADESH
MYANMAR

MONGOLIA

CHINA

NORTH KOREA
SOUTH KOREA
JAPAN

Hong Kong SAR
Macau SAR
LAOS
THAILAND
CAMBODIA
VIETNAM
PHILIPPINES

SUDAN
ERITREA
YEMEN
DJIBOUTI
SOUTH SUDAN
ETHIOPIA
SOMALIA
UGANDA
KENYA
M. OF GO
RWANDA
BURUNDI
TANZANIA

SRI LANKA
MALDIVES

SEYCHELLES

COMOROS

AMBIA
MALAWI
ZIMBABWE
TSWANA
MOZAMBIQUE
MADAGASCAR
MAURITIUS
SWAZILAND
LESOTHO

BRUNEI
MALAYSIA
SINGAPORE
INDONESIA
EAST TIMOR

PAPUA NEW GUINEA
SOLOMON ISLANDS

MICRONESIA, FED. STATES OF
PALAU
NAURU
KIRIBATI
TUVALU
SAMOA
VANUATU
FIJI
TONGA

AUSTRALIA

NEW ZEALAND

37

Urban dwellers

More than half of the world's people live in towns and cities and the number keeps growing. Back in 1800, some 3% lived in cities. In 2020, the corresponding figure is about 55%. And one projection is that by 2050 it will be 6.8 billion.

In 1950, the world's ten largest cities were in Europe and the Americas. But most major cities in Europe are now static in size, or declining, as improved transport and communications reduce the economic benefits of people living in highly concentrated urban environments.

The urbanization of recent years has happened largely in the poor, middle-income and developing countries, where people still move from the countryside to the cities in search of jobs and livelihoods.

Asia is leading the field in terms of megacities, but although it is these giant urban conglomerations that vie with each other to be the largest financial centre, or location of the world's tallest building, only one in eight of all urban residents actually lives in such cities. The majority of urban dwellers reside in small towns and cities of a more modest size and character.

Ten largest cities

In 1950 In 2018

👤 1 million people 👤 1 million people

Global urban population:
1950: 751 million
2020: 4,379 million

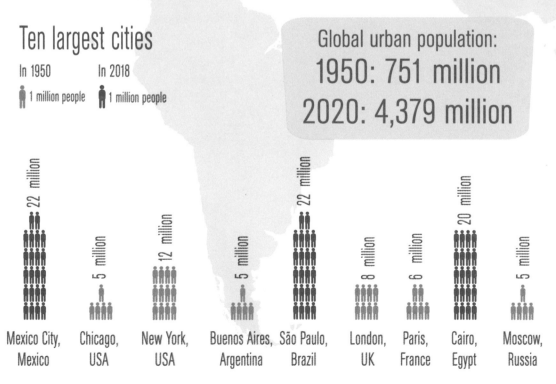

22 million	5 million	12 million	5 million	22 million	8 million	6 million	20 million	5 million
Mexico City, Mexico	Chicago, USA	New York, USA	Buenos Aires, Argentina	São Paulo, Brazil	London, UK	Paris, France	Cairo, Egypt	Moscow, Russia

City scale

Number of people living in different
sizes of urban conglomeration
2018

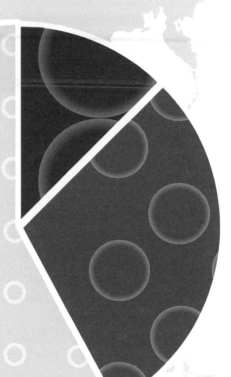

● 529 million people
living in megacities of
10 million or more

● 1.25 billion people
living in major cities
of 1–10 million

○ 2.4 billion people
living in towns and
cities of fewer than
1 million

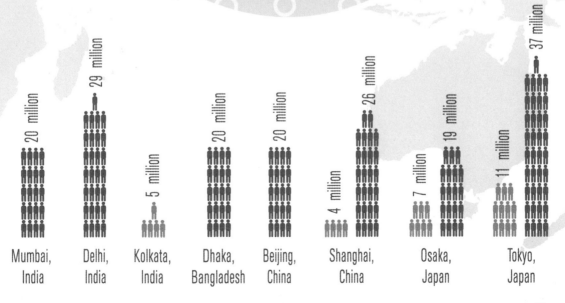

Mumbai, India	Delhi, India	Kolkata, India	Dhaka, Bangladesh	Beijing, China	Shanghai, China	Osaka, Japan	Tokyo, Japan
20 million	29 million	5 million	20 million	20 million	26 million	4 million / 7 million / 19 million	11 million / 37 million

Wealth and poverty

The 21st century opened with almost a decade of impressive economic growth worldwide during which global output nearly doubled. Since then, there have been two massive economic crises – 2008 to 2009, and 2020.

The crisis of 2008 to 2009 was financial – debt was too high and the collateral was inadequate. Finally, the party ended. Economic slowdown and recession were widespread. Public spending on health, education, and welfare was cut in many countries. Some countries remained in the grip of austerity a decade later but others had fared better and recovered during the 2010s.

Then, at the start of 2020, came Covid-19, a pandemic seemingly originating in the transfer of a virus from animal to human. Countries locked down. Many governments closed most workplaces along with schools and universities; they prevented most travel into, out of, and even within the country; almost all people stayed at home, coming out only for essential shopping; in many cases children were not allowed out of the home at all.

The full scale of the economic impact of Covid-19 will not be clear for some time. The short-term effects were a true economic shock. China's economy, which had grown steadily for almost 50 years, shrank in the first three months of 2020. In the USA 33 million people filed for unemployment benefit in March and April. Never, in modern times, had so many jobs disappeared so fast. Some governments footed part of the bill for workers' wages but could not keep that going long-term. Global airline travel collapsed by 99 per cent. Authoritative projections indicated world trade could slump by as much as one-third.

Evidence soon started to build that the effects of Covid-19 are not socially equal. The poor are hardest hit because they almost certainly lack savings, living hand to mouth, with no health insurance – or in some cases, with health insurance attached to their jobs, which they had lost. Statistics have revealed a general increase in inequality in the richer countries since the 1970s, and the effects of Covid-19 will be sharper in many places as a result. Without sustained counter-measures by governments, inequalities are likely to worsen. Extreme poverty has fallen sharply over the past three decades but there were signs in the first half of 2020 that this trend could reverse.

Income

Despite the economic crash in 2008–2009, growth in the world's economic output continued to outpace growth in its population. But then came the impact on trade, jobs, and incomes of Covid-19.

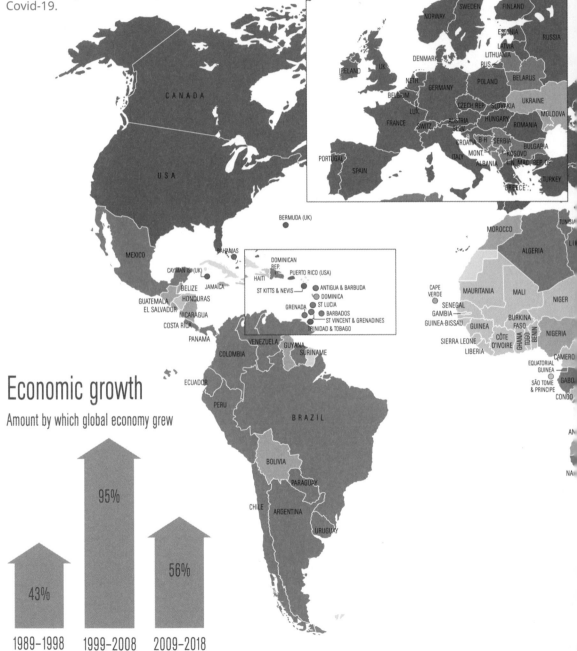

ICELAND
NORWAY
SWEDEN
FINLAND
ESTONIA
RUSSIA
LATVIA
DENMARK
LITHUANIA
RUS.
IRELAND
UK
NETH.
BELARUS
GERMANY
POLAND
BELGIUM
LUX.
CZECH REP.
SLOVAKIA
UKRAINE
FRANCE
SWITZ.
AUSTRIA
HUNGARY
MOLDOVA
SLOV.
ROMANIA
PORTUGAL
CROATIA
B-H
SERBIA
BULGARIA
ITALY
MONT.
KOSOVO
SPAIN
ALBANIA
N. MAC.
REP. OF
TURKEY
GREECE

CANADA

USA

MEXICO

BERMUDA (UK)

BAHAMAS

CAYMAN IS. (UK)

BELIZE
JAMAICA
GUATEMALA
HONDURAS
EL SALVADOR
NICARAGUA
COSTA RICA
PANAMA

DOMINICAN REP.
HAITI
PUERTO RICO (USA)
ST KITTS & NEVIS
ANTIGUA & BARBUDA
DOMINICA
GRENADA
ST LUCIA
BARBADOS
ST VINCENT & GRENADINES
TRINIDAD & TOBAGO

VENEZUELA
GUYANA
SURINAME
COLOMBIA
ECUADOR
PERU
BRAZIL
BOLIVIA
PARAGUAY
CHILE
ARGENTINA
URUGUAY

MOROCCO
TUNISIA
ALGERIA
LI

CAPE VERDE
MAURITANIA
MALI
NIGER
SENEGAL
GAMBIA
BURKINA FASO
GUINEA-BISSAU
GUINEA
NIGERIA
SIERRA LEONE
CÔTE D'IVOIRE
GHANA
TOGO
BENIN
LIBERIA
CAMERO
EQUATORIAL GUINEA
SÃO TOME & PRINCIPE
GABO
CONGO
AN
NA

Economic growth

Amount by which global economy grew

95%

56%

43%

1989–1998   1999–2008   2009–2018

Gross National Income

Per capita

2016 or latest available data

$25,000 or more
$10,000 – $24,999
$5,000 – $9,999
$1,000 – $4,999
less than $1,000
no data

RUSSIA

KAZAKHSTAN

MONGOLIA

UZBEKISTAN

KYRGYZSTAN

GEORGIA

ARMENIA AZER. TURKMEN.

TAJIKISTAN

JAPAN

SOUTH
KOREA

CYPRUS LEB.
ISRAEL
PALESTINE JORDAN

IRAQ

IRAN

AFGHANISTAN

CHINA

KUWAIT

EGYPT

BAHRAIN
QATAR
U.A.E.
SAUDI
ARABIA
OMAN

PAKISTAN

NEPAL BHUTAN

MACAO SAR (CHINA)

TAIWAN

HONG KONG SAR (CHINA)

INDIA

BANGLADESH

MYANMAR

LAOS

SUDAN

ERITREA YEMEN

THAILAND

VIETNAM

PHILIPPINES

CAMBODIA

SOUTH
SUDAN

ETHIOPIA

SRI LANKA

MICRONESIA, FED. ST. OF
MARSHALL ISLANDS
PALAU
NAURU
KIRIBATI
TUVALU

SAMOA

VANUATU
FIJI

TONGA

UGANDA

KENYA

D.R.
CONGO

RWANDA

BURUNDI

TANZANIA

SEYCHELLES

COMOROS

ZAMBIA MALAWI

MADAGASCAR

MAURITIUS

ZIMBABWE

BOTSWANA

MOZAMBIQUE

MALDIVES

BRUNEI

MALAYSIA

SINGAPORE

INDONESIA

TIMOR-LESTE

PAPUA
NEW
GUINEA

SOLOMON
ISLANDS

SOUTH
AFRICA

SWAZILAND

LESOTHO

AUSTRALIA

NEW
ZEALAND

Inequality

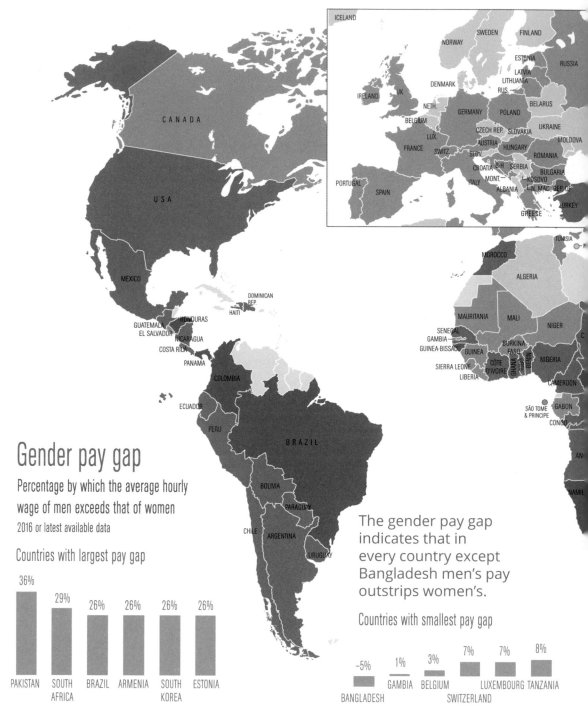

Gender pay gap

Percentage by which the average hourly wage of men exceeds that of women
2016 or latest available data

Countries with largest pay gap

36%	29%	26%	26%	26%	26%
PAKISTAN	SOUTH AFRICA	BRAZIL	ARMENIA	SOUTH KOREA	ESTONIA

The gender pay gap indicates that in every country except Bangladesh men's pay outstrips women's.

Countries with smallest pay gap

–5%	1%	3%	7%	7%	8%
BANGLADESH	GAMBIA	BELGIUM SWITZERLAND	LUXEMBOURG	TANZANIA	

Map labels: ICELAND, SWEDEN, FINLAND, NORWAY, ESTONIA, RUSSIA, LATVIA, DENMARK, LITHUANIA, RUS., IRELAND, UK, NETH., GERMANY, POLAND, BELARUS, BELGIUM, LUX., CZECH REP., SLOVAKIA, UKRAINE, FRANCE, SWITZ., AUSTRIA, HUNGARY, MOLDOVA, SLOV., ROMANIA, CROATIA, B-H, SERBIA, BULGARIA, PORTUGAL, ITALY, MONT., KOSOVO, N. MAC., REP. OF, SPAIN, ALBANIA, TURKEY, GREECE

CANADA, USA, MEXICO, GUATEMALA, EL SALVADOR, HONDURAS, NICARAGUA, COSTA RICA, PANAMA, HAITI, DOMINICAN REP., COLOMBIA, ECUADOR, PERU, BRAZIL, BOLIVIA, PARAGUAY, CHILE, ARGENTINA, URUGUAY

TUNISIA, MOROCCO, ALGERIA, MAURITANIA, MALI, NIGER, SENEGAL, GAMBIA, GUINEA-BISSAU, GUINEA, BURKINA FASO, NIGERIA, SIERRA LEONE, CÔTE D'IVOIRE, GHANA, TOGO, BENIN, LIBERIA, CAMEROON, SÃO TOME & PRINCIPE, GABON, CONGO, NAMIBIA

Distribution of wealth

Within a country

2017 or latest available data
Gini index

50 – 63 *most unequal*

40 – 49

30 – 39

22 – 29 *most equal*

no data

The Gini index measures the degree to which the distribution of wealth within a country is different from a perfectly equal distribution.

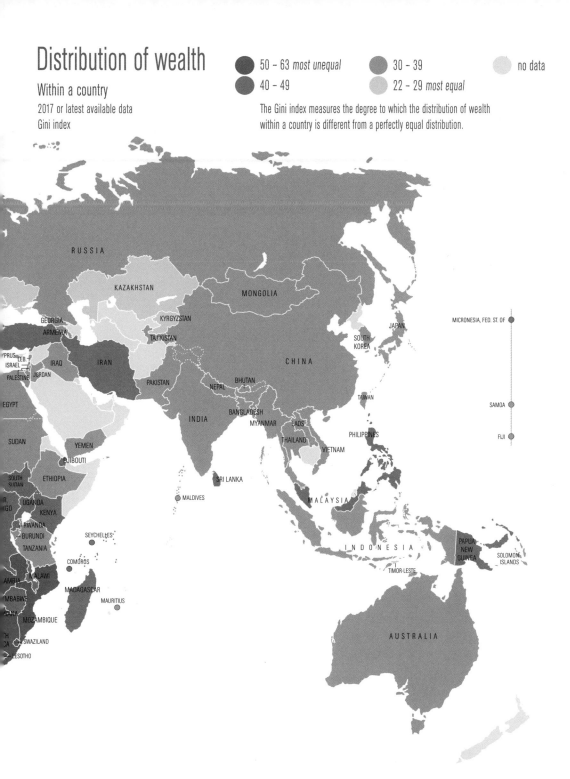

RUSSIA

KAZAKHSTAN

MONGOLIA

KYRGYZSTAN

GEORGIA

ARMENIA

TAJIKISTAN

CYPRUS

LEB.

ISRAEL

PALESTINE

JORDAN

IRAQ

IRAN

PAKISTAN

NEPAL

BHUTAN

JAPAN

SOUTH
KOREA

CHINA

TAIWAN

MICRONESIA, FED. ST. OF

EGYPT

SUDAN

YEMEN

DJIBOUTI

INDIA

BANGLADESH

MYANMAR

LAOS

THAILAND

VIETNAM

PHILIPPINES

SAMOA

FIJI

SOUTH
SUDAN

ETHIOPIA

SRI LANKA

MALDIVES

MALAYSIA

...GO

UGANDA

KENYA

RWANDA

BURUNDI

TANZANIA

SEYCHELLES

COMOROS

INDONESIA

PAPUA
NEW
GUINEA

SOLOMON
ISLANDS

TIMOR-LESTE

...AMBIA

MALAWI

MBABWE

...ANA

MADAGASCAR

MAURITIUS

MOZAMBIQUE

AUSTRALIA

...H

...A

SWAZILAND

LESOTHO

45

World poverty

Percentage of population
living on less than $1.90 a day

2017 or latest available data
PPP$

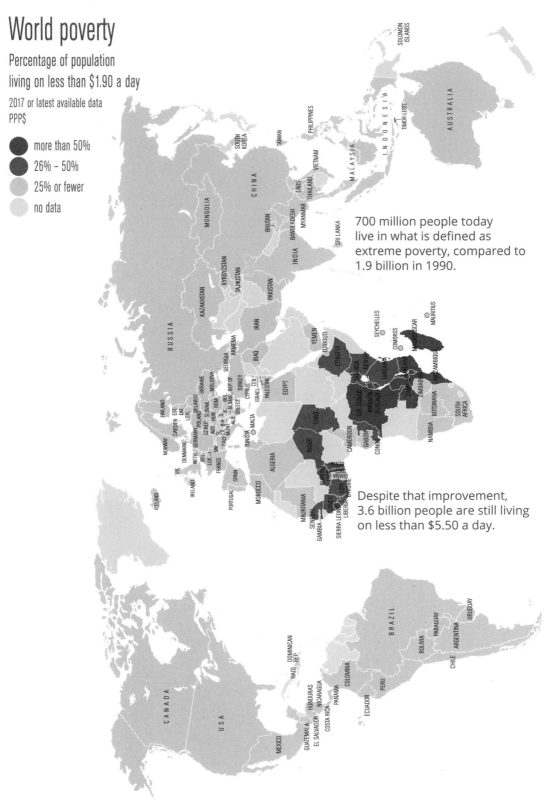

- more than 50%
- 26% – 50%
- 25% or fewer
- no data

700 million people today
live in what is defined as
extreme poverty, compared to
1.9 billion in 1990.

Despite that improvement,
3.6 billion people are still living
on less than $5.50 a day.

SOLOMON
ISLANDS

AUSTRALIA

INDONESIA

TIMOR-LESTE

PHILIPPINES

MALAYSIA

TAIWAN

SOUTH
KOREA

VIETNAM

THAILAND

LAOS

MYANMAR

BHUTAN

BANGLADESH

SRI LANKA

INDIA

CHINA

MONGOLIA

PAKISTAN

IRAN

KAZAKHSTAN

KYRGYZSTAN

TAJIKISTAN

MAURITIUS

MADAGASCAR

COMOROS

SEYCHELLES

YEMEN

DJIBOUTI

ETHIOPIA

UGANDA

KENYA

TANZANIA

ZAMBIA

RWANDA

BURUNDI

ZIMBABWE

MOZAMBIQUE

BOTSWANA

NAMIBIA

SOUTH
AFRICA

D.R. CONGO

GABON

CONGO

CAMEROON

CHAD

NIGER

BENIN

TOGO

GHANA

NIGERIA

BURKINA

CÔTE
D'IVOIRE

LIBERIA

GUINEA

SIERRA LEONE

GAMBIA

SENEGAL

MAURITANIA

MALI

ALGERIA

MOROCCO

EGYPT

PALESTINE

ISRAEL LEB.

CYPRUS

TURKEY

GREECE

MALTA

TUNISIA

IRAQ

ARMENIA

GEORGIA

MOLDOVA

UKRAINE

BELARUS

POLAND

CZECH

SLOVAK

HUN

ROM.

BUL

S.
M.

B-H.

ALB

MAC.
REP OF

ITALY

AUS

SLO

CR

MONT.

GERMANY

NETH.

BEL

LUX

SWI

FRANCE

SPAIN

PORTUGAL

IRELAND

UK

NORWAY

DENMARK

SWEDEN

FINLAND

EST.

LAT.

LITH.

ICELAND

RUSSIA

BRAZIL

URUGUAY

PARAGUAY

ARGENTINA

CHILE

BOLIVIA

PERU

COLOMBIA

ECUADOR

PANAMA

COSTA RICA

NICARAGUA

HONDURAS

EL SALVADOR

GUATEMALA

MEXICO

DOMINICAN
REP.

HAITI

USA

CANADA

46

The hands of a few

Countries with the most billionaires in 2019

👤 10 billionaires 2009   👥 10 billionaires 2019

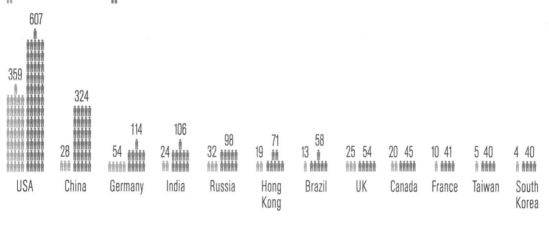

359 / 607	28 / 324	54 / 114	24 / 106	32 / 98	19 / 71	13 / 58	25 / 54	20 / 45	10 / 41	5 / 40	4 / 40
USA	China	Germany	India	Russia	Hong Kong	Brazil	UK	Canada	France	Taiwan	South Korea

Bouncing back

Number of billionaires and their total wealth

2008–2019

Billionaires were hit hard by the global crash in 2008. They recovered quickly.

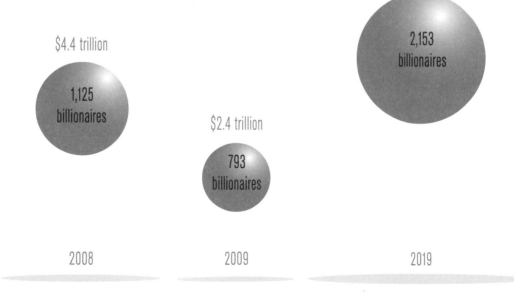

$4.4 trillion

1,125 billionaires

$2.4 trillion

793 billionaires

$8.7 trillion

2,153 billionaires

2008   2009   2019

Quality of life

There is more to happiness than wealth
alone – yet rich countries inevitably offer
a higher quality of life.

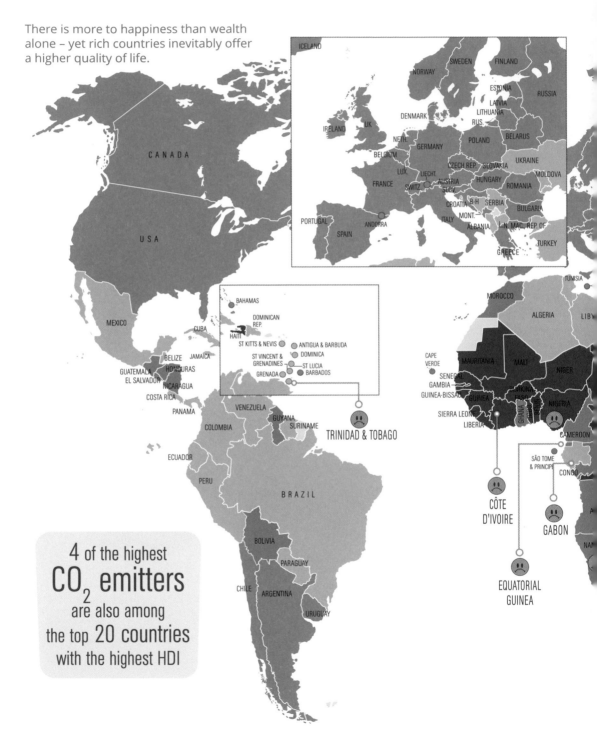

4 of the highest
CO_2 emitters
are also among
the top 20 countries
with the highest HDI

Relative human development

Score on the Human Development Index (HDI)

2017

very high
high
medium
low
no data

The Human Development Index (HDI) scores countries according to the life expectancy and educational level of their populations, and the national income per capita.

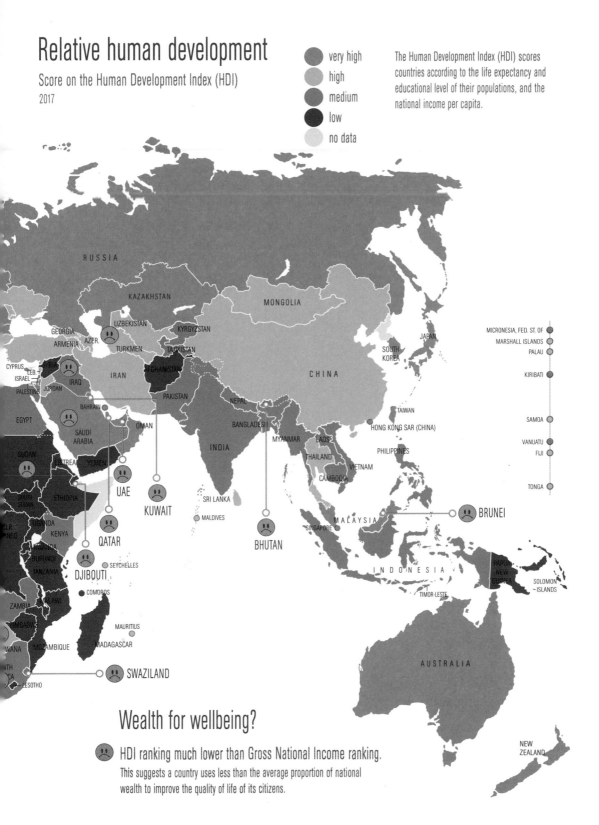

RUSSIA

KAZAKHSTAN

MONGOLIA

GEORGIA
ARMENIA
AZER.
UZBEKISTAN
KYRGYZSTAN
TURKMEN.
TAJIKISTAN

JAPAN
SOUTH KOREA

CYPRUS
LEB.
ISRAEL
PALESTINE
SYRIA
JORDAN
IRAQ
IRAN
AFGHANISTAN

CHINA

BAHRAIN
PAKISTAN
NEPAL

TAIWAN

EGYPT
SAUDI ARABIA
OMAN
BANGLADESH
HONG KONG SAR (CHINA)

SUDAN
ERITREA
YEMEN
INDIA
MYANMAR
LAOS
THAILAND
PHILIPPINES

UAE
VIETNAM
CAMBODIA

SOUTH SUDAN
ETHIOPIA
KUWAIT
SRI LANKA

UGANDA
D.R.
CONGO
KENYA
QATAR
MALDIVES
SINGAPORE
MALAYSIA
BRUNEI

RWANDA
BURUNDI
TANZANIA
DJIBOUTI
BHUTAN
SEYCHELLES

ZAMBIA
MALAWI
COMOROS

INDONESIA

PAPUA NEW GUINEA
SOLOMON ISLANDS

ZIMBABWE
MOZAMBIQUE
MAURITIUS
MADAGASCAR

TIMOR-LESTE

BWANA
TH CA
SWAZILAND
LESOTHO

AUSTRALIA

MICRONESIA, FED. ST. OF
MARSHALL ISLANDS
PALAU

KIRIBATI

SAMOA

VANUATU
FIJI

TONGA

NEW ZEALAND

Wealth for wellbeing?

HDI ranking much lower than Gross National Income ranking.
This suggests a country uses less than the average proportion of national wealth to improve the quality of life of its citizens.

Transnationals

Transnational corporations represent enormous wealth and therefore power. Operating in scores of countries, the largest companies have interests that reach far beyond any single national loyalty.

Winners and losers

Changes to Fortune magazine's ranking of largest corporations
2019

33 new to list:		
• 13 China, Hong Kong, Taiwan	• 5 USA, Canada	
• 5 South Korea, Japan	• 2 Mexico	
• 7 Europe	• 1 India	

Fortune Global 500 2019

Among 33 dropped from list	
• 9 Europe	
• 9 USA	
• 8 China	
• 2 South Korea	

Corporate wealth exceeds country wealth

Gross National Income (GNI) compared with annual revenue of selected transnationals

2017/18 or latest available GNI data
US$

GNI larger than revenue of any company
GNI smaller than Walmart ($500bn)
GNI smaller than Boeing ($93bn)
GNI smaller than Facebook ($41bn)
GNI smaller than McDonalds ($23bn)
no data

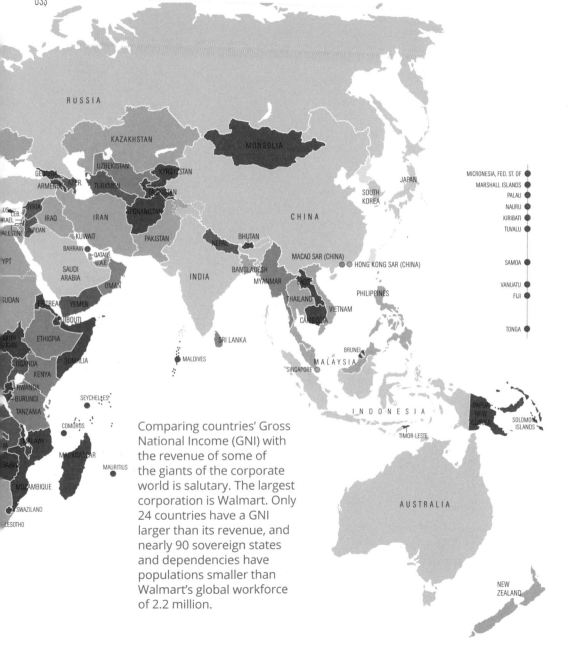

Comparing countries' Gross National Income (GNI) with the revenue of some of the giants of the corporate world is salutary. The largest corporation is Walmart. Only 24 countries have a GNI larger than its revenue, and nearly 90 sovereign states and dependencies have populations smaller than Walmart's global workforce of 2.2 million.

Banks

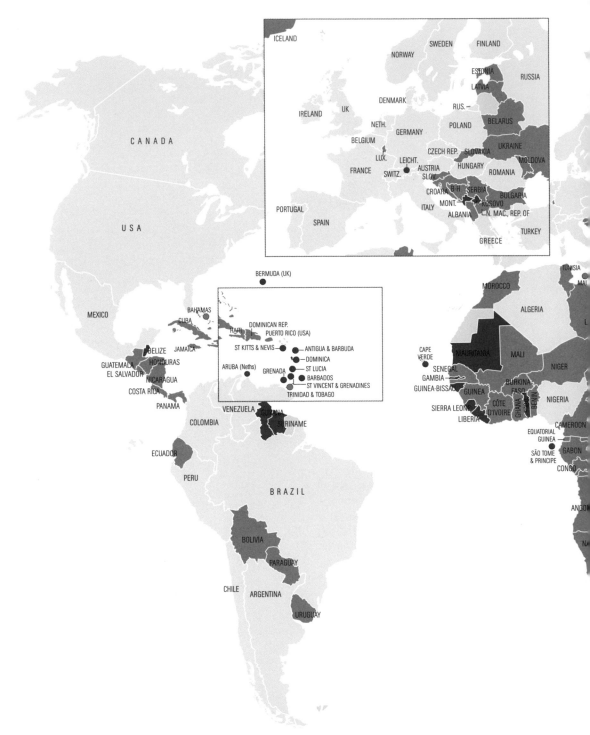

ICELAND

NORWAY SWEDEN FINLAND

ESTONIA
LATVIA RUSSIA

DENMARK RUS. —

IRELAND UK BELARUS

NETH. POLAND
GERMANY
BELGIUM CZECH REP. SLOVAKIA UKRAINE

LUX. LEICHT. MOLDOVA
FRANCE SWITZ. AUSTRIA HUNGARY ROMANIA
SLOV.
CROATIA B-H SERBIA BULGARIA
MONT. KOSOVO
PORTUGAL ITALY ALBANIA N. MAC., REP. OF
TURKEY
SPAIN
GREECE

CANADA

USA

MEXICO

BERMUDA (UK)

BAHAMAS
CUBA DOMINICAN REP.
HAITI PUERTO RICO (USA)
ST KITTS & NEVIS ANTIGUA & BARBUDA
BELIZE JAMAICA DOMINICA
GUATEMALA HONDURAS ARUBA (Neths) ST LUCIA
EL SALVADOR GRENADA BARBADOS
NICARAGUA ST VINCENT & GRENADINES
COSTA RICA TRINIDAD & TOBAGO
PANAMA

VENEZUELA GUYANA
COLOMBIA SURINAME

ECUADOR

PERU

BRAZIL

TUNISIA
MOROCCO MALI

ALGERIA

L

CAPE
VERDE MAURITANIA MALI
SENEGAL NIGER
GAMBIA BURKINA
GUINEA-BISSAU GUINEA FASO BENIN NIGERIA
SIERRA LEONE CÔTE GHANA
D'IVOIRE
LIBERIA
CAMEROON
EQUATORIAL
GUINEA GABON
SÃO TOME CONGO
& PRINCIPE

ANGOL

NA

BOLIVIA

PARAGUAY

CHILE ARGENTINA

URUGUAY

Comparative wealth

Gross National Income (GNI) compared with JPMorgan Chase
annual revenue of $131.4bn

2017 2018 or latest available date
for GNI

● GNI greater than annual revenue of JPMorgan Chase
● GNI smaller than annual revenue of JPMorgan Chase
● GNI smaller than annual revenue of JPMorgan Chase
as is the combined GNI of these 48 countries
● no data

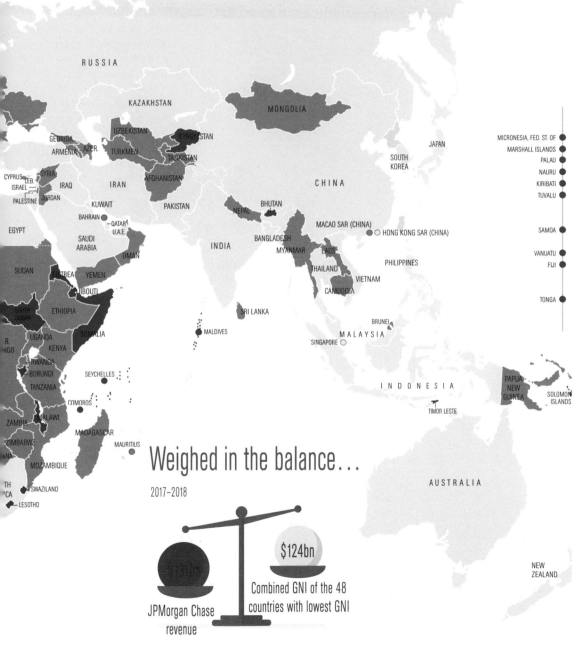

RUSSIA
KAZAKHSTAN
MONGOLIA
UZBEKISTAN
KYRGYZSTAN
GEORGIA
ARMENIA AZER. TURKMEN
TAJIKISTAN
CYPRUS SYRIA
LEB.
ISRAEL IRAQ IRAN
PALESTINE JORDAN
AFGHANISTAN
JAPAN
SOUTH
KOREA
CHINA
KUWAIT PAKISTAN
BAHRAIN ● NEPAL BHUTAN
–QATAR
EGYPT U.A.E.
SAUDI BANGLADESH
ARABIA OMAN INDIA MYANMAR LAOS
MACAO SAR (CHINA)
○ HONG KONG SAR (CHINA)
SUDAN ERITREA YEMEN THAILAND PHILIPPINES
DJIBOUTI VIETNAM
SOUTH ETHIOPIA CAMBODIA
SUDAN SRI LANKA BRUNEI
R. UGANDA SOMALIA MALDIVES MALAYSIA
GO KENYA SINGAPORE ○
RWANDA
BURUNDI SEYCHELLES INDONESIA PAPUA
TANZANIA NEW SOLOMON
COMOROS GUINEA ISLANDS
ZAMBIA MALAWI TIMOR LESTE
MADAGASCAR
ZIMBABWE MAURITIUS
NA
MOZAMBIQUE
TH AUSTRALIA
CA SWAZILAND
LESOTHO

MICRONESIA, FED. ST. OF ●
MARSHALL ISLANDS ●
PALAU ●
NAURU ●
KIRIBATI ●
TUVALU ●

SAMOA ●

VANUATU ●
FIJI ●

TONGA ●

NEW
ZEALAND

Weighed in the balance...

2017–2018

$124bn

JPMorgan Chase
revenue

Combined GNI of the 48
countries with lowest GNI

Corruption

Rate of corruption

Score according to
Corruption Perceptions Index
2018

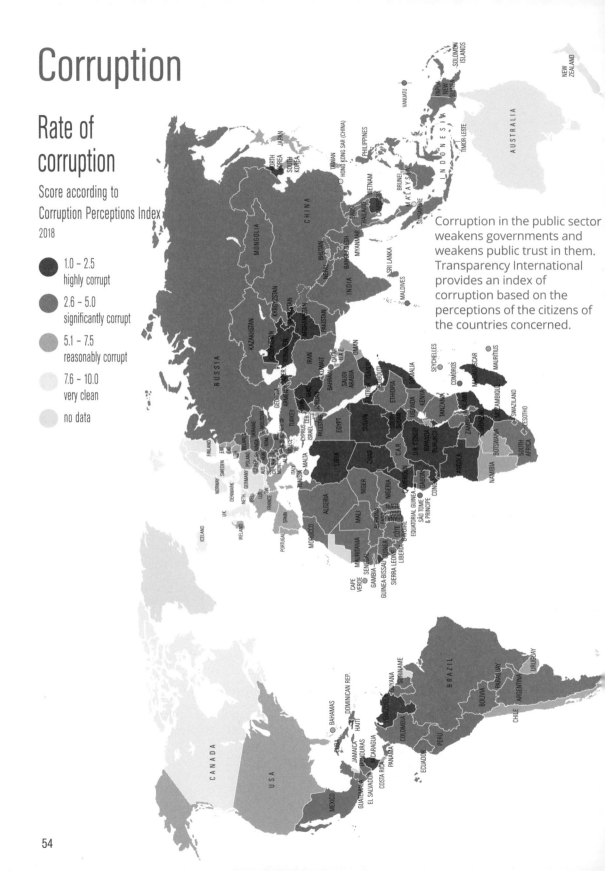

- **1.0 – 2.5** highly corrupt
- **2.6 – 5.0** significantly corrupt
- **5.1 – 7.5** reasonably corrupt
- **7.6 – 10.0** very clean
- no data

Corruption in the public sector weakens governments and weakens public trust in them. Transparency International provides an index of corruption based on the perceptions of the citizens of the countries concerned.

Shadow economy

Value of legal economic
activities unreported
to authorities as
percentage
of formal economy
average of 2004–15

- 51% – 67%
- 36% – 50%
- 21% – 35%
- 7% – 20%
- no data

The strength of the shadow
economy is one indicator of
a corrupt society. Although it
may involve activities that are
themselves legal, the failure to
report the financial gains from
those activities to the country's tax
authorities – tax evasion – is illegal.

Taxes worth at least
$500 billion
are lost annually – more
than one-fifth of corporate
tax revenues.

Panama and Paradise Papers

The Panama Papers are the biggest ever text dump in history – the result not of hacking but of a leak from an anonymous source. It offered up for global public scrutiny internal documents of Mossack Fonseca, a Panama-based law firm specializing in "offshore services" for rich individuals and corporate clients. The core of the service is how best to hide money from tax authorities. The following year came the Paradise Papers, a similar leak, with documents from three companies, headquartered in Bermuda and Singapore.

The global trade in offshore financial services is not a minor or marginal part of the world's economic and financial system. It is at the core of it. What the two document dumps revealed is that many of the world's political and corporate leaders, celebrities and stars, and people closely connected to them have turned to this industry to handle their wealth.

The essence of democracy is transparency and accountability: we see what governments do and every few years we hold them to account in an election. The essence of the offshore financial services sector is the very opposite. They keep their work secret and are accountable to nobody but their clients as they move legitimately earned (or inherited) wealth outside any national system of regulation or taxation.

The heart of the story revealed by the leaks is a struggle between governments that want tax income to fund vital public services, and rich individuals who don't want to provide it. The latter are aided by individuals, companies and a few governments that profit from the trade in non-accountability and opacity.

Scale of the leaks

Panama Papers

2.6
terabytes

11.5m
files

Paradise Papers

1.4
terabytes

13.4m
files

The struggle is an unequal one, and not just because powerful people in countries that need tax income are among those who use offshore financial services. The struggle is unequal because states and governments have borders and, in the modern world, money does not. For the rich, it is easy to move money outside the scope of government regulation and oversight, into a quiet, safe place – a haven – calling on it when needed. But the scrutiny the offshore trade has come under since 2016 has made the havens less comfortable.

Offshore financial services

Top ten providers based on number of companies registered there
that appeared in Mossack Fonseca's files (Panama Papers)
1977–2015

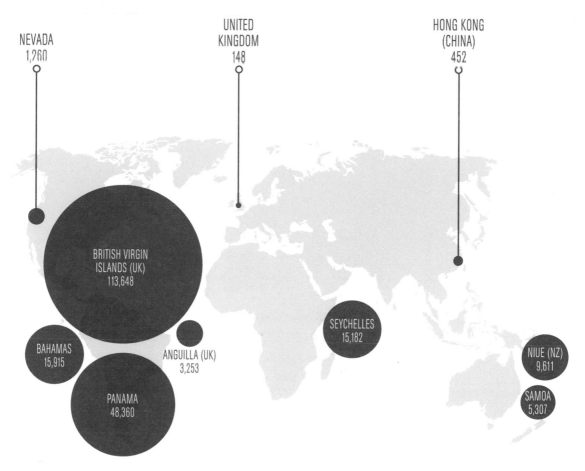

NEVADA
1,260

UNITED
KINGDOM
148

HONG KONG
(CHINA)
452

BRITISH VIRGIN
ISLANDS (UK)
113,648

BAHAMAS
15,915

ANGUILLA (UK)
3,253

PANAMA
48,360

SEYCHELLES
15,182

NIUE (NZ)
9,611

SAMOA
5,307

Many companies are no more than convenient fictions to hide money. In the Caribbean island of Nevis, population 11,000, there are more than 18,000 registered companies. There are individuals elsewhere in the region who are on the books as directors or company secretaries to thousands of firms.

These fictions are not the speciality of the Caribbean alone. In a smart street in London, one address is the registered HQ of over 2,000 companies. Few of them use the building for office space. One company that does is in the business of creating other companies. It has brought into existence over 10 million companies.

Panama and Paradise – power players

Country to which individual named in Panama Papers (1977–2016)
and Paradise Papers (1950–2016) had political links

- current or former country leader
- relative or associate of current or former country leader
- current or former politician or public official
- relative or associate of current or former politician or public official
- no data

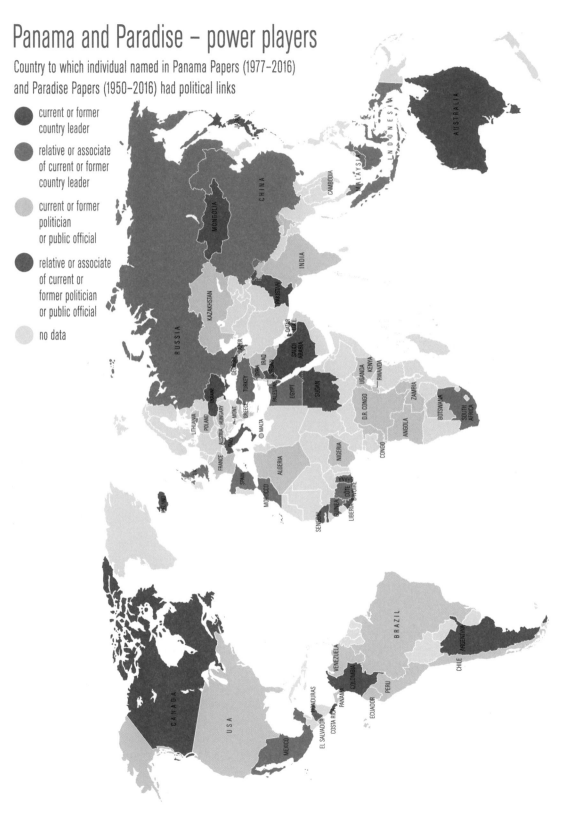

Panama Papers – effects of leak

as of March 2019

- **substantive** (changes to rules and regulations)
- **individual consequences** (civil or criminal action, political outcome)
- **deliberative** (legislative commissions, public protest)
- no data

Backlash

- countries where there has been a backlash against journalists or media organizations

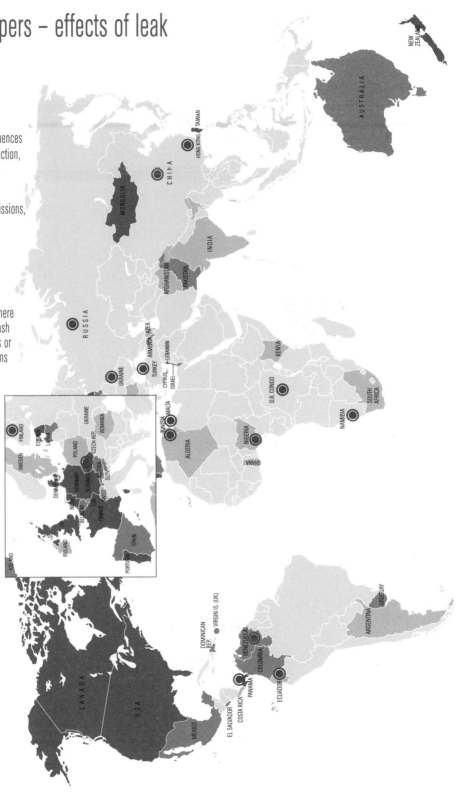

Debt

Government debt

Gross debt as
a percentage of GDP

2018

- 150% or more
- 100% – 149%
- 50% – 99%
- less than 50%
- no data

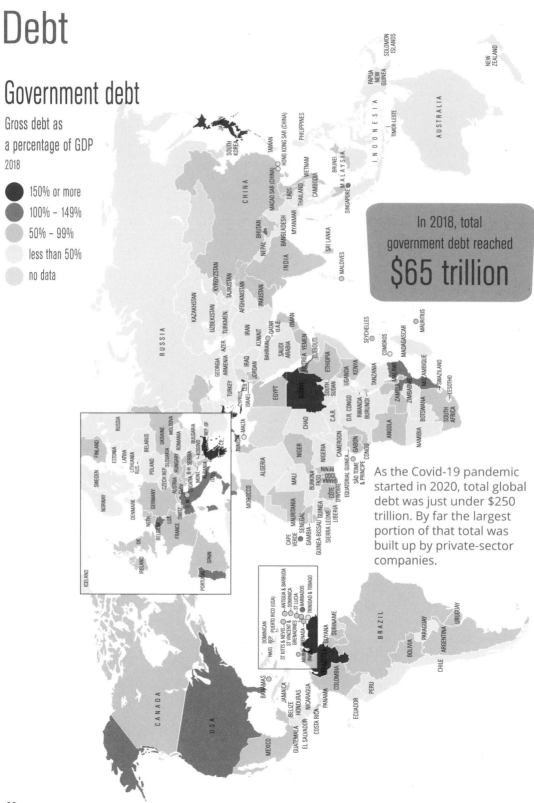

In 2018, total
government debt reached

$65 trillion

As the Covid-19 pandemic
started in 2020, total global
debt was just under $250
trillion. By far the largest
portion of that total was
built up by private-sector
companies.

Household debt

Private debt, loans, and debt securities as percentage of GDP

2017

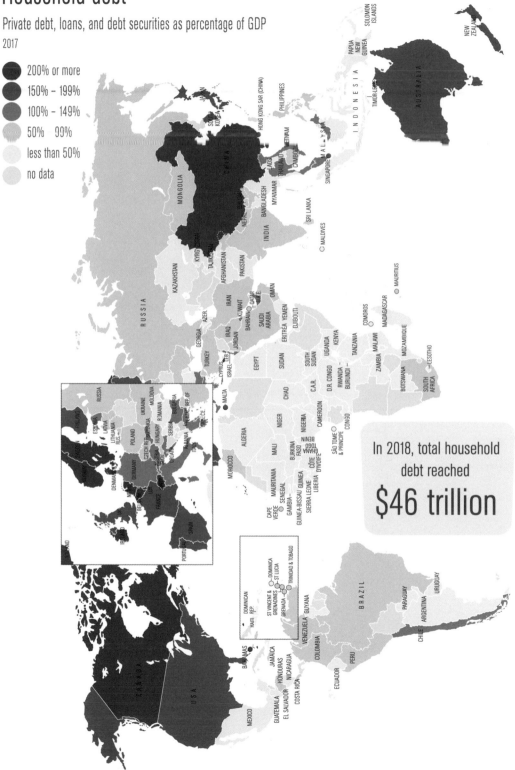

- 200% or more
- 150% – 199%
- 100% – 149%
- 50% – 99%
- less than 50%
- no data

In 2018, total household debt reached

$46 trillion

How the money's made

The route to a sophisticated modern economy passes from agriculture, to mass-production industry, to hi-tech manufacture, and finally to knowledge and services.

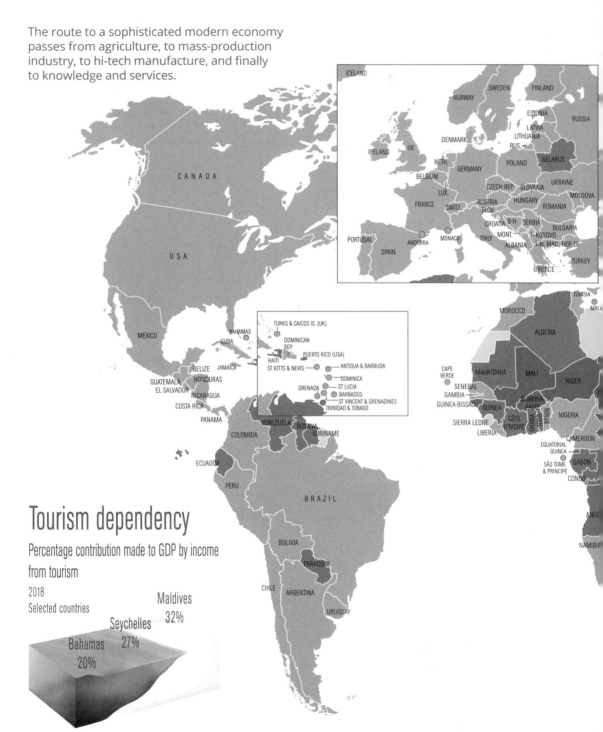

Tourism dependency

Percentage contribution made to GDP by income from tourism

2018
Selected countries

Maldives
32%

Seychelles
27%

Bahamas
20%

Which sector dominates a country's economy?

Contribution to GDP at least 20% higher
than that of other sector(s)

2018 or latest available data

services

agricultural and services

agriculture

industry

industry and services

sectors within 20% of each other

no data

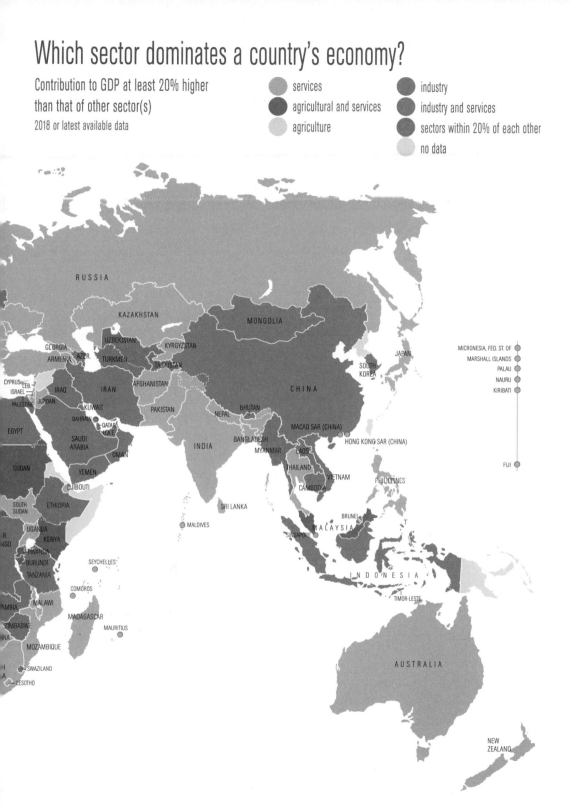

RUSSIA

KAZAKHSTAN

MONGOLIA

GEORGIA
ARMENIA   AZER.
UZBEKISTAN
KYRGYZSTAN
TURKMEN.
TAJIKISTAN

JAPAN

SOUTH
KOREA

CYPRUS
LEB.
ISRAEL
PALESTINE   JORDAN
IRAQ
IRAN
AFGHANISTAN

CHINA

KUWAIT
BAHRAIN
EGYPT
QATAR
U.A.E.
SAUDI
ARABIA
OMAN
PAKISTAN

NEPAL
BHUTAN

MACAO SAR (CHINA)

HONG KONG SAR (CHINA)

BANGLADESH

INDIA
MYANMAR
LAOS

SUDAN

YEMEN

DJIBOUTI

THAILAND

VIETNAM

PHILIPPINES

CAMBODIA

SOUTH
SUDAN   ETHIOPIA

SRI LANKA

MALDIVES

BRUNEI

MALAYSIA

SINGAPORE

UGANDA
KENYA
R.
NGO
RWANDA
BURUNDI
TANZANIA

SEYCHELLES

COMOROS

INDONESIA

TIMOR-LESTE

AMBIA   MALAWI

MADAGASCAR

MAURITIUS

ZIMBABWE
NA

MOZAMBIQUE

AUSTRALIA

HA
A
SWAZILAND
LESOTHO

MICRONESIA, FED. ST. OF
MARSHALL ISLANDS
PALAU
NAURU
KIRIBATI

FIJI

NEW
ZEALAND

63

Rights and respect

Protection from both economic depredation and the threat of violent conflicts derives from laws made for the common good. When laws are made by a process that represents and responds to the interests of the majority, and are accepted rather than imposed, then social order is based on the rule of law and the contract between citizen and state upholds accountable authority. Such societies are more resilient, and the majority of people fare better, than when power is arbitrary and laws are made by an elite minority for their own interests.

Ours is an age of growing democracy – at least when measured by the number of countries that are now established democracies, and the percentage of the world population that lives in them. This is a relatively new development. The world has only been moving in that direction for one or two centuries, and until the last 20 to 30 years democratic government was not the global norm.

The transition from dictatorship to democracy is perilous. Those who expect to be disadvantaged by that transition almost always resist the change if they can. It is hard to end the ensuing conflict peacefully when the institutions that might keep it peaceful are themselves being fought over. The democratic wave that swept the Middle East in 2011 and 2012 was accompanied everywhere by violence, with open civil war in Libya and Syria.

Once a democracy is established that is not always the whole story. In Europe, Asia, and the Americas, democracies have witnessed a fragmentation of political norms and social consensus in the past decade. The trend is not uniform but it is real, and where it unfolds it weakens democracy. In large part, it results from economic problems and feeds on a slow erosion of democracy's vitality. In many established democracies, despite surges of political energy on issues such as the climate crisis, political participation is not high. Voting is as far as most citizens' political participation goes, and even then a large turnout cannot always be counted on.

In 2020, the emergency measures required to meet the challenge of the Covid-19 pandemic were used by some governments to restrict political freedoms. It is a tragic irony that this will weaken their countries' ability to bounce back from the effects of the pandemic and other major shocks.

Political systems

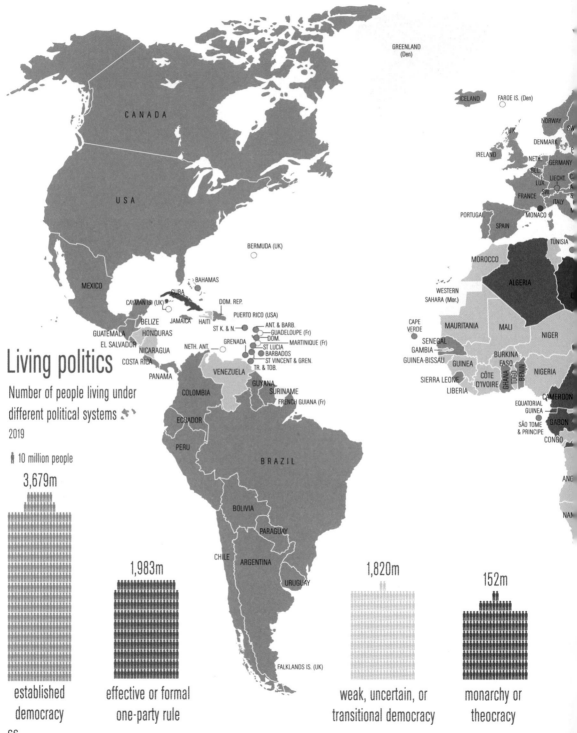

Living politics

Number of people living under different political systems 🔍
2019

👤 10 million people

3,679m
established democracy

1,983m
effective or formal one-party rule

1,820m
weak, uncertain, or transitional democracy

152m
monarchy or theocracy

Map labels:

GREENLAND (Den)
ICELAND
FAROE IS. (Den)
NORWAY
SW
UK
DENMARK
IRELAND
NETH.
GERMANY
BEL.
LIECHT.
LUX
SW.
FRANCE
ITALY
PORTUGAL
MONACO
SPAIN
TUNISIA
MOROCCO
WESTERN SAHARA (Mor.)
ALGERIA
CAPE VERDE
MAURITANIA
MALI
NIGER
SENEGAL
GAMBIA
BURKINA FASO
GUINEA-BISSAU
GUINEA
CÔTE D'IVOIRE
GHANA
TOGO
BENIN
NIGERIA
SIERRA LEONE
LIBERIA
CAMEROON
EQUATORIAL GUINEA
SÃO TOME & PRINCIPE
GABON
CONGO
ANG
NAM

CANADA
USA
MEXICO
BERMUDA (UK)
BAHAMAS
CUBA
CAYMAN IS. (UK)
DOM. REP.
BELIZE
JAMAICA
HAITI
PUERTO RICO (USA)
GUATEMALA
HONDURAS
ST K. & N.
ANT. & BARB.
EL SALVADOR
GUADELOUPE (Fr)
NICARAGUA
NETH. ANT.
GRENADA
DOM.
MARTINIQUE (Fr)
ST LUCIA
COSTA RICA
BARBADOS
ST VINCENT & GREN.
PANAMA
TR. & TOB.
VENEZUELA
GUYANA
COLOMBIA
SURINAME
FRENCH GUIANA (Fr)
ECUADOR
PERU
BRAZIL
BOLIVIA
PARAGUAY
CHILE
ARGENTINA
URUGUAY
FALKLANDS IS. (UK)

66

Current political systems

2019

- ● established democracy
- ● weak, uncertain, or transitional democracy
- ● effective or formal one-party rule
- ● monarchy or theocracy
- ● state of disorder
- ● dependent territory

RUSSIA

KAZAKHSTAN

MONGOLIA

UKRAINE

MOLDOVA

GEORGIA

UZBEKISTAN

KYRGYZSTAN

NORTH KOREA

JAPAN

TURKEY

ARMENIA

AZER.

TURKMEN.

TAJIKISTAN

SOUTH KOREA

MAC. REP OF

N. CYPRUS (Turk)

CYPRUS

LEB.

SYRIA

IRAQ

IRAN

AFGHANISTAN

CHINA

TAIWAN

ISRAEL

JORDAN

KUWAIT

BAHRAIN

PALESTINE

QATAR

U.A.E.

EGYPT

SAUDI ARABIA

OMAN

PAKISTAN

NEPAL

BHUTAN

INDIA

BANGLADESH

MYANMAR

LAOS

PHILIPPINES

SUDAN

ERITREA

YEMEN

DJIBOUTI

THAILAND

VIETNAM

CAMBODIA

ETHIOPIA

SRI LANKA

SOUTH SUDAN

C.A.R.

SOMALIA

MALDIVES

BRUNEI

UGANDA

KENYA

MALAYSIA

SINGAPORE

D.R. CONGO

RWANDA

BURUNDI

SEYCHELLES

TANZANIA

COMOROS

INDONESIA

PAPUA NEW GUINEA

SOLOMON ISLANDS

ZAMBIA

MALAWI

MADAGASCAR

TIMOR-LESTE

ZIMBABWE

MAURITIUS

BOTSWANA

MOZAMBIQUE

SWAZILAND

LESOTHO

AUSTRALIA

NEW ZEALAND

MICRONESIA, FED. ST. OF ○
MARSHALL IS. ○
PALAU ○
NAURU ○
KIRIBATI ○
TUVALU ●
SAMOA ●
VANUATU ●
FIJI ●
COOK IS. (NZ) ○
TONGA ●
NEW CALEDONIA (Fr) ○
FRENCH POLYNESIA (Fr) ○

In **2019,**
for the first time,
there were
**no military
dictatorships**

62m
state of
disorder

6m
dependent
territory

67

Transition to and from democracy

Most recent transition to weak or established democracy
with universal suffrage

2019

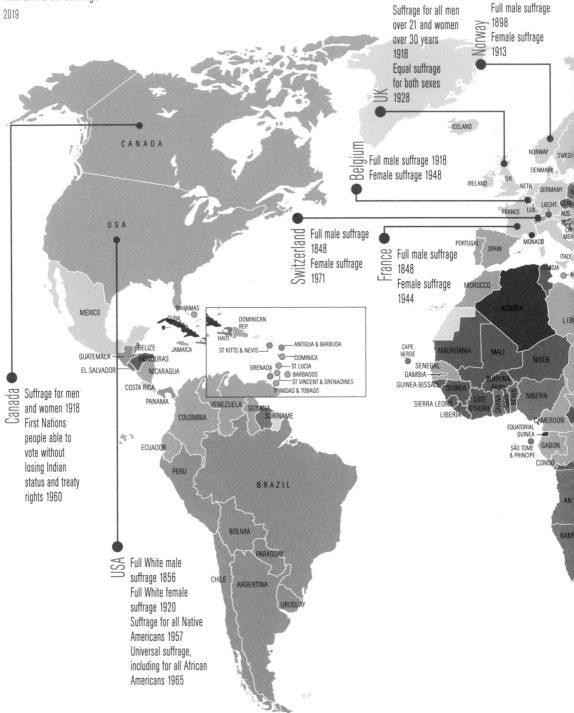

Norway
Full male suffrage 1898
Female suffrage 1913

UK
Suffrage for all men over 21 and women over 30 years 1918
Equal suffrage for both sexes 1928

Belgium
Full male suffrage 1918
Female suffrage 1948

Switzerland
Full male suffrage 1848
Female suffrage 1971

France
Full male suffrage 1848
Female suffrage 1944

Canada
Suffrage for men and women 1918
First Nations people able to vote without losing Indian status and treaty rights 1960

USA
Full White male suffrage 1856
Full White female suffrage 1920
Suffrage for all Native Americans 1957
Universal suffrage, including for all African Americans 1965

CANADA

USA

MEXICO

BAHAMAS
CUBA
HAITI
DOMINICAN REP.
ST KITTS & NEVIS
ANTIGUA & BARBUDA
DOMINICA
GRENADA
ST LUCIA
BARBADOS
ST VINCENT & GRENADINES
TRINIDAD & TOBAGO
JAMAICA

BELIZE
GUATEMALA
HONDURAS
EL SALVADOR
NICARAGUA
COSTA RICA
PANAMA

VENEZUELA
COLOMBIA
GUYANA
SURINAME
ECUADOR
PERU
BRAZIL
BOLIVIA
PARAGUAY
CHILE
ARGENTINA
URUGUAY

ICELAND
NORWAY
SWED
DENMARK
IRELAND
UK
NETH
GERMANY
FRANCE
LUX
LIECHT
L
CZ.R
SI
AUS
CH
MO
MONACO
PORTUGAL
SPAIN
ITALY
TUNISIA
MOROCCO
ALGERIA
LIB

CAPE VERDE
MAURITANIA
MALI
NIGER
SENEGAL
GAMBIA
GUINEA-BISSAU
GUINEA
BURKINA FASO
NIGERIA
SIERRA LEONE
CÔTE D'IVOIRE
GHANA
TOGO
BENIN
LIBERIA
CAMEROON
EQUATORIAL GUINEA
SÃO TOME & PRINCIPE
GABON
CONGO
AN
NAM

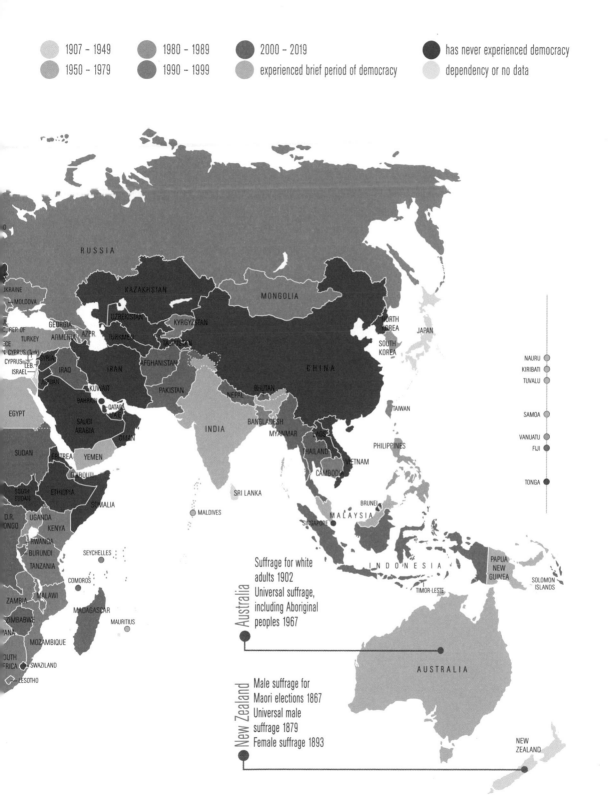

1907 – 1949
1950 – 1979
1980 – 1989
1990 – 1999
2000 – 2019
experienced brief period of democracy
has never experienced democracy
dependency or no data

RUSSIA

UKRAINE
MOLDOVA
GEORGIA
REP OF
TURKEY
CYPRUS (Turk)
CYPRUS
LEB.
ISRAEL
SYRIA
IRAQ
EGYPT
SUDAN
ERITREA
YEMEN
DJIBOUTI
SOUTH SUDAN
ETHIOPIA
SOMALIA
D.R. CONGO
UGANDA
KENYA
RWANDA
BURUNDI
TANZANIA
ZAMBIA
MALAWI
ZIMBABWE
MOZAMBIQUE
SOUTH AFRICA
SWAZILAND
LESOTHO
MADAGASCAR
MAURITIUS
SEYCHELLES
COMOROS

KAZAKHSTAN
UZBEKISTAN
TURKMEN.
KYRGYZSTAN
TAJIKISTAN
AZER.
ARMENIA
IRAN
AFGHANISTAN
KUWAIT
BAHRAIN
QATAR
U.A.E.
SAUDI ARABIA
OMAN
PAKISTAN

MONGOLIA

CHINA

NORTH KOREA
SOUTH KOREA
JAPAN

NEPAL
BHUTAN
INDIA
BANGLADESH
MYANMAR
LAOS
THAILAND
VIETNAM
CAMBODIA
SRI LANKA
MALDIVES

TAIWAN

PHILIPPINES

BRUNEI
MALAYSIA
SINGAPORE
INDONESIA
TIMOR-LESTE

PAPUA NEW GUINEA
SOLOMON ISLANDS

NAURU
KIRIBATI
TUVALU
SAMOA
VANUATU
FIJI
TONGA

Australia
Suffrage for white adults 1902
Universal suffrage, including Aboriginal peoples 1967

AUSTRALIA

New Zealand
Male suffrage for Maori elections 1867
Universal male suffrage 1879
Female suffrage 1893

NEW ZEALAND

69

Religious rights

Faith is often a matter of government policy, and in some countries is the cornerstone of the state. Almost a quarter of the world's states have a formal link to a religion enshrined in their constitution or laws. What this means in practice varies widely.

An official religion can mean intolerance, discrimination, or repression for other faiths – but a state-backed religion has also proved to be compatible with secularism in the state and tolerance in society. The greatest intolerance and violence can spring from religious groups that are, or were at one time, marginalized by the state.

Sharia

The Islamic system of law (Sharia) derives from four sources – the Quran, accounts of the life of the Prophet, reasoning, and the established consensus of juridical opinion. It reaches more widely than Western ideas of law, and covers how to live virtuously as well as legal norms and crimes.

Sharia has largely been replaced by secular (Western) law in most countries, with the exception of family law. Towards the end of the 20th century, some movements and some governments in Islamic countries started to give increased weight to Sharia. Only two countries exclusively rely on it today.

State attitude towards religion

2018 or most recent available data

- discriminates against all religions
- favours religion of majority and interferes with others
- favours religion of majority, tolerates all others
- tolerates all religions
- no data
- • state religion established in law

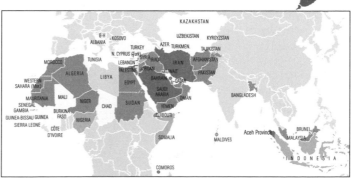

Legal system in Muslim majority states

2019

- Islamic law only – based on Sharia
- combination of Islamic and secular laws
- co-existence of Islamic and secular laws
- in flux
- secular law only

Human rights

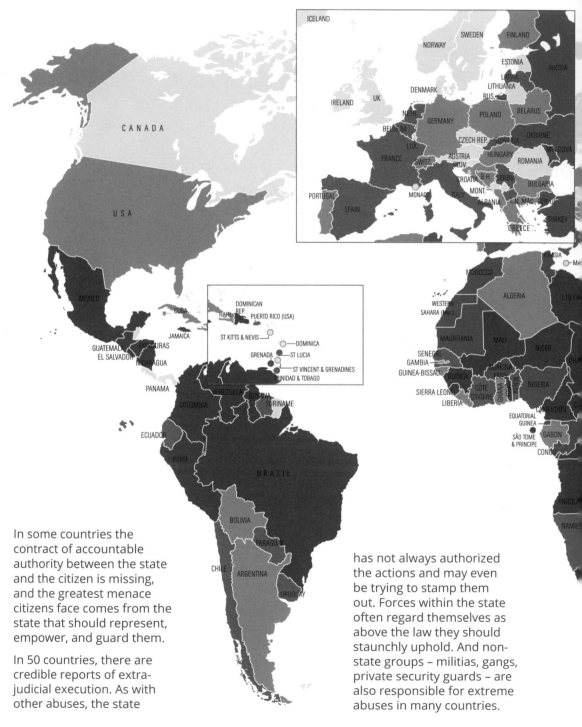

In some countries the contract of accountable authority between the state and the citizen is missing, and the greatest menace citizens face comes from the state that should represent, empower, and guard them.

In 50 countries, there are credible reports of extra-judicial execution. As with other abuses, the state has not always authorized the actions and may even be trying to stamp them out. Forces within the state often regard themselves as above the law they should staunchly uphold. And non-state groups – militias, gangs, private security guards – are also responsible for extreme abuses in many countries.

Extreme abuses of human rights

Worst form of abuse for which there are credible reports

2017 and 2018

● extra-judicial executions and other lethal force

● torture

● arbitrary arrest and detention

● mistreatment by police and/or prison authorities

● violent and/or abusive treatment of refugees, asylum seekers, or immigrants

● no human rights abuses recorded

● no data available

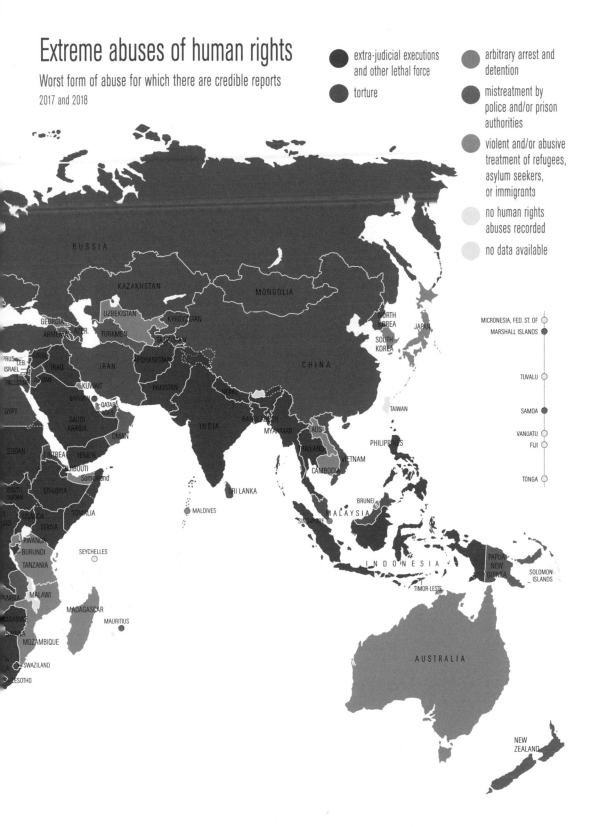

73

Judicial killings

Status of death penalty
As of 31 December 2018
USA, 2019

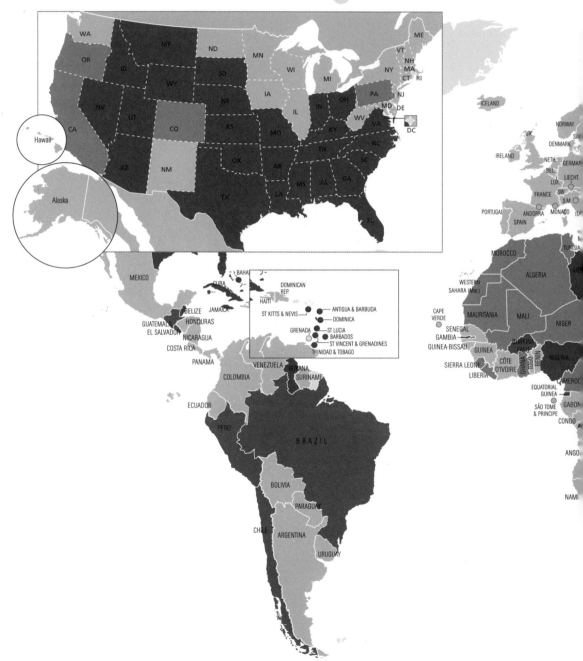

retentionist
retains death penalty for ordinary crimes

abolitionist for ordinary crimes only
law provides for death penalty only for exceptional crimes such as crimes under military law or crimes committed in exceptional circumstances

abolitionist in practice
retains death penalty for ordinary crimes such as murder but has not executed anyone during past 10 years and is believed to have a policy or established practice of not carrying out executions

abolitionist for all crimes
law does not provide for the death penalty for any crime

no data

The foundational idea of human rights is that there is something special and deserving of respect about every person.

Killing people, whether done according to that country's laws or illegally and arbitrarily, reveals an erosion of that respect.

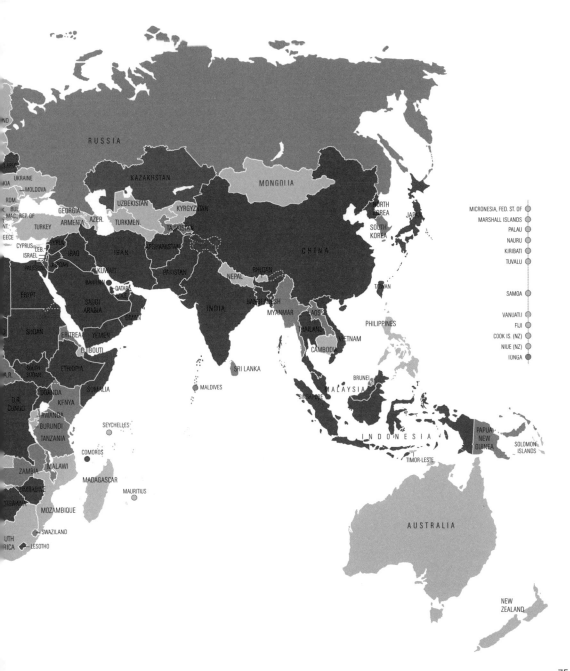

RUSSIA

KAZAKHSTAN

MONGOLIA

UZBEKISTAN

KYRGYZSTAN

UKRAINE

MOLDOVA

ROM.

BUL.

MAC. REP. OF

GEORGIA

ARMENIA

AZER.

TURKMEN.

TAJIKISTAN

NORTH KOREA

JAPAN

EECE

TURKEY

CYPRUS

LEB.

ISRAEL

PALESTINE

SYRIA

IRAQ

IRAN

AFGHANISTAN

SOUTH KOREA

CHINA

JORDAN

KUWAIT

BAHRAIN

QATAR

PAKISTAN

NEPAL

BHUTAN

TAIWAN

MICRONESIA, FED. ST. OF

MARSHALL ISLANDS

PALAU

NAURU

KIRIBATI

TUVALU

EGYPT

SAUDI ARABIA

OMAN

INDIA

BANGLADESH

MYANMAR

LAOS

SAMOA

SUDAN

ERITREA

YEMEN

THAILAND

VIETNAM

PHILIPPINES

VANUATU

FIJI

COOK IS. (NZ)

NIUE (NZ)

TONGA

DJIBOUTI

CAMBODIA

C.A.R.

SOUTH SUDAN

ETHIOPIA

SRI LANKA

MALDIVES

BRUNEI

UGANDA

SOMALIA

MALAYSIA

D.R. CONGO

KENYA

SINGAPORE

RWANDA

SEYCHELLES

INDONESIA

PAPUA NEW GUINEA

SOLOMON ISLANDS

BURUNDI

TANZANIA

COMOROS

TIMOR-LESTE

ZAMBIA

MALAWI

MADAGASCAR

MAURITIUS

MOZAMBIQUE

AUSTRALIA

ZIMBABWE

TSWANA

SWAZILAND

UTH

RICA

LESOTHO

NEW ZEALAND

Sex trafficking

Number of victims detected by police on selected international and domestic routes
2014–2017

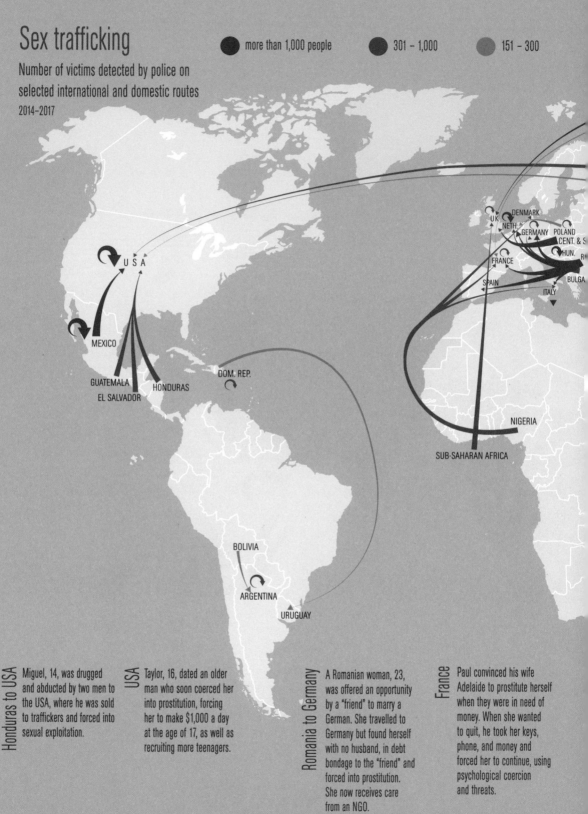

Honduras to USA Miguel, 14, was drugged and abducted by two men to the USA, where he was sold to traffickers and forced into sexual exploitation.

USA Taylor, 16, dated an older man who soon coerced her into prostitution, forcing her to make $1,000 a day at the age of 17, as well as recruiting more teenagers.

Romania to Germany A Romanian woman, 23, was offered an opportunity by a "friend" to marry a German. She travelled to Germany but found herself with no husband, in debt bondage to the "friend" and forced into prostitution. She now receives care from an NGO.

France Paul convinced his wife Adelaide to prostitute herself when they were in need of money. When she wanted to quit, he took her keys, phone, and money and forced her to continue, using psychological coercion and threats.

Sex trafficking is a global industry generating annual profits each year worth about $100 billion. It is estimated that 4.8 million people, 99% of them women and girls, were forced into sexual exploitation in 2016. In many countries, victims of sex trafficking are arrested, tried, and punished for acts they were forced to carry out.

CHINA

EAST ASIA & PACIFIC

MYANMAR
THAILAND
CAMBODIA
VIETNAM
PHILIPPINES

MALAYSIA

INDONESIA

1 million
children forced into sexual exploitation in 2016

Nigeria to Italy
Promised a job in Italy, when Faith arrived she was informed she had to pay back a debt of $50,000. Threatened and forced into prostitution, she managed to escape.

Syria to Lebanon
Maya, 22, fled Syria due to conflict, was promised a job in a factory but forced into prostitution along with 70 other Syrian women in Lebanon. A victim of severe physical and psychological violence.

Cambodia
When in debt, Lai's mother started to sell her 12-year-old daughter to men. This went on for about two years until Lai fled and found security in a residence for victims of sex trafficking.

Children's rights

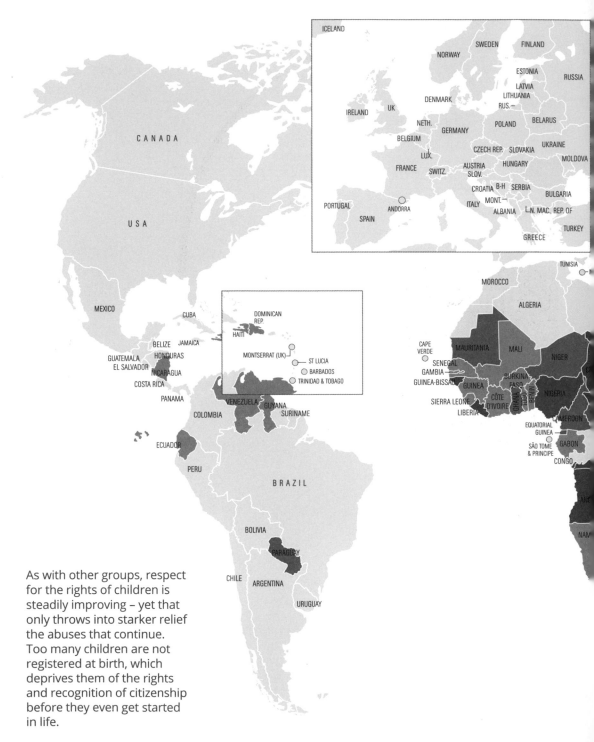

As with other groups, respect for the rights of children is steadily improving – yet that only throws into starker relief the abuses that continue. Too many children are not registered at birth, which deprives them of the rights and recognition of citizenship before they even get started in life.

Unregistered children

Unregistered births as percentage of all births

2018 or latest available data

70% or more **30% – 49%** **19% or fewer**

50% – 69% **10% – 29%** **no data**

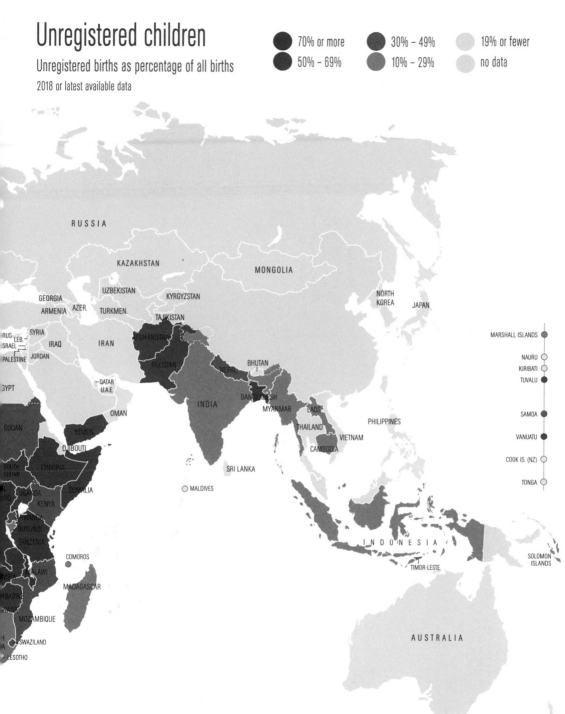

RUSSIA

KAZAKHSTAN

MONGOLIA

UZBEKISTAN KYRGYZSTAN

NORTH KOREA

JAPAN

GEORGIA AZER. TURKMEN. TAJIKISTAN

ARMENIA

SYRIA AFGHANISTAN MARSHALL ISLANDS

NUS LEB. IRAQ IRAN

SRAEL JORDAN PAKISTAN BHUTAN NEPAL NAURU

PALESTINE KIRIBATI

QATAR TUVALU

GYPT U.A.E.

OMAN INDIA BANGLADESH MYANMAR LAOS

SUDAN YEMEN THAILAND PHILIPPINES SAMOA

DJIBOUTI VIETNAM VANUATU

SOUTH ETHIOPIA CAMBODIA COOK IS. (NZ)

SUTAN SRI LANKA

SOMALIA TONGA

UGANDA MALDIVES

KENYA

RWANDA

BURUNDI

TANZANIA

COMOROS INDONESIA

MALAWI SOLOMON ISLANDS

MADAGASCAR TIMOR-LESTE

MBABWE

MOZAMBIQUE

SWAZILAND AUSTRALIA

LESOTHO

NEW ZEALAND

Children at work

Economically active children aged 5–17 years
as percentage of age-group
2019

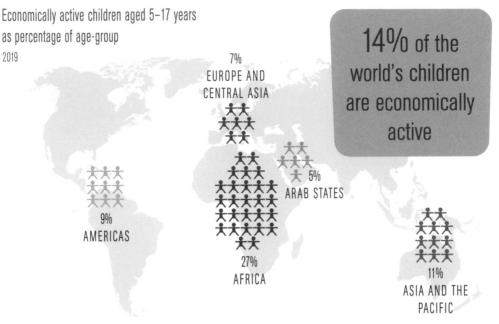

7%
EUROPE AND
CENTRAL ASIA

14% of the world's children are economically active

5%
ARAB STATES

9%
AMERICAS

27%
AFRICA

11%
ASIA AND THE
PACIFIC

Nearly one child in ten is economically active, and half of them are doing hazardous work, involving tasks that will cripple them in later years. Although the situation is improving, the rate of progress has slowed. Of those children aged 5 to 14 years who work, a third do not attend school.

Children at risk

Number of children employed in hazardous work

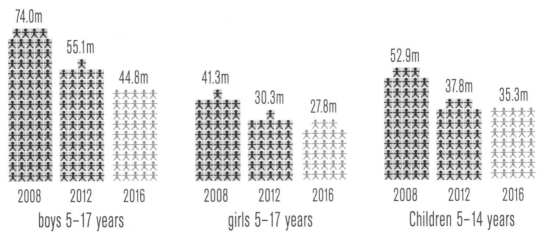

74.0m   55.1m   44.8m
2008   2012   2016
boys 5–17 years

41.3m   30.3m   27.8m
2008   2012   2016
girls 5–17 years

52.9m   37.8m   35.3m
2008   2012   2016
Children 5–14 years

Children not in school

Percentage of children of primary-school age not attending school by region
2017

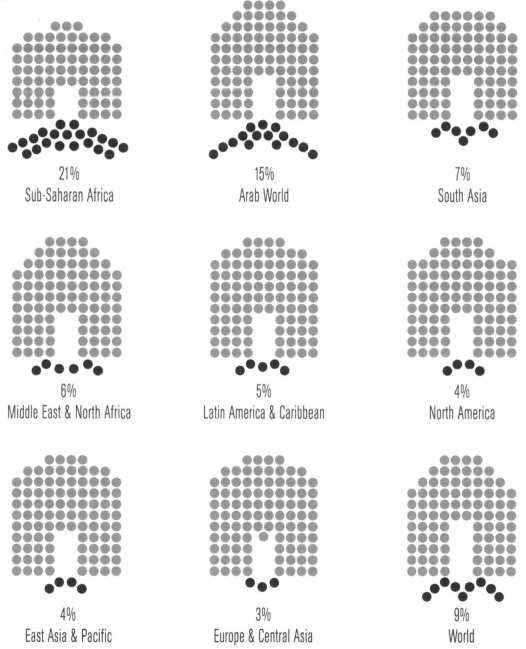

● 1% in school
● 1% not in school

21%
Sub-Saharan Africa

15%
Arab World

7%
South Asia

6%
Middle East & North Africa

5%
Latin America & Caribbean

4%
North America

4%
East Asia & Pacific

3%
Europe & Central Asia

9%
World

Nearly one child in ten who should be attending primary school does not –
more than 63 million absentees between the ages of 5 and 11.

Women's rights

Equal rights

Gender Inequality Index score

2017

| ● 71 or more *least equal* | ● 31 – 50 | ● 4 – 10 *most equal* |
| ● 51 – 70 | ● 11 – 30 | ● no data |

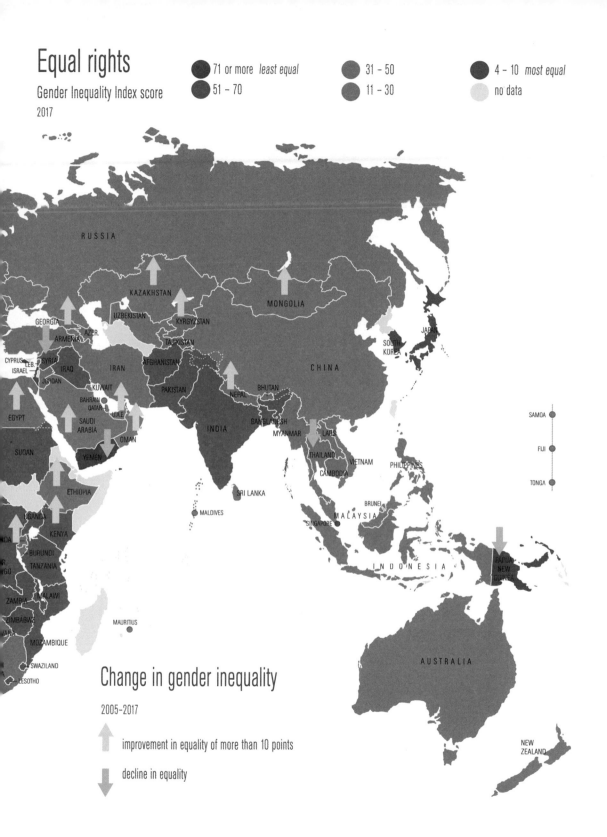

Change in gender inequality

2005–2017

⬆ improvement in equality of more than 10 points

⬇ decline in equality

Women in parliament

Percentage of seats in parliament held by women

2017 or latest available data

- more than 30%
- 21% – 30%
- 11% – 20%
- 10% or fewer
- no data

Included: all heads of government and acting heads of government in power for 100 days or more.

Excluded: heads of state and acting heads of government in power for fewer than 100 days.
2018

In the 1950s, women as heads of democratic governments were unknown; in the 1960s and 1970s, they were a rarity; in the 1980s and 1990s they were uncommon but getting steadily less so. Yet today the question remains, why so few? Only 60 democratic countries have ever had a woman head of government, even counting appointed prime ministers in presidential systems.

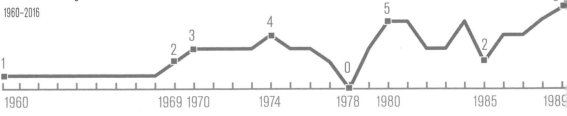

Powerful women

Number of countries with female heads of government

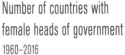

1960–2016

RUSSIA

KAZAKHSTAN

MONGOLIA

GEORGIA
UZBEKISTAN
KYRGYZSTAN
TURKEY
ARMENIA
AZER.
TURKMEN.
TAJIKISTAN

NORTH
KOREA
JAPAN

SOUTH
KOREA

CYPRUS
SYRIA
LEB.
IRAQ
AFGHANISTAN
ISRAEL
JORDAN
IRAN

CHINA

PALESTINE

KUWAIT
PAKISTAN
NEPAL
BHUTAN

EGYPT
BAHRAIN
QATAR
U.A.E.
SAUDI
ARABIA
OMAN

INDIA
BANGLADESH
MYANMAR
LAOS
THAILAND

SUDAN
ERITREA
YEMEN
VIETNAM
CAMBODIA

PHILIPPINES

DJIBOUTI

SOUTH
SUDAN
ETHIOPIA

SRI LANKA

A.R.

R. CONGO
UGANDA
SOMALIA
MALDIVES
BRUNEI
M A L A Y S I A

RWANDA
KENYA
SINGAPORE

URUNDI

TANZANIA
SEYCHELLES

COMOROS
I N D O N E S I A
PAPUA
NEW
GUINEA

ZAMBIA
MALAWI
MADAGASCAR
SOLOMON
ISLANDS

ZIMBABWE
TIMOR-LESTE

MAURITIUS

TSWANA
MOZAMBIQUE

SWAZILAND

UTH
LESOTHO
RICA

MICRONESIA, FED. ST. OF ●
MARSHALL ISLANDS ●
PALAU ◉
NAURU ◉
KIRIBATI ●
TUVALU ◉

SAMOA ●

VANUATU ●
FIJI ◉

TONGA ●

A U S T R A L I A

18

16

17

16

20

NEW
ZEALAND

15

16

15

17

12

13

10

10

8

7

6

3

00 1992   1998 2000 2003   2011 2014   2019

85

LGBTQ+ rights

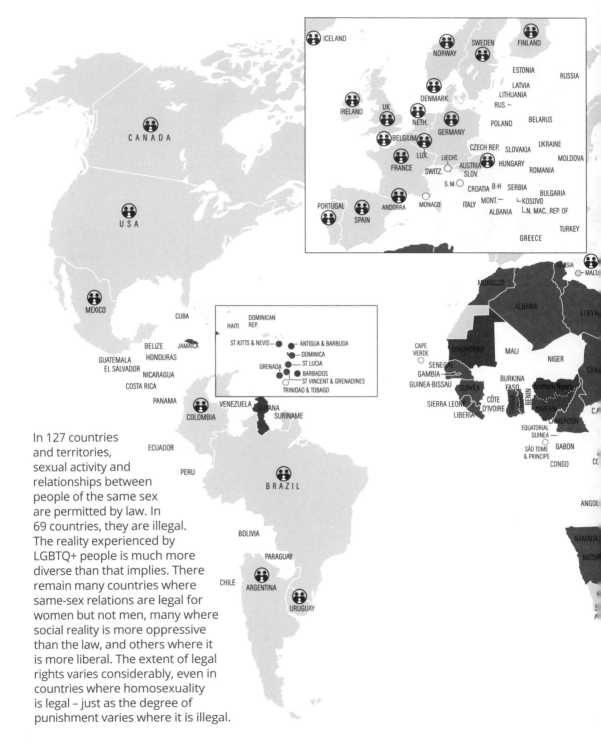

ICELAND

NORWAY SWEDEN FINLAND

ESTONIA RUSSIA
LATVIA
LITHUANIA
DENMARK RUS.—

IRELAND UK NETH. POLAND BELARUS

BELGIUM GERMANY
LUX. CZECH REP. SLOVAKIA UKRAINE
FRANCE LIECHT. MOLDOVA
SWITZ. AUSTRIA HUNGARY ROMANIA
SLOV.
S.M. CROATIA B-H SERBIA BULGARIA
PORTUGAL ANDORRA MONACO MONT.— └KOSOVO
ITALY ALBANIA ⌐N. MAC. REP. OF
SPAIN
TURKEY
GREECE

CANADA

USA

MEXICO

TUNISIA MALT
MOROCCO
ALGERIA LIBYA

CUBA

HAITI DOMINICAN CAPE
REP. VERDE MAURITANIA MALI NIGER
BELIZE JAMAICA ST KITTS & NEVIS ANTIGUA & BARBUDA SENEGAL CHA
GUATEMALA HONDURAS DOMINICA GAMBIA BURKINA
EL SALVADOR GRENADA ST LUCIA GUINEA-BISSAU FASO BENIN
NICARAGUA BARBADOS GUINEA CÔTE NIGERIA
COSTA RICA ST VINCENT & GRENADINES SIERRA LEONE D'IVOIRE CA
PANAMA TRINIDAD & TOBAGO LIBERIA CAMEROON
VENEZUELA GUYANA EQUATORIAL
COLOMBIA SURINAME GUINEA —
SÃO TOME GABON
& PRINCIPE CONGO CO
ECUADOR

PERU ANGOL

BRAZIL

BOLIVIA NAMIBIA BOTSW

PARAGUAY

CHILE ARGENTINA

URUGUAY

In 127 countries
and territories,
sexual activity and
relationships between
people of the same sex
are permitted by law. In
69 countries, they are illegal.
The reality experienced by
LGBTQ+ people is much more
diverse than that implies. There
remain many countries where
same-sex relations are legal for
women but not men, many where
social reality is more oppressive
than the law, and others where it
is more liberal. The extent of legal
rights varies considerably, even in
countries where homosexuality
is legal – just as the degree of
punishment varies where it is illegal.

Legal status

Of same-sex sexual
acts & relationships
2019

Punishment where illegal:
- death penalty
- prison sentence over 10 years
- prison sentence up to 10 years

Extent of right where legal:
- same-sex acts legal but no legal status for same-sex relationships
- civil partnership/union allowed
- full marriage rights for same-sex couples
- legal status unclear
- no data

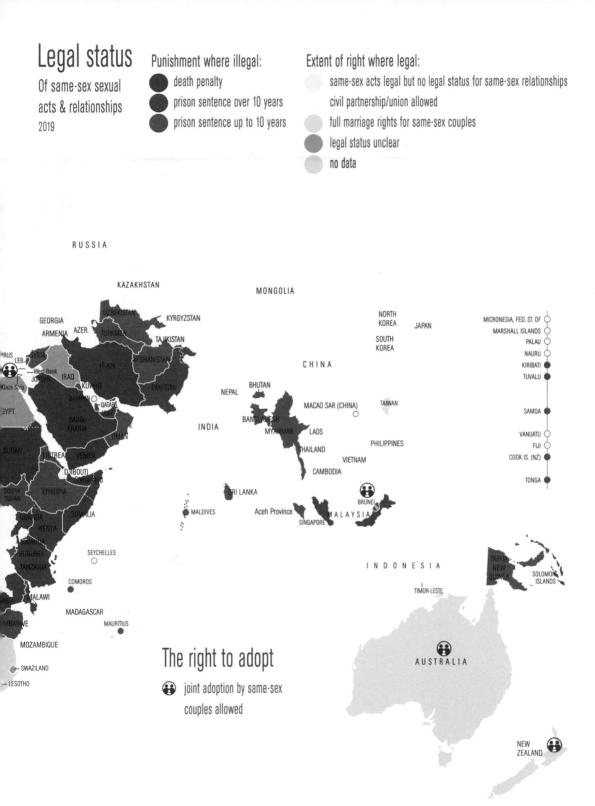

The right to adopt

😊 joint adoption by same-sex
couples allowed

Acceptance of LGB people in military

2019

Lesbian, gay, and bisexual people:

 may serve in the military   may not serve in the military   no data

The acceptability or not of LGB people serving in the military is an interesting litmus test of the degree to which acceptance of homosexuality is normalized and people are treated as citizens – with the same rights, duties, and choices – regardless of sexual preference.

Minorities

RUSSIA

RUS.

BELARUS

UKRAINE

MOLDOVA

CROATIA B-H SERBIA

KOSOVO

ALBANIA N. MAC., REP. OF

TUNISIA

MOROCCO

ALGERIA

LIBYA

MEXICO

CUBA

DOMINICAN REP.

JAMAICA

HAITI

GUATEMALA

EL SALVADOR

HONDURAS

NICARAGUA

MAURITANIA MALI NIGER

SENEGAL

GAMBIA

GUINEA-BISSAU GUINEA

SIERRA LEONE

LIBERIA CÔTE D'IVOIRE

BURKINA FASO

NIGERIA

TOGO BENIN

CHAD

C.A.R.

CAMEROON

VENEZUELA GUYANA

COLOMBIA

SURINAME

EQUATORIAL GUINEA

SÃO TOME & PRINCIPE GABON

CONGO

D.R. CON

ECUADOR

PERU

ANGOLA

The Peoples under Threat index produced by Minorities Rights Group International identifies country situations where communities face the risk of genocide, mass killing, or systematic violent repression. It is based on a range of indicators of conflict, prior genocide or politicide, flight, group division, and democracy or governance indicators, as well as the OECD country risk classification.

BOLIVIA

PARAGUAY

ARGENTINA

Peoples under threat

Index of risk to communities
of genocide and mass killing

2019 score

- **20.0 or more** *highest risk*
- **15.0 – 19.9**
- **10.0 – 14.9**
- **5.0 – 9.9**
- **less than 5.0** *lowest risk*
- **no data or** *extremely low risk*

Freedom

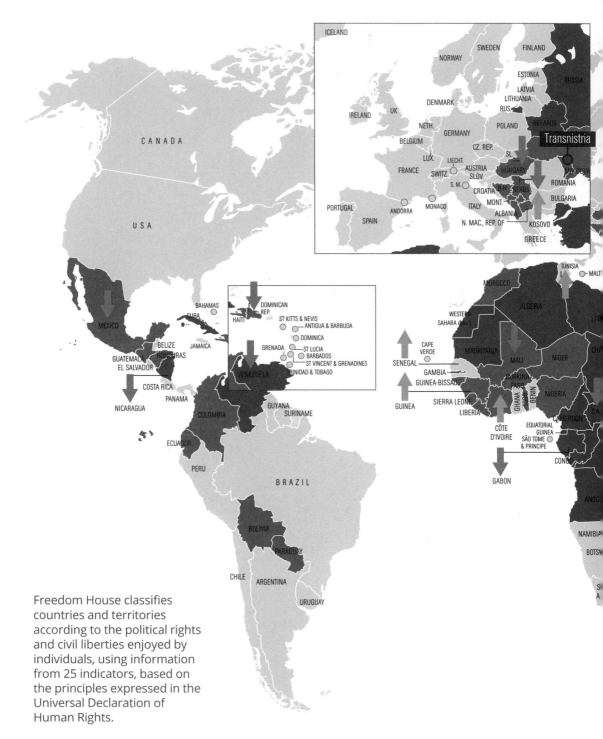

Freedom House classifies countries and territories according to the political rights and civil liberties enjoyed by individuals, using information from 25 indicators, based on the principles expressed in the Universal Declaration of Human Rights.

Freedom in the world

Freedom House rating

2018

● free ● partly free ● not free

○ disputed territories

RUSSIA

UKRAINE

KAZAKHSTAN

MONGOLIA

NORTH KOREA

JAPAN

South Ossetia

Crimea

GEORGIA

ARMENIA

AZER.

UZBEKISTAN

KYRGYZSTAN

Pakistani Kashmir

SOUTH KOREA

CHINA

TURKEY

CYPRUS LEB.

ISRAEL

PALESTINE

JORDAN

SYRIA

IRAQ

IRAN

TURKMEN.

TAJIKISTAN

Nagorno-Karabakh

AFGHANISTAN

Indian Kashmir

EGYPT

KUWAIT

BAHRAIN

QATAR

SAUDI ARABIA

OMAN

PAKISTAN

NEPAL

BHUTAN

TAIWAN

HONG KONG SAR (CHINA)

SUDAN

ERITREA

YEMEN

Somaliland

INDIA

BANGLADESH

MYANMAR

LAOS

VIETNAM

PHILIPPINES

SOUTH SUDAN

ETHIOPIA

DJIBOUTI

SOMALIA

UGANDA

SRI LANKA

THAILAND

CAMBODIA

BRUNEI

MALAYSIA

MALDIVES

SINGAPORE

DR CONGO

KENYA

RWANDA

BURUNDI

SEYCHELLES

COMOROS

TANZANIA

INDONESIA

PAPUA NEW GUINEA

ZAMBIA

MADAGASCAR

MAURITIUS

TIMOR-LESTE

SOLOMON ISLANDS

ZIMBABWE

MOZAMBIQUE

AUSTRALIA

SWAZILAND

LESOTHO

NEW ZEALAND

MICRONESIA, FED. ST. OF ○

MARSHALL ISLANDS ○

PALAU ○

NAURU ○

KIRIBATI ○

TUVALU ○

SAMOA ○

VANUATU ○

FIJI ●

TONGA ○

Changing times

Increase or decrease in freedom

2008–2018

↑ increase

↓ decrease

War and peace

Any war is too much war. That said, from 1995 to 2010 there were fewer, less lethal wars each year. This was the peace dividend from the end of the Cold War in 1990, along with a reduced risk of nuclear conflagration and the use of more economic resources for peaceful purposes. It was possible because international cooperation increased and helped end wars and monitor peace agreements.

But those gains have not been sustained. Since 2010, the number of wars has increased, the number of international peace operations has declined, the number of new peace agreements has fallen away, and the rate of casualties from war has risen sharply.

Military spending also picked up pace in 1999, increasing every year until 2012, when it stabilised following the 2008 to 2009 financial and economic crisis, before starting to increase again in 2015. The global total is now as high as just before the end of the Cold War. Whether the economic impact of the Covid-19 pandemic will slow spending again has yet to be seen.

There are still around 13,000 nuclear warheads in the world. Even a handful striking a country would be a disaster so these arsenals are hardly insignificant, but compared to 65,000 or so warheads at the height of the Cold War, the reduction has been a real achievement. Unfortunately, it is unclear how strong the commitment is to further reductions. The USA and Russia each claimed the other cheated over the Intermediate Nuclear Forces Treaty of 1987; the USA announced it would abandon the treaty in 2018 and Russia followed suit. During 2019 and 2020, neither country would commit to continuing a treaty that limits long-range missiles and bombers.

All this reflects the increasingly toxic nature of geopolitics, both at the global level – USA vs China, NATO vs Russia – and in regional rivalries such as between Iran and Saudi Arabia, and India and Pakistan. That toxin hinders cooperation to end armed conflicts. It is the reason why the global system of conflict management is weaker than at any time since 1990. And it means that the appetite for cooperation is declining at the very moment when the world faces a range of challenges – climate change, pandemics, potential cyber vulnerability – to which responding cooperatively is the realistic way forward.

Wars this century

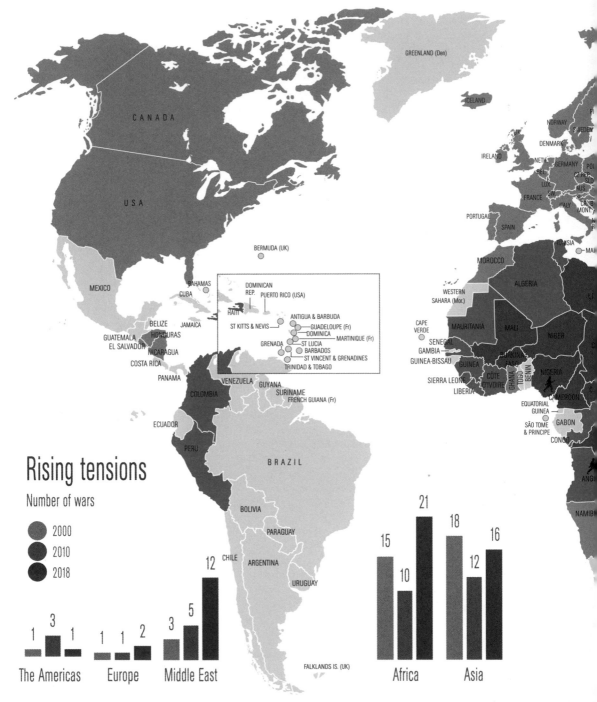

GREENLAND (Den)

ICELAND

CANADA

NORWAY
SWEDEN

DENMARK

IRELAND
NETH.
GERMANY
POL
BEL.
CZECH REP.
SLO
LUX.
AUS
FRANCE
SW
ITALY
CRO
MONT.

USA

PORTUGAL
SPAIN

TUNISIA MAL

BERMUDA (UK)

MOROCCO
WESTERN
SAHARA (Mor.)
ALGERIA
LI

MEXICO
BAHAMAS
CUBA

DOMINICAN
REP.
PUERTO RICO (USA)

HAITI

CAPE
VERDE
MAURITANIA
MALI
NIGER

ANTIGUA & BARBUDA
ST KITTS & NEVIS
GUADELOUPE (Fr)
DOMINICA
MARTINIQUE (Fr)
GRENADA
ST LUCIA
BARBADOS
ST VINCENT & GRENADINES
TRINIDAD & TOBAGO

SENEGAL
GAMBIA
GUINEA-BISSAU
BURKINA
FASO
GUINEA
CÔTE
D'IVOIRE
GHANA
TOGO
BENIN
NIGERIA

BELIZE
JAMAICA
GUATEMALA
HONDURAS
EL SALVADOR
NICARAGUA
COSTA RICA
PANAMA

SIERRA LEONE
LIBERIA
CAMEROON

EQUATORIAL
GUINEA
SÃO TOME
& PRINCIPE
GABON
CONGO

VENEZUELA
GUYANA
SURINAME
FRENCH GUIANA (Fr)
COLOMBIA

ECUADOR

PERU
BRAZIL
ANG

Rising tensions

Number of wars

NAMIB

○ 2000
● 2010
● 2018

BOLIVIA

PARAGUAY

CHILE
ARGENTINA

URUGUAY

FALKLANDS IS. (UK)

The Americas
1 3 1

Europe
1 1 2

Middle East
3 5 **12**

Africa
15 10 **21**

Asia
18 12 16

At war

Presence of open armed conflict for political goals
2000–2019

● has experienced armed conflict within national borders

● armed conflict active within national borders as of 2 November 2019

🏃 has *also* sent 500 or more troops to fight in war outside national borders

● has *only* fought war outside national borders

● has not experienced armed conflict

RUSSIA

KAZAKHSTAN

MONGOLIA

UZBEKISTAN

KYRGYZSTAN

TURKMEN.

TAJIKISTAN

NORTH KOREA

JAPAN

SOUTH KOREA

GEORGIA
ARMENIA AZER.
TURKEY

RUS
ISRAEL
LEB.
SYRIA
IRAQ
IRAN
AFGHANISTAN

CHINA

TAIWAN

PALESTINE
JORDAN
KUWAIT
BAHRAIN
QATAR
UAE

PAKISTAN

NEPAL

BHUTAN

BANGLADESH

EGYPT

SAUDI ARABIA

OMAN

INDIA

MYANMAR

LAOS

THAILAND

VIETNAM

PHILIPPINES

SUDAN
ERITREA
YEMEN
DJIBOUTI
SOMALILAND

CAMBODIA

BRUNEI

SOUTH SUDAN
ETHIOPIA
PUNTLAND

MALDIVES

SRI LANKA

MALAYSIA

SINGAPORE

UGANDA
KENYA
SOMALIA

SEYCHELLES

INDONESIA

PAPUA NEW GUINEA

SOLOMON ISLANDS

RWANDA
BURUNDI
TANZANIA

COMOROS

TIMOR-LESTE

MALAWI

MADAGASCAR

MAURITIUS

MBIA
MBABWE
ANA
MOZAMBIQUE

SWAZILAND

LESOTHO

MICRONESIA, FED. ST. OF ○
MARSHALL ISLANDS ○

KIRIBATI ○

SAMOA ○

FIJI ○

TONGA ○

AUSTRALIA

NEW ZEALAND

For 20 years after the US–Soviet Cold War ended in 1990, the world experienced a peace dividend. Though warfare continued, often on a horrifying scale – Rwanda in 1994, Bosnia and Herzegovina in 1992–95, Sudan until 2011, Iraq in 1991 and again from 2003 on – there were actually fewer wars and fewer fatalities. Compared to 50 armed conflicts in 1990, by 2010 there were 31. But then the number increased again, to 52 by 2019.

97

Fighting outside borders

Afghanistan

Countries involved at some point since 2001

as of 2018

location of war

NATO members

other participating
countries

NATO members: Albania, Belgium, Bulgaria, Canada, Croatia, Czech Republic, Denmark, Estonia, France, Germany, Greece, Hungary, Iceland, Italy, Latvia, Lithuania, Luxembourg, Montenegro, Netherlands, Norway, Poland, Portugal, Romania, Slovakia, Slovenia, Spain, Turkey, UK, USA

Other participants: Armenia, Australia, Austria, Azerbaijan, Bahrain, Bosnia-Herzegovina, El Salvador, Finland, Georgia, Iran, Ireland, Jordan, North Macedonia, Malaysia, Mongolia, New Zealand, Pakistan, Singapore, South Korea, Sweden, Switzerland, Tonga, Ukraine, United Arab Emirates

Iraq

Countries involved at some point since 2003

as of end 2018

location of war

participating countries

Albania, Armenia, Australia, Azerbaijan, Bahrain, Belgium, Bosnia-Herzegovina, Bulgaria, Canada, Czech Republic, Denmark, Estonia, France, Georgia, Honduras, Italy, Jordan, Kazakhstan, Latvia, Lithuania, North Macedonia, Moldova, Mongolia, Netherlands, Nicaragua, Norway, Philippines, Poland, Portugal, Romania, Saudi Arabia, Slovakia, South Korea, Spain, Tonga, Ukraine, UAE, UK, USA

D.R. Congo

Countries involved in 2000, 2013, 2017

 location of war

participating countries

Angola, Burundi, Chad, Namibia, Rwanda, Sudan, Uganda, Zimbabwe

Somalia

Countries involved at some point since 2007

 location of war

participating countries

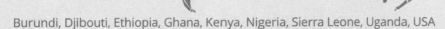

Burundi, Djibouti, Ethiopia, Ghana, Kenya, Nigeria, Sierra Leone, Uganda, USA

Yemen

Countries involved at some point since 2011

as of end 2018

 location of war

participating countries

Bahrain, Egypt, Jordan, Kuwait, Morocco, Qatar, Saudi Arabia, Sudan, UAE, USA

Warlords, ganglords, and militias

Non-state armed forces

Estimated strength of non-state armed forces in all countries

latest available data 2010–2019

10,000 or more

fewer than 10,000

unknown strength

no known non-state armed force

armed conflict fought between non-state forces

Non-state wars

Armed conflicts do not only occur within or between states. The number of armed conflicts in which no state has any part is now greater than the number of armed conflicts involving states – 80 without states in 2019 compared to 52 with states.

Along with that, there has been a marked proliferation of non-state armed forces. By one estimate, the number of armed groups active per armed conflict was 8 in 1950, increasing to 14 in 2010. But even that figure is modest by current standards: in warfare in Syria since 2011, over 1,000 separate armed groups have been identified – in Libya in the same period some 2,000.

The power of private armies and the risk of non-state wars grow when and where the state's ability to impose order is weak. In some parts of some countries the state is essentially absent for extended periods, sometimes because of war, sometimes corruption, and sometimes because the state simply cannot afford to obtain the equipment and train the forces it would need in order to control its territory.

Many militias continue to operate long after the war is over. In those circumstances, local leaders emerge, often enriching themselves by controlling key economic activities: small-scale mining, as in eastern DRC, or the narcotics trade, as in Colombia, Mexico, and Central Asia. If the state does try to restore its authority, its soldiers all too often become part of the problem, terrorizing civilians with theft, rape, and other human rights abuses.

One common abuse in which militias lead the way is recruiting children to fight, often forcibly, always with a brutal, traumatizing impact on the children's lives – even if they survive the war.

Colombia

Colombia   293 children
used

Children at war

Used by non-state armed forces as verified by the UN

2018

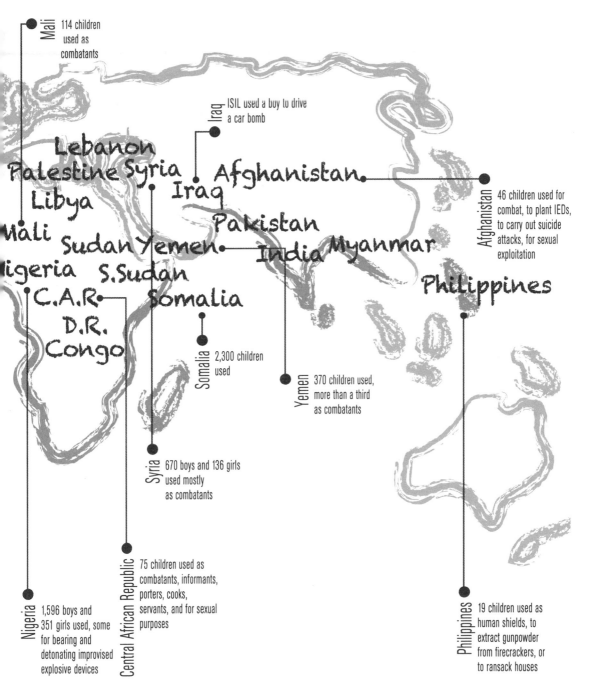

Mali
114 children used as combatants

Iraq
ISIL used a boy to drive a car bomb

Lebanon
Palestine Syria
Libya
Mali
Nigeria
Sudan Yemen
S.Sudan
C.A.R.
D.R.
Congo
Iraq
Afghanistan.
Pakistan
India Myanmar
Philippines
Somalia

Afghanistan
46 children used for combat, to plant IEDs, to carry out suicide attacks, for sexual exploitation

Somalia
2,300 children used

Yemen
370 children used, more than a third as combatants

Syria
670 boys and 136 girls used mostly as combatants

Central African Republic
75 children used as combatants, informants, porters, cooks, servants, and for sexual purposes

Nigeria
1,596 boys and 351 girls used, some for bearing and detonating improvised explosive devices

Philippines
19 children used as human shields, to extract gunpowder from firecrackers, or to ransack houses

Military muscle

ICELAND

NORWAY   SWEDEN   FINLAND

ESTONIA

RUSSIA

LATVIA

DENMARK   LITHUANIA

IRELAND   UK   RUS.—

NETH.   POLAND   BELARUS

BELGIUM   GERMANY

LUX.   CZECH REP.   SLOVAKIA   UKRAINE

FRANCE   AUSTRIA   HUNGARY   MOLDOVA

SWITZ.   SLOV.   ROMANIA

CROATIA   B-H   SERBIA   BULGARIA

PORTUGAL   ITALY   MONT.—   KOSOVO

SPAIN   ALBANIA   N. MAC. REP. OF

GREECE   TURKEY

CANADA

USA

MEXICO

CUBA

DOMINICAN REP.

BELIZE   JAMAICA   HAITI

GUATEMALA   HONDURAS

EL SALVADOR

COSTA RICA   NICARAGUA

PANAMA   TRINIDAD & TOBAGO

COLOMBIA   VENEZUELA   GUYANA

ECUADOR

PERU

BRAZIL

BOLIVIA

PARAGUAY

CHILE   ARGENTINA

URUGUAY

TUNISIA   MALTA

MOROCCO

ALGERIA

LIBYA

CAPE VERDE

MAURITANIA   MALI   NIGER   CHAD

SENEGAL

GAMBIA

GUINEA-BISSAU   GUINEA   BURKINA FASO   NIGERIA

SIERRA LEONE   CÔTE D'IVOIRE   GHANA TOGO BENIN

LIBERIA   CAMEROON   C.A.R.

EQUATORIAL GUINEA

GABON   D.R. CONGO

CONGO

ANGOLA

NAMIBIA

BOTSWANA

SOU AFF

World military spending in 2019 was approximately

$1.9 trillion

Military spending

Military expenditure as a percentage of GDP

2019 or latest available data

- 4.0% or more
- 3.0% – 3.9%
- 2.0% – 2.9%
- 1.0% – 1.9%
- less than 1.0%
- no data

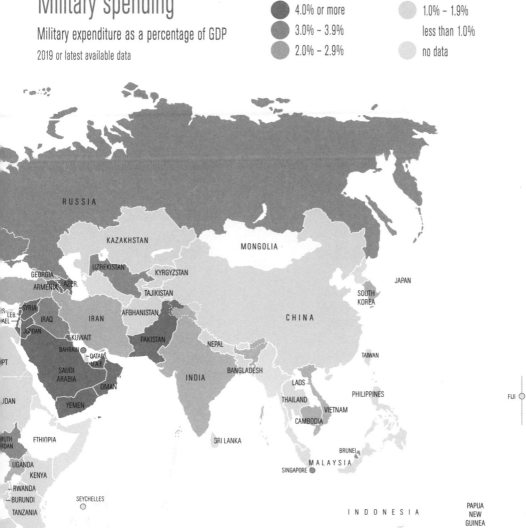

Top military spenders

US$ at 2018 constant prices

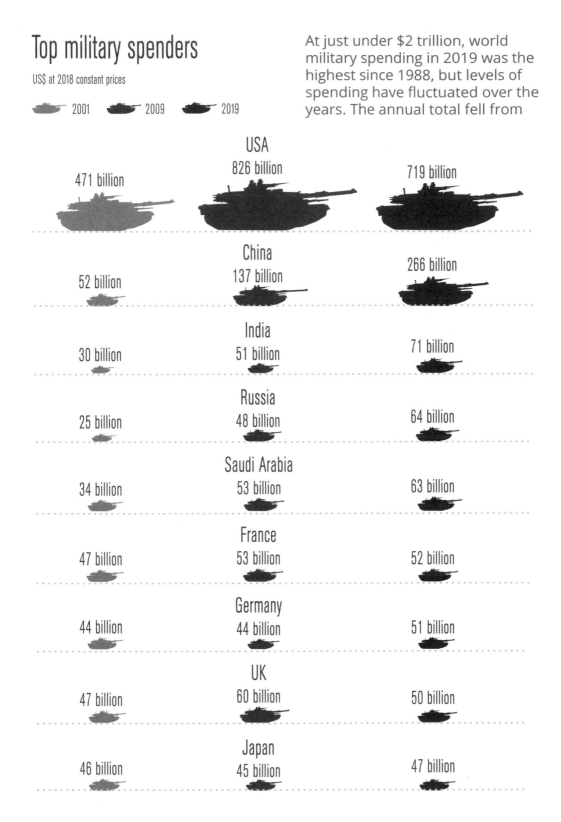

At just under $2 trillion, world military spending in 2019 was the highest since 1988, but levels of spending have fluctuated over the years. The annual total fell from

🔹 2001   🔹 2009   🔹 2019

USA
471 billion   826 billion   719 billion

China
52 billion   137 billion   266 billion

India
30 billion   51 billion   71 billion

Russia
25 billion   48 billion   64 billion

Saudi Arabia
34 billion   53 billion   63 billion

France
47 billion   53 billion   52 billion

Germany
44 billion   44 billion   51 billion

UK
47 billion   60 billion   50 billion

Japan
46 billion   45 billion   47 billion

2011 through 2014 in the wake of the 2008–09 global economic and financial crisis. From 2015, military spending increased steadily. The economic impact of the Covid-19 pandemic means 2019 might turn out to have been a peak year.

Levels of military spending – as of all government spending – reflect priorities and choices about where to use resources. More military spending does not automatically mean more military power, let alone more real security.

Armed forces top ten

Largest regular armed forces

2020

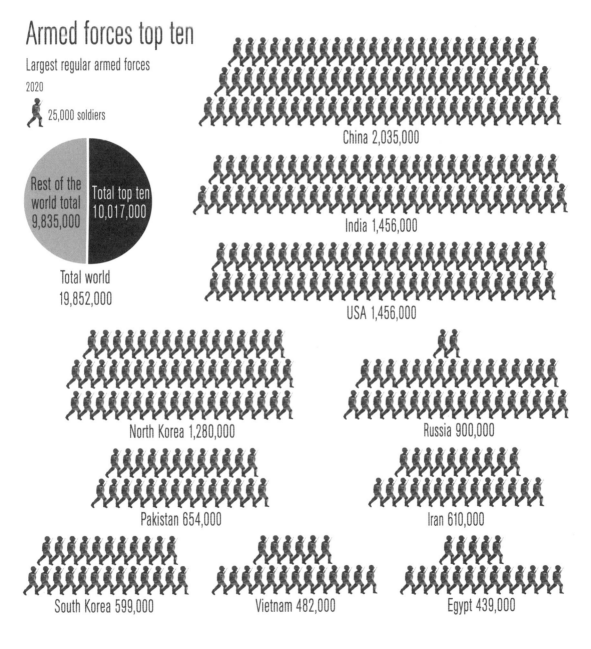

25,000 soldiers

Rest of the world total 9,835,000

Total top ten 10,017,000

Total world 19,852,000

China 2,035,000

India 1,456,000

USA 1,456,000

North Korea 1,280,000

Russia 900,000

Pakistan 654,000

Iran 610,000

South Korea 599,000

Vietnam 482,000

Egypt 439,000

Mass destruction

Declining stockpiles of nuclear warheads

1985–2019

— USA   — USSR

45,000
39,197
24,237
37,000
21,004
27,000
21,000
12,144
17,000
10,577
10,295
12,000
9,600
7,500
7,260
6,500
6,185

1985 1986 1990 1995 2000 2005 2010 2015 2019

In 2019, the global nuclear stockpile amounted to 13,850 warheads and bombs. This was dramatically fewer than the 65,000 to 70,000 bombs and warheads stockpiled in the mid-1980s at the height of the Cold War. Two-thirds of each of the US and Russian stockpiles today are inactive – either in storage or waiting to be dismantled.

Nuclear accidents

Officially or unofficially reported incident

1950–2000

Responsibility of UK
Responsibility of USA
Responsibility of USSR

Many accidents with nuclear weapons and waste have been recorded, including: accidental or unauthorized firing; nuclear detonation; non-nuclear detonation or burning of a nuclear weapon or radioactive component; radioactive contamination; theft, accidental jettisoning; public hazard; false alerts of incoming nuclear attack.

YEAR	LOCATION
1950	British Columbia, Canada
	New Mexico, USA
	Ohio, USA
	California, USA
	Quebec, Canada
1952	Alaska, USA
1956	Mediterranean Sea
	UK
1957	New Mexico, USA
	New Mexico, USA
	Florida, USA
	Atlantic Ocean
	Florida, USA
1958	overseas base
	off Georgia coast, USA
	Greenham Common, UK
	off Georgia coast, USA
	Georgia, USA
	Texas, USA
	Louisiana, USA
	South Carolina, USA
	Urals, USSR
1959	unspecified Pacific base
	Louisiana, USA
	Washington, USA
	Kentucky, USA
	Florida, USA
1960	New Jersey, USA
1961	Utah, USA
	North Carolina, USA
	California, USA
	North Sea
1962	US Pacific Test Range

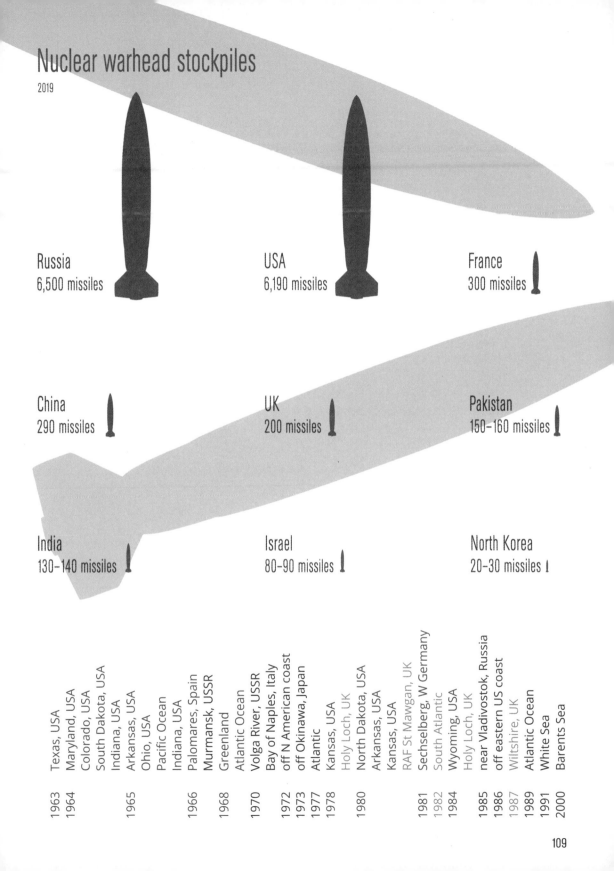

Nuclear warhead stockpiles

2019

Russia
6,500 missiles

USA
6,190 missiles

France
300 missiles

China
290 missiles

UK
200 missiles

Pakistan
150–160 missiles

India
130–140 missiles

Israel
80–90 missiles

North Korea
20–30 missiles

1963	Texas, USA
	Maryland, USA
1964	Colorado, USA
	South Dakota, USA
	Indiana, USA
1965	Arkansas, USA
	Ohio, USA
	Pacific Ocean
	Indiana, USA
1966	Palomares, Spain
	Murmansk, USSR
1968	Greenland
	Atlantic Ocean
1970	Volga River, USSR
1972	Bay of Naples, Italy
	off N American coast
1973	off Okinawa, Japan
1977	Atlantic
1978	Kansas, USA
	Holy Loch, UK
1980	North Dakota, USA
	Arkansas, USA
	Kansas, USA
	RAF St Mawgan, UK
1981	Sechselberg, W Germany
1982	South Atlantic
1984	Wyoming, USA
	Holy Loch, UK
1985	near Vladivostok, Russia
1986	off eastern US coast
1987	Wiltshire, UK
1989	Atlantic Ocean
1991	White Sea
2000	Barents Sea

Chemical weapons in Syria

2012	July: Syrian Foreign Ministry confirms that Syria has chemical weapons.
2012	Dec: **Allegation of use of chemical weapons in Syria.**
2013	Mar: **Allegation of use of chemical weapons.** UN announces investigation in collaboration with WHO and OPCW.
2013	Apr: **Two allegations of use of chemical weapons.**
2013	Aug: **Allegation of use of chemical weapons.** UN investigators attacked by snipers in Syria.
2013	Sept: USA & Russia agree plan for accounting, inspection, control, and elimination of Syria's chemical weapons. Syria submits declaration of stockpiles of chemical weapons to the OPCW.
2013	Oct: Destruction of Syria's stockpiles of chemical weapons begins. All declared facilities for mixing and producing chemical weapons are destroyed, or rendered inoperable.
2013	Nov: OPCW approves plan for removal of Syria's chemical weapons by ship from country.
2014	Jan–April: 80% of chemical weapons and 92% of chemical agents removed.
2014	April: **Allegation of use of chemical weapons.**
2014	June: OPCW confirms use of chlorine gas in earlier attacks.
2014	June: OPCW announces removal of all chemical weapons from Syria.
2014	Sept: OPCW confirms use of chlorine gas.
2015	Mar: UN Security Council adopts resolution condemning use of chlorine as a weapon in Syria's civil war and threatening action under Chapter VII of the UN Charter if action repeated.
2015	Apr: **Allegation of use of chemical weapons.**

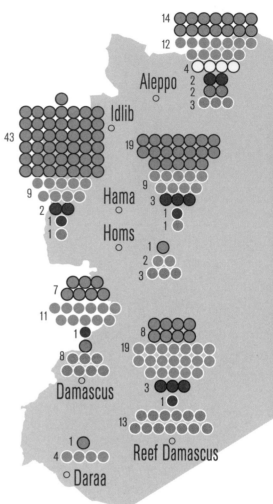

Use of chemical agents in warfare has been rare since World War I, when they caused 1.3 million casualties, including 90,000 deaths. They were allegedly used in Yemen by Egyptian forces in the 1960s and were used by Iraq against Iranian forces and Kurdish civilians in the 1980s. They were used in terrorism in Japan in the 1990s and for political assassinations in the UK in 2006 and 2018, and in Malaysia in 2017. And they have been used in Syria since 2012. Their production, stockpiling, and use is outlawed by the Chemical Weapons Convention of 1997.

1 ◯
Al-Hasakah

SYRIA

Deir Ezzor

Chemical attacks in Syria

Number of incidents in each governate of Syria
as of 23 January 2019

Perpetrator: Assad regime, except for releases of
mustard gas by ISIS in Aleppo and Al-Hasakah

◯ incident comprehensively confirmed
investigated and confirmed by competent international
bodies or backed up by at least three highly reliable
independent sources

◯ incident confirmed
backed up by at least two highly reliable sources or
three or more independent secondary sources

● chlorine

● sarin

mustard gas/sulfur mustard

● unknown

2016	Aug: **Allegation of use of chemical weapons.**
2016	Aug: OPCW finds Syrian government responsible for chemical weapons attacks in April 2014 & March 2015, Islamic State responsible for use of sulfur mustard in August 2015.
2016	Sept: **Allegation of use of chemical weapons.**
2016	Oct: OPCW finds Syrian regime responsible for chlorine gas use in March 2015
2016	Dec: **Allegation of use of chemical weapons.**
2017	Apr: **Allegation of use of chemical weapons.** USA uses Tomahawk cruise missiles to attack Syrian airbase from which it believes chemical weapons attack was launched.
2017	Apr: OPCW confirms that sarin was used.
2017	June: OPCW finds Syrian regime responsible for April 2017 attack, and Islamic State responsible for use of sulfur mustard in Sept 2016.
2018	Feb: **Allegation of use of chemical weapons.**
2018	Apr: **Allegation of use of chemical weapons.**
2018	May: OPCW finds it likely that chemical weapons were used in February 2018.
2018	June: OPCW finds it very likely that sarin was used twice in March 2017.
2018	Sept: Independent International Commission of Inquiry on the Syrian Arab Republic, appointed by UN, finds that Syrian government used chlorine as a weapon four times from Jan–July 2018.
2019	Mar: **OPCW reports that chemical weapons were used in April 2018.**

Casualties of war

Death toll this century

Best estimates of deaths from violent conflict
2000–2018
For Iraq, Yemen, Syria and Palestine/Israel,
deaths in 2019 are included.

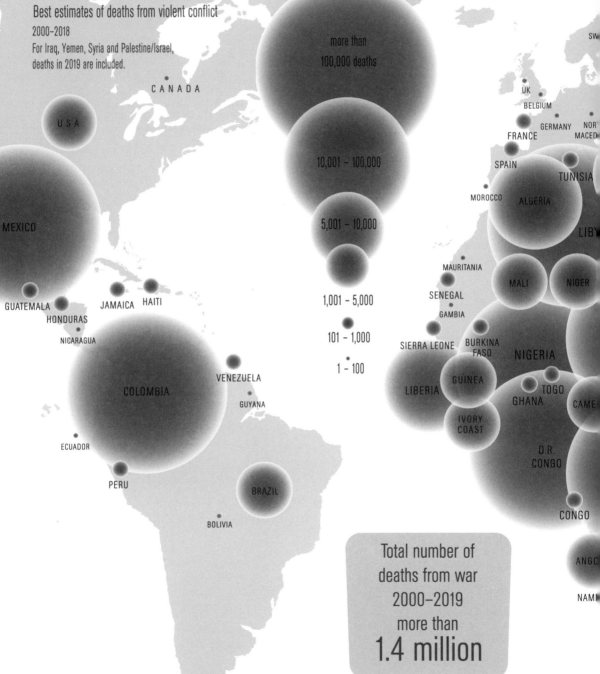

more than
100,000 deaths

10,001 – 100,000

5,001 – 10,000

1,001 – 5,000

101 – 1,000

1 – 100

CANADA

USA

MEXICO

GUATEMALA
HONDURAS
NICARAGUA

JAMAICA   HAITI

COLOMBIA

VENEZUELA

GUYANA

ECUADOR

PERU

BRAZIL

BOLIVIA

UK
BELGIUM
GERMANY   NOR
FRANCE   MACED

SPAIN

TUNISIA

MOROCCO   ALGERIA

LIB

MAURITANIA

SENEGAL

GAMBIA

MALI   NIGER

SIERRA LEONE   BURKINA
FASO

NIGERIA

LIBERIA   GUINEA
                         TOGO
             GHANA   CAME

IVORY
COAST

D.R.
CONGO

CONGO

ANGO

NAM

SW

Total number of
deaths from war
2000–2019
more than
1.4 million

KRAINE

RUSSIA

AFGHANISTAN

KEY

SYRIA

UZBEKISTAN   KYRGYZSTAN

GEORGIA

ARMENIA   AZERBAIJAN   TAJIKISTAN

LEBANON

IRAQ

CHINA

L &
INE

JORDAN   IRAN

PAKISTAN   NEPAL

PT

SAUDI
ARABIA

SUDAN

ERITREA   KUWAIT

AD   BAHRAIN
                                UAE

LAOS

DJIBOUTI   YEMEN

THAILAND

JTH
JAN   BANGLADESH

ETHIOPIA   INDIA   MYANMAR   CAMBODIA   PHILIPPINES

MALAYSIA

UGANDA

KENYA   PAPUA
                                    NEW GUINEA

TRAL   RWANDA
ICAN
JBLIC   TANZANIA   SOMALIA   SRI LANKA   INDONESIA

BURUNDI

MADAGASCAR

ZAMBIA

MOZAMBIQUE   AUSTRALIA

MBABWE

113

Increasing death toll

Reliable statistics on deaths in war do not exist. There are several reasons why. The figures are manipulated up or down for competing propaganda purposes. In many wars the dangers and complexities of compiling reliable data are simply too great. Though the number of people who die in battle, whether they are fighters or civilians, can sometimes be counted or well estimated, it is often impossible to know anything about the numbers who die through indirect effects – such as from the spread of disease because water systems are destroyed, or from injuries or illnesses that cannot be medically treated because hospitals are destroyed.

Regional toll

Best estimates of combat deaths in armed conflict

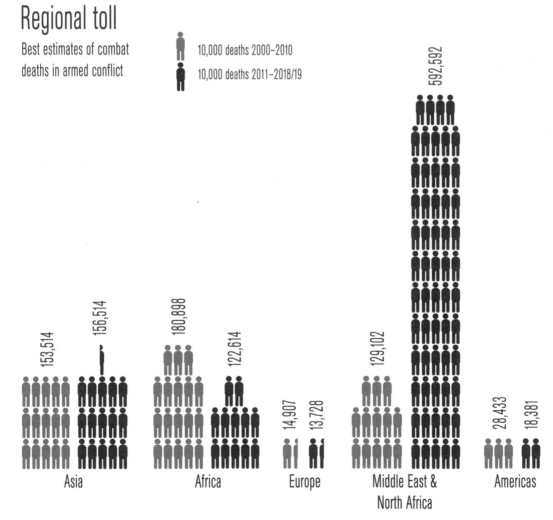

10,000 deaths 2000–2010
10,000 deaths 2011–2018/19

153,514
156,514
Asia

180,898
122,614
Africa

14,907
13,728
Europe

129,102
592,592
Middle East & North Africa

28,433
18,381
Americas

Estimates are nonetheless available. Of varying reliability in detail, the big picture trends they show tend to be more dependable. The Middle East and North Africa has been a crucible of war and violence this century. The biggest element of the region's death toll in the first decade (2000–2010) was the war in Iraq, starting with the US-led invasion in 2003. The biggest element in the second decade has been warfare in Syria. Meanwhile, in Africa, though armed conflict persists in many countries, the toll has reduced by about one-third from the century's first to second decades.

Type of conflict

Best estimates of combat deaths in armed conflict

1,000 deaths 2000–2010
1,000 deaths 2011–2018/19

Total combat deaths
2000–2010
507,000
2011–2019:
904,000

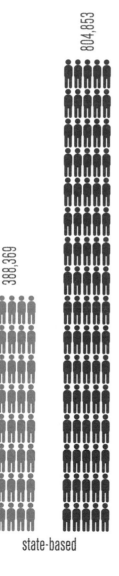

804,853

388,369

state-based

50,214

53,237

non-state

68,271

45,739

one-sided

Terrorism

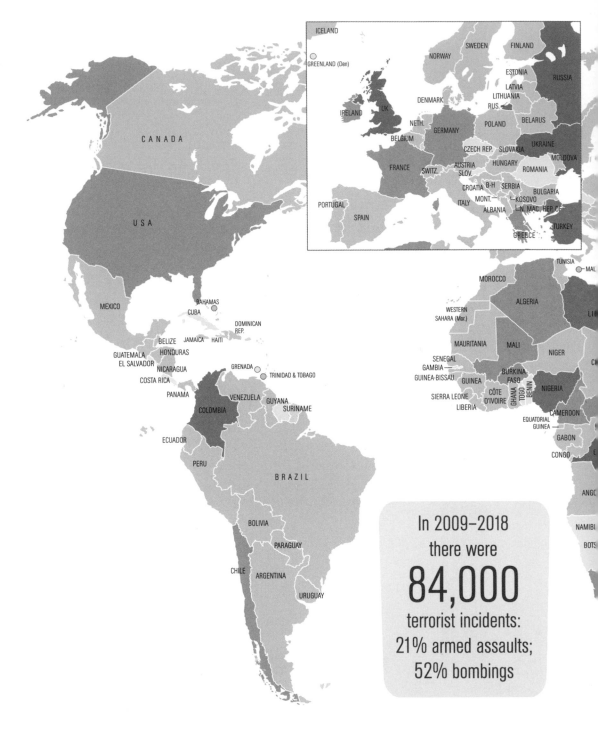

ICELAND
GREENLAND (Den)
NORWAY
SWEDEN
FINLAND
ESTONIA
RUSSIA
LATVIA
LITHUANIA
DENMARK
RUS.
IRELAND
UK
NETH.
POLAND
BELARUS
BELGIUM
GERMANY
UKRAINE
CZECH REP.
SLOVAKIA
MOLDOVA
FRANCE
SWITZ.
AUSTRIA
HUNGARY
ROMANIA
SLOV.
CROATIA
B-H
SERBIA
BULGARIA
PORTUGAL
MONT.
KOSOVO
ITALY
ALBANIA
N. MAC, REP. OF
SPAIN
TURKEY
GREECE

CANADA

USA

MEXICO
BAHAMAS
CUBA
DOMINICAN REP.
BELIZE JAMAICA HAITI
GUATEMALA HONDURAS
EL SALVADOR
NICARAGUA
GRENADA
COSTA RICA
TRINIDAD & TOBAGO
PANAMA
VENEZUELA GUYANA
COLOMBIA
SURINAME
ECUADOR
PERU
BRAZIL
BOLIVIA
PARAGUAY
CHILE
ARGENTINA
URUGUAY

TUNISIA
MAL
MOROCCO
ALGERIA
LI
WESTERN
SAHARA (Mor.)
MAURITANIA
MALI
NIGER
SENEGAL
GAMBIA
CH
GUINEA-BISSAU
BURKINA
FASO
NIGERIA
GUINEA
SIERRA LEONE
CÔTE
D'IVOIRE
GHANA
TOGO
BENIN
LIBERIA
CAMEROON
EQUATORIAL
GUINEA
GABON
CONGO
ANGO
NAMIBI
BOTS

In 2009–2018
there were
84,000
terrorist incidents:
21% armed assaults;
52% bombings

Incidents

Number of intentional violent
attacks by non-state actors
2009–2018

- more than 10,000
- 1,001 – 10,000
- 501 – 1,000
- 101 – 500
- 1 – 100
- no incident

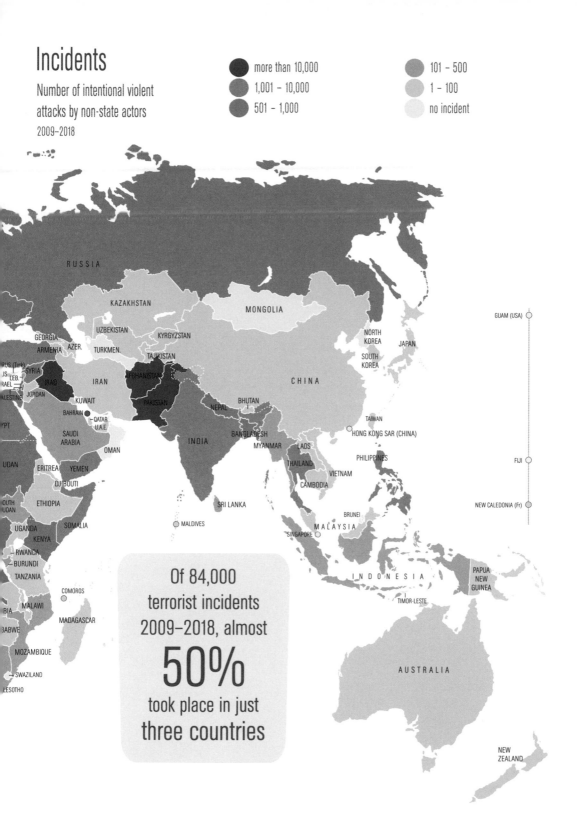

RUSSIA

KAZAKHSTAN

MONGOLIA

UZBEKISTAN

KYRGYZSTAN

GEORGIA
ARMENIA   AZER.
TURKMEN.

RUS (Turk)
JS   LEB.
AEL
JORDAN
PALESTINE
PT
SYRIA
IRAQ
IRAN
KUWAIT
BAHRAIN   QATAR
U.A.E

TAJIKISTAN

AFGHANISTAN

PAKISTAN

NEPAL   BHUTAN

CHINA

NORTH
KOREA   JAPAN

SOUTH
KOREA

GUAM (USA)

SAUDI
ARABIA
OMAN

INDIA

BANGLADESH
MYANMAR

LAOS

TAIWAN

HONG KONG SAR (CHINA)

UDAN
ERITREA   YEMEN
DJIBOUTI

THAILAND

VIETNAM

PHILIPPINES

FIJI

OUTH
UDAN
ETHIOPIA

SRI LANKA

CAMBODIA

UGANDA
KENYA

SOMALIA

MALDIVES

BRUNEI

MALAYSIA

SINGAPORE

NEW CALEDONIA (Fr)

RWANDA
BURUNDI
TANZANIA

COMOROS

BIA
MALAWI   MADAGASCAR
3ABWE

INDONESIA

PAPUA
NEW
GUINEA

TIMOR-LESTE

MOZAMBIQUE

SWAZILAND
LESOTHO

AUSTRALIA

NEW
ZEALAND

Of 84,000
terrorist incidents
2009–2018, almost

50%

took place in just
three countries

117

Refugees

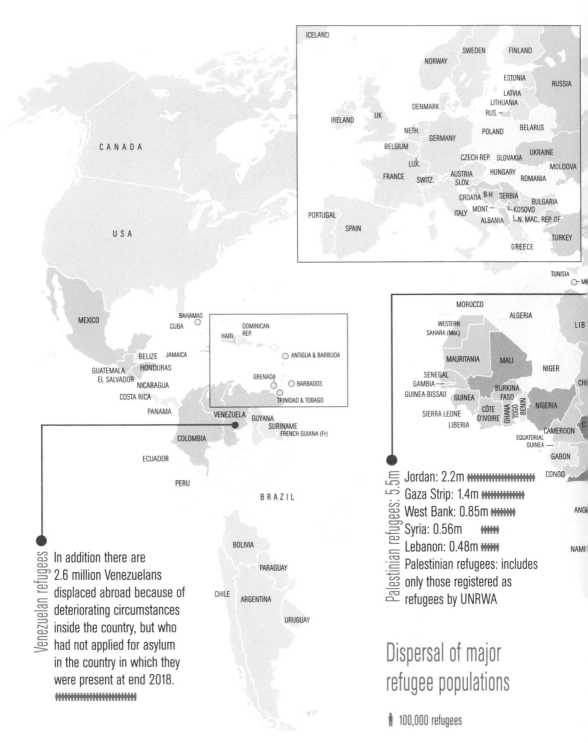

ICELAND · NORWAY · SWEDEN · FINLAND · ESTONIA · RUSSIA · LATVIA · LITHUANIA · RUS. · DENMARK · IRELAND · UK · NETH. · GERMANY · POLAND · BELARUS · BELGIUM · LUX. · CZECH REP. · SLOVAKIA · UKRAINE · FRANCE · SWITZ. · AUSTRIA · SLOV. · HUNGARY · ROMANIA · MOLDOVA · CROATIA · B-H · SERBIA · BULGARIA · PORTUGAL · ITALY · MONT. · KOSOVO · N. MAC. · REP. OF · ALBANIA · SPAIN · GREECE · TURKEY

CANADA · USA · MEXICO · CUBA · BAHAMAS · HAITI · DOMINICAN REP. · BELIZE · JAMAICA · ANTIGUA & BARBUDA · GUATEMALA · HONDURAS · EL SALVADOR · NICARAGUA · GRENADA · BARBADOS · COSTA RICA · TRINIDAD & TOBAGO · PANAMA · VENEZUELA · GUYANA · SURINAME · FRENCH GUIANA (Fr) · COLOMBIA · ECUADOR · PERU · BRAZIL · BOLIVIA · PARAGUAY · CHILE · ARGENTINA · URUGUAY

TUNISIA · MOROCCO · ALGERIA · LIB · WESTERN SAHARA (Mor.) · MAURITANIA · MALI · NIGER · SENEGAL · GAMBIA · GUINEA-BISSAU · GUINEA · BURKINA FASO · NIGERIA · CH · SIERRA LEONE · CÔTE D'IVOIRE · GHANA · TOGO · BENIN · LIBERIA · CAMEROON · C · EQUATORIAL GUINEA · GABON · CONGO · ANG · NAMI

Venezuelan refugees

In addition there are 2.6 million Venezuelans displaced abroad because of deteriorating circumstances inside the country, but who had not applied for asylum in the country in which they were present at end 2018.

Palestinian refugees: 5.5m

Jordan: 2.2m

Gaza Strip: 1.4m

West Bank: 0.85m

Syria: 0.56m

Lebanon: 0.48m

Palestinian refugees: includes only those registered as refugees by UNRWA

Dispersal of major refugee populations

👤 100,000 refugees

Where refugees come from

Number of refugees by country origin

end 2018 or latest available data

- 1 million or more
- 500,000 – 999,999
- 100,000 – 499,999
- 10,000 – 99,999
- 1,000 – 9,999
- fewer than 1,000
- no data

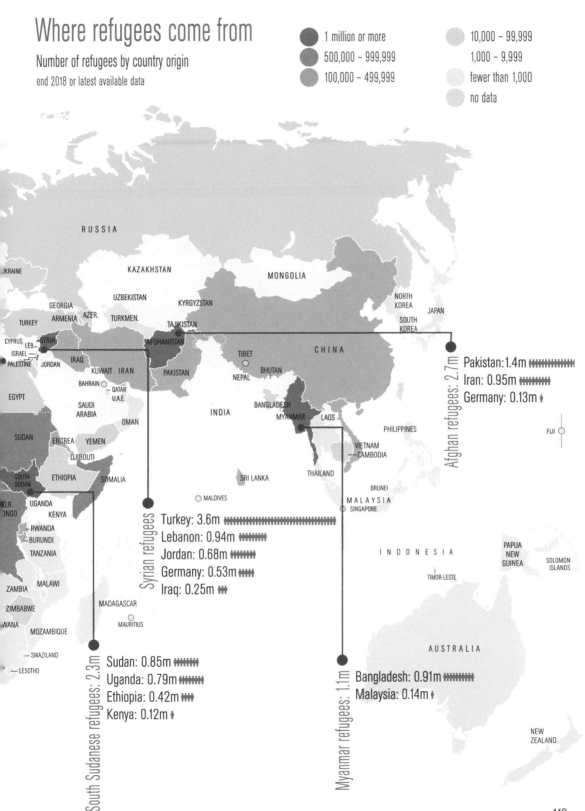

Afghan refugees: 2.7m
Pakistan: 1.4m
Iran: 0.95m
Germany: 0.13m

Syrian refugees
Turkey: 3.6m
Lebanon: 0.94m
Jordan: 0.68m
Germany: 0.53m
Iraq: 0.25m

South Sudanese refugees: 2.3m
Sudan: 0.85m
Uganda: 0.79m
Ethiopia: 0.42m
Kenya: 0.12m

Myanmar refugees: 1.1m
Bangladesh: 0.91m
Malaysia: 0.14m

Where refugees go to

Number of refugees in country
of asylum

end 2018 or latest available data

- 1 million or more
- 500,000 – 999,999
- 100,000 – 499,999
- 10,000 – 99,999
- 1,000 – 9,999
- fewer than 1,000
- no data

In 2019 there were 71 million forcibly displaced people. The number of has never been greater and it increases at an average rate of 37,000 people per day.

Many refugees are second or third generation – born in exile. Many are twice-over refugees having had to flee from the refuge to which they fled.

Internally displaced people

Number of IDPs due to conflict and violence

end 2018 or latest available data

- 1 million or more
- 500,000 – 999,999
- 100,000 – 499,999
- 10,000 – 99,999
- 1,000 – 9,999
- fewer than 1,000
- no data

Stateless people

Number of stateless people

end 2018

Most refugees find shelter in countries neighbouring their own. Some attempt longer, perilous journeys to seek a better future in a richer country.

Many, despite their hardships, and despite all states' legal responsibilities under the 1951 Refugee Convention, receive little or no comfort upon arrival.

Keeping the peace

Cost of violence ... and what it could be spent on

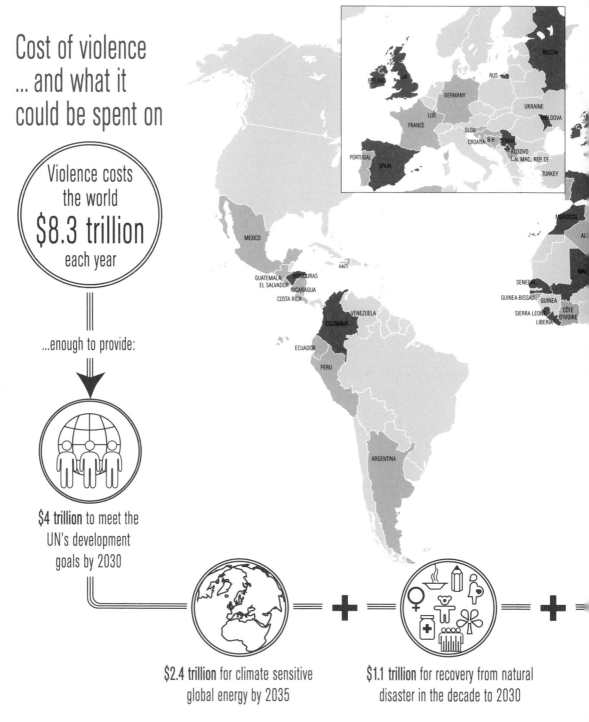

Violence costs the world **$8.3 trillion** each year

...enough to provide:

$4 trillion to meet the UN's development goals by 2030

$2.4 trillion for climate sensitive global energy by 2035

$1.1 trillion for recovery from natural disaster in the decade to 2030

RUSSIA
IRELAND
UK
RUS.
GERMANY
UKRAINE
LUX.
MOLDOVA
FRANCE
SLOV.
CROATIA
B-H
SERBIA
PORTUGAL
KOSOVO
SPAIN
N. MAC. REP. OF
TURKEY

MEXICO
HAITI
GUATEMALA
HONDURAS
EL SALVADOR
NICARAGUA
COSTA RICA
VENEZUELA
COLOMBIA
ECUADOR
PERU
ARGENTINA

MOROCCO
AL
MAL
SENEGAL
GUINEA-BISSAU
GUINEA
SIERRA LEONE
CÔTE D'IVOIRE
LIBERIA

Peace agreements since 1990

Signed multiparty agreements

1990–2019

At least one agreement signed in:

- 1990s, 2000s, 2010s
- 1990s, 2000s
- 1990s, 2010s
- 2000s, 2010s
- 1990s
- 2000s
- 2010s
- no data

Number of international peace agreements on intra-state wars since 1990:

206

$0.2 trillion to cover costs of humanitarian assistance needed as response to climate change by 2030

And in the second violence-free year, the world could...

Peacekeeping trends

A UN study found that in the first 12 or so years after the end of the Cold War, as many peace agreements were signed as in the previous 200 years.

The number of peace missions also increased, because the end of the confrontation between the USA and the Soviet Union freed the United Nations to do more.

UN peacekeeping missions

Number of active missions
1950–2019

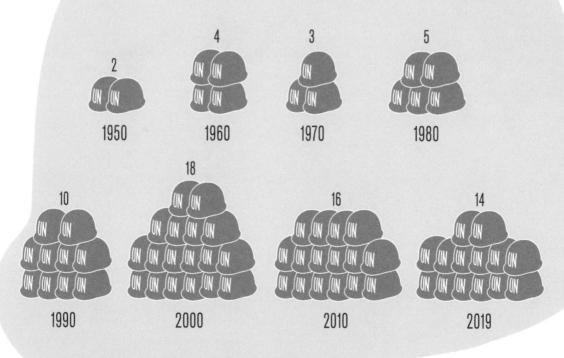

2
1950

4
1960

3
1970

5
1980

10
1990

18
2000

16
2010

14
2019

Peacekeeping missions

December 2019

⬤ active mission in country

Type of mission:

🪖 UN

🪖 African Union

🪖 Economic Community of West African States

🪖 EU

🪖 NATO

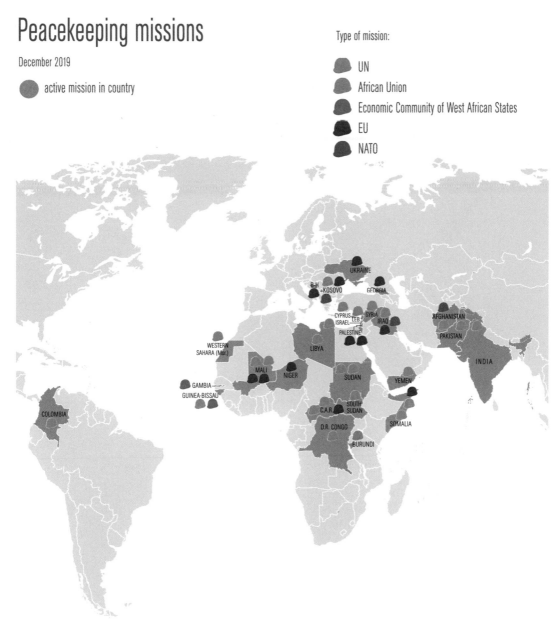

The number of peacekeeping missions plateaued in the mid-2000s and, although the trend is not yet clear, it looks as though it is now tailing off. This is partly an indication that several peacekeeping missions have been successfully accomplished – but may also be a sign that rich states are less willing to pay for peacekeeping in tougher economic times.

Forces for peace

Type of force
2019

🪖 1,000 troops

🚶 1,000 military observers

🚶 1,000 police

🚶 1,000 international civilian personnel

1948–2019
3,890 deaths among UN forces for peace

71,830 troops

Contributing to peace

Number of military and police personnel
committed to UN peacekeeping operations

October 2019

- 5,000 or more
- 1,000 – 4,999
- 500 – 999
- 1 – 499
- none

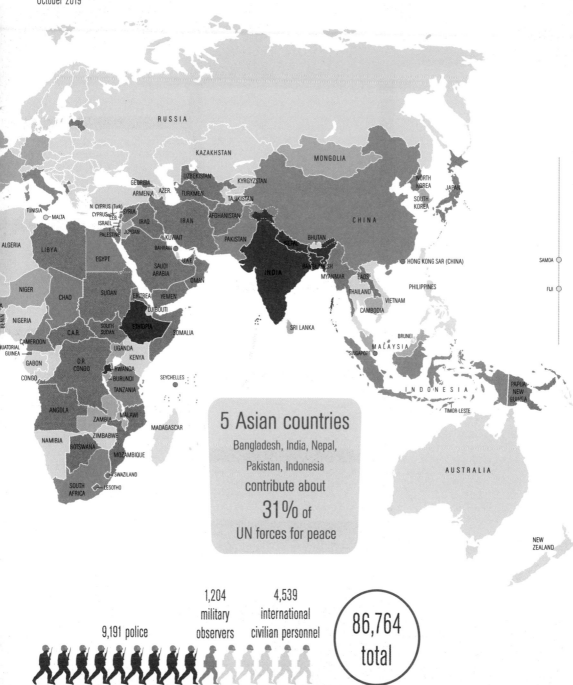

5 Asian countries
Bangladesh, India, Nepal,
Pakistan, Indonesia
contribute about
31% of
UN forces for peace

9,191 police

1,204
military
observers

4,539
international
civilian personnel

86,764
total

The new front line

Cyber warfare

selected incidents

Global cyber attack, 2011: The biggest reported series of cyber attacks to date hit 72 organizations including:
- The governments of Canada, India, S. Korea, Taiwan, Vietnam, USA
- The UN secretariat in Geneva
- The Association of South-East Asian Nations
- The International Olympic Committee and the World Anti-Doping Agency
- Defence contractors and hi-tech companies.

Worldwide, Capital One, 2019: Credit card company revealed a hacker accessed data on 100 million credit card applications, including applicants' bank account numbers.

Worldwide, Play Station, 2011: Cyber penetration of PlayStation network accessed personal data of more than 80 million users.

Worldwide, WannaCry, 2017: 150 countries hit by WannaCry ransomware that locked files and demanded ransom payment in Bitcoin. Russia, Ukraine, India, and Taiwan were most affected. UK health service, German railways and telecom companies in Argentina, Portugal, and Spain also hit hard.

Worldwide, Yahoo, 2013: The biggest ever (known) impact of a cyber breach: 3 billion personal records compromised in hack attack on Yahoo.

US Navy, June 2018: Chinese government hackers compromised the networks of a US Navy contractor, stealing 614 GB of data related to weapons, sensor, and communication systems under development for US submarines.

USA, Congressional elections, 2018: US Cyber Command blocked internet access of Russian company The Internet Research Agency, reportedly involved in disinformation operations during 2016 US Presidential election.

USA, Sony Corp, 2014: Cyber intrusion presumed to originate from North Korea broke into Sony emails and employee files and dumped them online.

USA, Cyber Command, 2010: New US Military Command was established under a Four Star General. 30,000 troops initially assigned; number as high as 60,000 by 2020.

USA, 2009: For the first time, Chinese government is identified as source of hacking attack on Google and 45 other US companies.

UK, Easyjet airline, May 2020: Chinese hackers accessed the travel records of 9 million customers of UK airline EasyJet.

Estonia, 2007: A series of a "distributed denial of service" (DDoS) attacks originating from Russia disrupted government departments and interrupted access to emergency services.

Copenhagen, NotPetya, 2017: Maersk shipping was the main target of NotPetya malware that temporarily shut down 76 ports and 800 ships, representing 18% of global cargo. The following year, UK and USA officially blamed NotPetya on Russia.

Brussels, European Union, 2018: The EU acknowledged China has had access to sensitive EU communications for several years.

London, UK, 2012: UK's counter-intelligence director illustrated cyber threat by reference to an unnamed major UK company that lost around $1.35bn in a hostile cyber attack.

Georgia, 2008: As the Russian–Georgian war started, Russian nationalists mounted a "distributed denial of service" (DDoS) attack on Georgia – flooding government websites with bogus enquiries so as to overwhelm and crash them.

Airbus, Europe, 2012: EADS (Airbus) and German steelmaker Thyssenkrupp recorded major attacks by Chinese hackers.

US military, Middle East, 2008: At a US military base in the Middle East, memory sticks containing a self-propagating worm were deliberately left in a washroom. One or more soldiers broke regulations by putting one in a military laptop. US Central Command was infected; the clean up took 14 months.

Egypt, 2019: Journalists, academics, lawyers, human rights activists, and opposition politicians suffered cyberattacks – widely assumed to be carried out by the government.

Syria, 2007: Syria defenceless against Israeli air strike because US Air Force software disabled Syrian air defence.

Saudi Arabia, 2012: Iranian Shamoon virus attacked Saudi Aramco oil company, shutting thousands of computers and hard drives, leaving image of burning American flag on many screens. Repeat attack in 2016.

Hong Kong, June 2019: A denial-of-service attack on encrypted messaging service Telegram disrupted communications among HK protesters.

Ukraine, 2016: Cyberattack on national power company shut down electricity in northern Kiev for 30 minutes.

Western Intelligence, 2018: Russian internet search company Yandex penetrated by hackers using software known to be used by the Five Eyes intelligence alliance of Australia, Canada, New Zealand, UK, and USA.

Iran, 2019: Allegations surfaced that Iranian hackers targeted over 170 universities worldwide, 2013–2017, stealing $3.4 billion worth of intellectual property.

Iran, 2010: US–Israeli-designed Stuxnet virus deactivated 30,000 Iranian government computers and a quarter of Iran's enrichment centrifuges.

Iran, 2012: Israel's Flamer cyber worm wiped out Iranian hard drives and forced cut in oil production.

Virtual manoeuvres, 2011, 2012: US and Chinese officials jointly played cyber war games.

South Korean military, 2016: US and South Korean contingency plans in the event of war accessed by hackers, allegedly from North Korea.

South Korea, Seoul, 2013: Computer networks of major banks and broadcasters were attacked by a virus designed to wipe out their stored data. North Korea widely blamed for attack, which occurred during joint US and South Korean military manoeuvres.

Huawei, 2019: Chinese telecoms mega-corporation accused US government of hacking into its internal information systems to disrupt business operations.

China, 2019: China's National Computer Network Emergency Response Technical Team claimed so many cyberattacks came from USA it was like all-out cyber war against China.

China, 2010: The government claimed it was hit by almost 500,000 cyberattacks – 15% from USA, 8% from India, approx. 25% from elsewhere outside China.

3D printing

Additive manufacturing (AM), generally known as 3D printing, creates three-dimensional objects. It is especially useful for producing prototypes, for making quick design changes, and potentially for making components that are no longer commercially available. 3D printing has been used to manufacture parts for weapons (see below), but during the Covid-19 crisis of 2020, the 3D printing community was quick to offer their technology for the rapid production of parts for ventilators and PPE.

Developments reported during 2010s

YEAR

2010s	50lb-warhead for hypersonic missile like the X51A Waverider is 3D-printed.
2010s	Los Alamos National Laboratory (site of original atomic bomb research in 1940s) pioneers 3D printing for high explosives to be used in US nuclear weapons.
2010s	Dutch researchers 3D-print TNT.
2013	A US student makes the first 3D-printed gun out of plastic and calls it "Liberator".
2013	NASA successfully tests a 3D-printed engine injector for a rocket – extra thrust with fewer components.
2014	The Sellafield (UK) nuclear plant 3D-prints a custom-designed lid for a nuclear waste container.
2015	Raytheon Corp (US) announces it has produced a missile in which 80% of components are 3D-printed.

The future:

- Bioprinting of human tissues offers medical opportunities but could also be used to transmit toxins for use as weapons.

- If digital files of small arms can be transmitted instead of the physical object having to be transported from one place to another, how will they be controlled?

Artificial intelligence and the arms race

Artificial intelligence (AI) and machine learning mean huge amounts of information can be handled much, much faster. Whether that is good or bad depends on how it is used.

For pre-emptive response to threats? For armed robots? For greater accuracy in missile strikes? For ensuring agreements and treaties are properly implemented? All are possible.

AI in attack and defence

Examples of areas in which it can be used

Early warning and intelligence, surveillance, reconnaissance (ISR)

- detection of enemy attack

- data processing and analysis

- predicting enemy's nuclear-related activity

Cyber security and attack

- better defence mechanisms against cyberattacks

- enhanced capability for cyberattacks

Nuclear and conventional weapons Autonomous:

- drones

- hypersonics

- surface and underwater vehicles

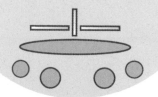

Defensive mechanisms

- better targeting of defensive systems

- better detection of enemy signals

- better jamming capabilities

- autonomous anti-submarine and counter-mine systems

- autonomous robots for protection of nuclear assets

Health of the people

The health of the people reflects the health of a society. Good health is a basic need and access to good healthcare a basic right, a central part of the contract between state and citizen in many parts of the world. And the health of the people is a significant success story in the last century and a half of human development and progress. Despite the many flaws of modern society, more people live longer today than ever before, mainly because of better public health systems, clean water and safe sewage treatment, improved nutrition, and more medical knowledge and care. And yet...

It is not just the Covid-19 pandemic of 2020 that presses pause on relative optimism about the global health horizon. It is, however, an enormous wake-up call. Preparations were generally deficient, though warnings had been sounded. Some governments' response to the pandemic has been tragically poor. Even where the response has been relatively effective, most countries have revealed their lack of resilience, often due to spending cuts in the previous decade. Care for the elderly, as a prime example, has been done as cheaply as possible.

The Covid-19 pandemic is the latest episode in a series of novel infectious diseases this century: SARS, MERS, H1N1, Ebola. The increasing tempo is worrying. And now the World Health Organization, riven by disputes, has been weakened by the USA deciding to withdraw its membership and funding.

The big killing diseases of our time, however, are lifestyle-related. While malnutrition and hunger are increasing again, the food-related epidemic is obesity. Carrying too much body weight is a major health risk. Likewise smoking, also increasing, and a major cause of heart disease, respiratory disease and some kinds of cancer.

Yet cancer is in some ways a story that reflects progress; if caught early, most kinds of cancer are treatable. With HIV/AIDS, there has been progress; it cannot be cured but can be managed. But mental health remains a taboo issue in many countries – impossible to discuss and therefore impossible to manage, even if resources were available.

Overall, however, huge advances have been registered in public health and the treatment of diseases. The way we live continues to generate problems that medical science has to solve. The next step, surely, is to figure out how to live better.

Pandemics

The first identified cases of illness caused by a novel corona virus surfaced in Wuhan province in China in December 2019. In January 2020 it spread beyond China. At the end of the month, the World Health Organization called it a Public Health Emergency of International Concern. In February it named the new virus Covid-19 and during March labelled the outbreak a global pandemic.

Every day people read the Covid-19 statistics – the numbers of cases and deaths – watching them mount. All were misleading and incomplete. Much official data was an understatement and even when that was not

deliberate, counting methodologies differed markedly from one country to another.

Indirect consequences were also striking. Many countries introduced lockdowns, which slowed the rate of infection but had other consequences including a globally recorded upsurge in domestic violence. And with Covid-19 taking priority, many patients with other debilitating diseases went untreated.

Like the 21st century's other pandemics – and like 60% of known diseases and 75% of new ones – Covid-19 is probably zoonotic, meaning it was transmitted from animals to people.

The age of epidemics and pandemics

Countries worst affected

SARS: Severe Acute Respiratory Syndrome (2002–2003)

H1N1 (Swine flu) (2009–2010)

MERS: Middle East Respiratory Syndrome (2012–2020)

Ebola (2014–2016)

Ebola (2018–2020)

no data

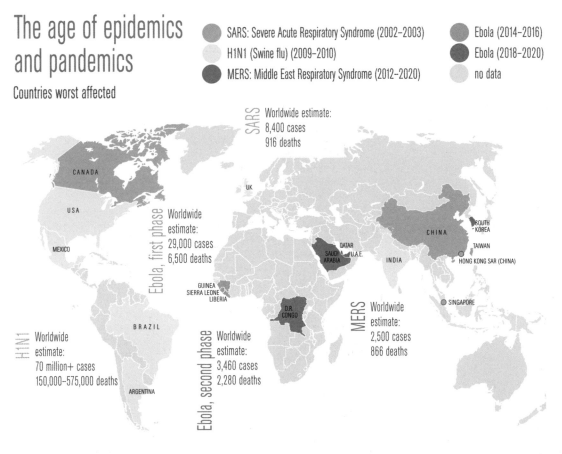

SARS Worldwide estimate:
8,400 cases
916 deaths

Ebola, first phase Worldwide estimate:
29,000 cases
6,500 deaths

MERS Worldwide estimate:
2,500 cases
866 deaths

H1N1 Worldwide estimate:
70 million+ cases
150,000–575,000 deaths

Ebola, second phase Worldwide estimate:
3,460 cases
2,280 deaths

CANADA

USA

MEXICO

UK

CHINA

SOUTH KOREA

TAIWAN

QATAR

SAUDI ARABIA U.A.E.

INDIA

HONG KONG SAR (CHINA)

GUINEA SIERRA LEONE LIBERIA

D.R. CONGO

SINGAPORE

BRAZIL

ARGENTINA

Covid-19

Epicentres of the Covid-19 pandemic
January – June 2020

- epicentres
- other countries with confirmed cases of Covid-19

April – May
USA

June
Mexico

May – June
Brazil

March – April
Europe & the Eastern Mediterranean

January – March
Asia

June
South Africa

Covid-19 confirmed cases

By region
January – June 2020

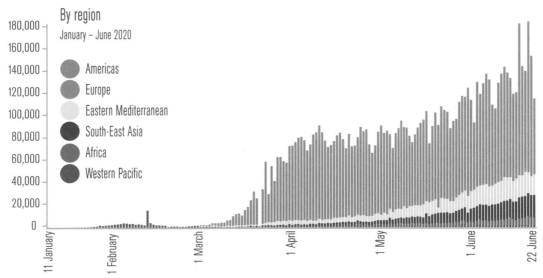

- Americas
- Europe
- Eastern Mediterranean
- South-East Asia
- Africa
- Western Pacific

180,000
160,000
140,000
120,000
100,000
80,000
60,000
40,000
20,000
0

11 January · 1 February · 1 March · 1 April · 1 May · 1 June · 22 June

Malnutrition

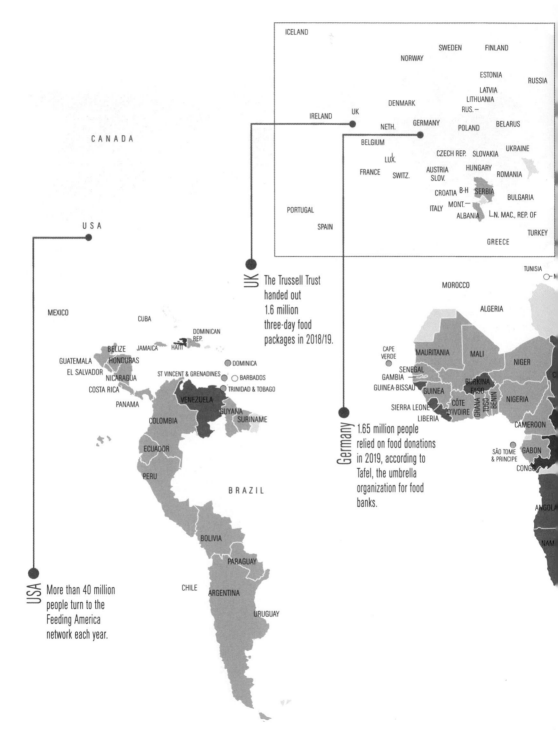

ICELAND

NORWAY SWEDEN FINLAND

ESTONIA RUSSIA
LATVIA
DENMARK LITHUANIA
RUS. —
IRELAND UK NETH. GERMANY POLAND BELARUS
BELGIUM UKRAINE
LUX. CZECH REP. SLOVAKIA
FRANCE SWITZ. AUSTRIA HUNGARY ROMANIA
SLOV.
CROATIA B-H SERBIA BULGARIA
PORTUGAL ITALY MONT.—
ALBANIA L N. MAC., REP. OF
SPAIN TURKEY
GREECE

CANADA

USA

MEXICO

CUBA
DOMINICAN
REP.
BELIZE JAMAICA HAITI
GUATEMALA HONDURAS DOMINICA
EL SALVADOR NICARAGUA ST VINCENT & GRENADINES BARBADOS
COSTA RICA TRINIDAD & TOBAGO
PANAMA VENEZUELA
GUYANA
COLOMBIA SURINAME

ECUADOR

PERU BRAZIL

BOLIVIA

PARAGUAY

CHILE ARGENTINA

URUGUAY

TUNISIA
MOROCCO
ALGERIA

CAPE MAURITANIA MALI NIGER
VERDE
SENEGAL
GAMBIA BURKINA
GUINEA-BISSAU GUINEA FASO BENIN NIGERIA
CÔTE GHANA TOGO
SIERRA LEONE D'IVOIRE
LIBERIA CAMEROON
SÃO TOMÉ GABON
& PRINCIPE CONGO

ANGOLA

NAM

UK
The Trussell Trust
handed out
1.6 million
three-day food
packages in 2018/19.

Germany
1.65 million people
relied on food donations
in 2019, according to
Tafel, the umbrella
organization for food
banks.

USA
More than 40 million
people turn to the
Feeding America
network each year.

Undernourished people

Percentage of population whose food intake
is insufficient to meet dietary energy requirements
2017

40% or more
20% – 39%

5% – 19%
fewer than 5%

no data

Undernourishment

From 2005 to 2015, the number of undernourished people worldwide decreased steadily. In 2015 that trend stopped and the number started to increase again, in line with the growing world population.

The main factors behind this reversal are climate change and violent conflict. However, shortages of food are caused by a range of different factors. People's ability to grow enough food can be hit by changes such as the length and timing of the rainy season due to climate change. People's ability to buy enough food can be hit by volatility in world food prices as a result of developments in far distant

countries. Crop failure, natural disasters, and war have a heavy impact, as do structural economic deficiencies such as supply problems and poor local transport infrastructure.

Deficiencies in diet are as serious a problem as insufficiencies of food. The absence of vitamins in daily intake can lead to crushing ailments. Vitamin A deficiency, for instance, affects an estimated 250 million pre-school children and is the leading cause of preventable blindness in children as well as increasing the risk of disease and death from severe infections.

Hunger

Number of undernourished people
2005–2018

Latin America & Caribbean   Asia   Africa   — prevalence of global undernourishment

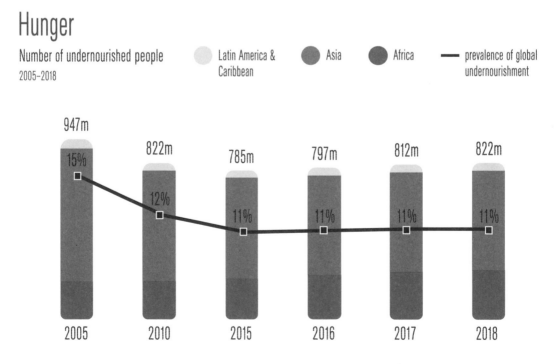

Food shortages

Requiring external assistance

as of September 2019

 exceptional shortage in food production/supplies

 severe but localized food insecurity

 widespread lack of access to basic food

 no food shortage requiring external assistance

NORTH KOREA

SYRIA

IRAQ

AFGHANISTAN

PAKISTAN

LIBYA

HAITI

CAPE VERDE

MAURITANIA

MALI

SENEGAL

GUINEA

SIERRA LEONE

LIBERIA

BURKINA FASO

NIGER

CHAD

SUDAN

ERITREA

YEMEN

DJIBOUTI

NIGERIA

CAMEROON

C.A.R.

SOUTH SUDAN

ETHIOPIA

SOMALIA

VENEZUELA

CONGO

D.R. OF CONGO

UGANDA

KENYA

BURUNDI

BANGLADESH

MYANMAR

MALAWI

ZIMBABWE

MADAGASCAR

MOZAMBIQUE

SWAZILAND

LESOTHO

Vitamin A deficiency affects around

250 million

pre-school children worldwide

Obesity

Overweight adults

Percentage of adults with Body Mass
Index (BMI) of 25 or more

2016

66% or more

51% – 65%

31% – 50%

30% or fewer

no data

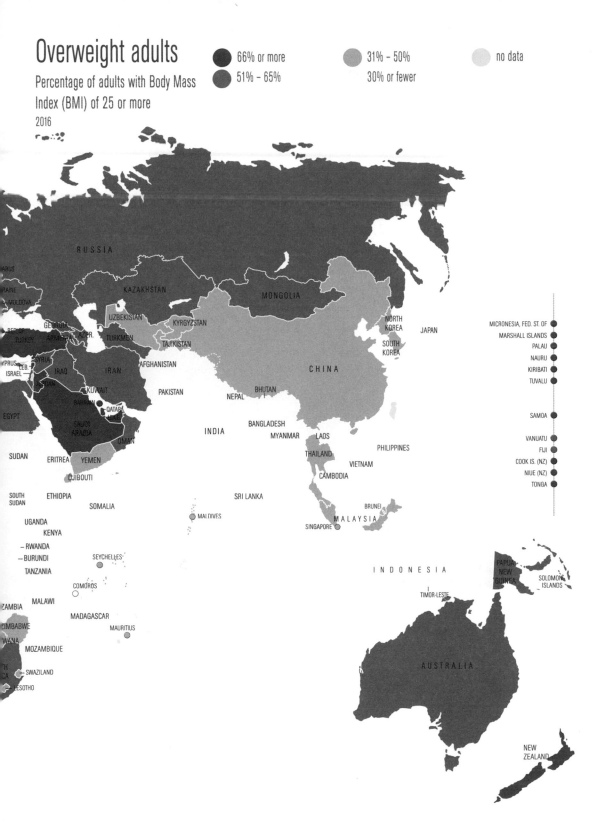

Impact of obesity

The incidence of obesity has more than trebled since 1975. An estimated 1.9 billion adults in the world are overweight or obese. Most people live in countries where there are more deaths from excess weight than from undernourishment. A person carrying excessive body weight risks contracting a range of debilitating and life-threatening health conditions.

The problem is not just the amount of food that people eat but, to a much greater extent, what we eat. Cheap processed foods are particularly high in animal fats and sugars. They make an affordable diet for people on low incomes but directly fuel the obesity epidemic. Worldwide, health services are struggling to cope with the strain.

Overweight as cause of death

Percentage of deaths from common causes
attributable to a Body Mass Index (BMI) of 25 or more
2017

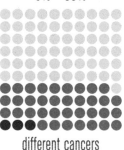
18%

ischemic heart-disease

31%

diabetes

3% – 39%

different cancers

17%

stroke

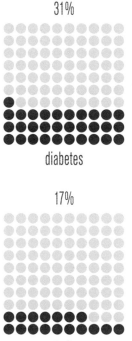

America's growing obesity problem

Percentage of population in each state
reported as having a BMI of 30 or more

2012, 2015, 2018

● 35.0% or more   ● 30.0% – 34.9%   ● 25.0% – 29.9%   less than 25.0%

2012

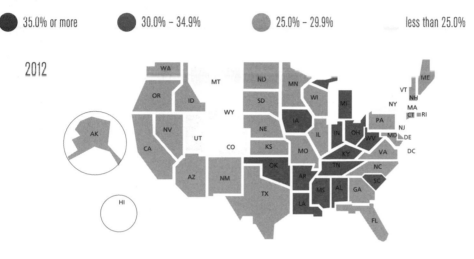

2015

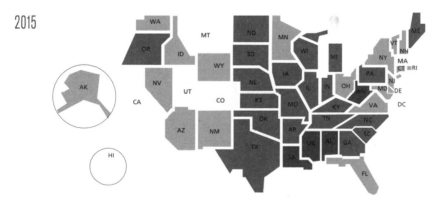

2018

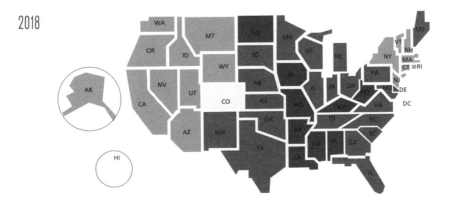

Smoking

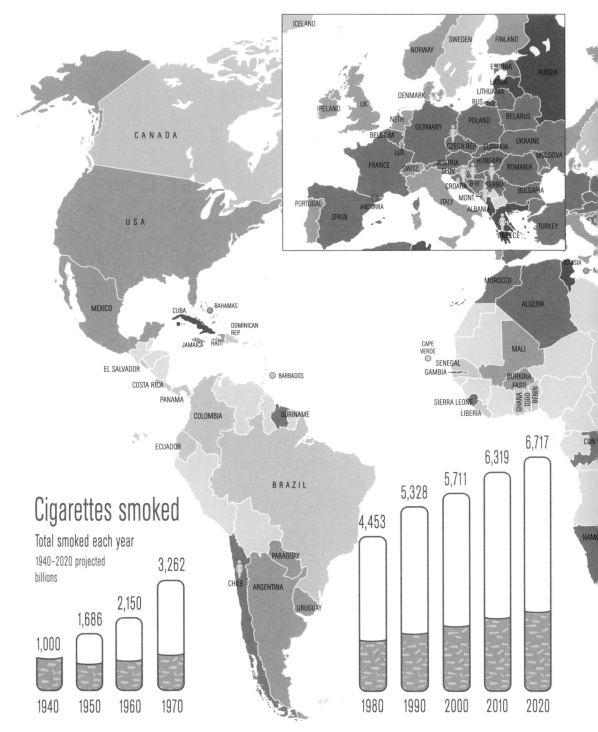

Cigarettes smoked

Total smoked each year

1940–2020 projected
billions

1,000	1940
1,686	1950
2,150	1960
3,262	1970
4,453	1980
5,328	1990
5,711	2000
6,319	2010
6,717	2020

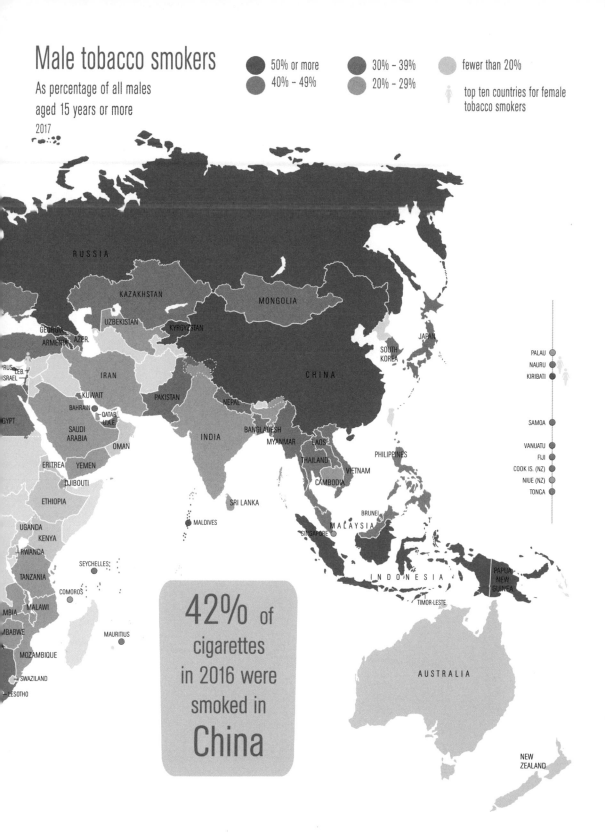

Male tobacco smokers

As percentage of all males
aged 15 years or more

2017

- 50% or more
- 40% – 49%
- 30% – 39%
- 20% – 29%
- fewer than 20%
- top ten countries for female tobacco smokers

RUSSIA

KAZAKHSTAN

MONGOLIA

UZBEKISTAN

KYRGYZSTAN

JAPAN

GEORGIA
ARMENIA   AZER.

SOUTH
KOREA

CHINA

CYPRUS
LEB.
ISRAEL

IRAN

KUWAIT
BAHRAIN
QATAR
UAE

PAKISTAN

NEPAL

EGYPT

SAUDI
ARABIA

OMAN

INDIA

BANGLADESH

MYANMAR

LAOS

PHILIPPINES

ERITREA   YEMEN

THAILAND

VIETNAM

DJIBOUTI

CAMBODIA

ETHIOPIA

SRI LANKA

UGANDA

KENYA

MALDIVES

BRUNEI

RWANDA

MALAYSIA

SINGAPORE

SEYCHELLES

TANZANIA

COMOROS

INDONESIA

PAPUA
NEW
GUINEA

MALAWI

TIMOR-LESTE

MAURITIUS

ZIMBABWE

MOZAMBIQUE

SWAZILAND

LESOTHO

AUSTRALIA

NEW
ZEALAND

PALAU
NAURU
KIRIBATI

SAMOA

VANUATU
FIJI
COOK IS. (NZ)
NIUE (NZ)
TONGA

42% of cigarettes in 2016 were smoked in China

145

Smoke-free legislation

March 2019

- all public places smoke-free, or at least 90% of population covered by complete subnational smoke-free legislation
- comprehensive smoke-free law, including bars and restaurants
- no effective legislation

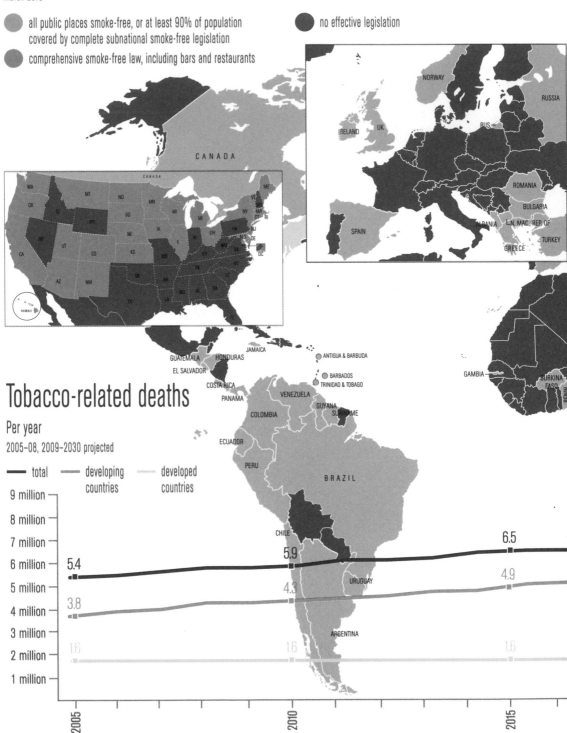

Tobacco-related deaths

Per year

2005–08, 2009–2030 projected

— total   — developing countries   — developed countries

9 million
8 million
7 million
6 million
5 million
4 million
3 million
2 million
1 million

5.4
3.8
1.6

5.9
4.3
1.6

6.5
4.9
1.6

2005   2010   2015

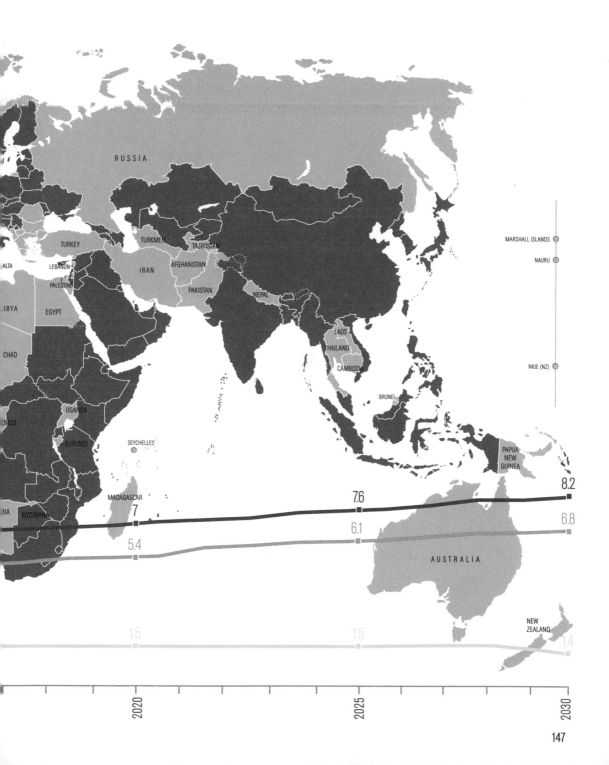

RUSSIA

MARSHALL ISLANDS ●

NAURU ●

TURKEY

TURKMEN.   TAJIKISTAN

ALTA

LEBANON   IRAN   AFGHANISTAN

PALESTINE

.IBYA   EGYPT   PAKISTAN

NEPAL

NIUE (NZ) ●

CHAD   LAOS
                                            THAILAND

                                            CAMBODIA

UGANDA   BRUNEI

)NGO

BURUNDI   SEYCHELLES ●

                                                              PAPUA
                                                              NEW
                                                              GUINEA

MADAGASCAR   8.2

                                    7.6

3IA BOTSWANA   7

                            6.1   6.8

                5.4

                                                    AUSTRALIA

1.5   1.5

                                            NEW
                                            ZEALAND
                                                              1.4

2020   2025   2030

Cancer

Cancer is a generic name for diseases characterized by the growth and spread of abnormal cells. It is the second leading cause of death, responsible for 16 per cent of all deaths. Though treatments and preventive strategies are improving, the incidence of cancer more than doubled from 1975 to 2008 and grew by 42 per cent in the subsequent 10 years.

As the world's population grows, and improvements in general health mean that people live longer on average, cancer looms ever larger. In countries where prosperity is advancing, bringing with it changes in lifestyle, diet, and tobacco use, the incidence of cancer is rising. Although the rate of cancer is currently 2.5 times greater in high-income countries than elsewhere, rates in poorer countries are increasing rapidly.

Cancer is most treatable when caught early. On a large scale, early diagnosis requires education and active screening programmes as part of comprehensive health care – more likely prospects in richer than in poorer countries.

Cancer on the increase

Number of new cases globally per year
1975, 2008, 2012, 2018, 2040 projected

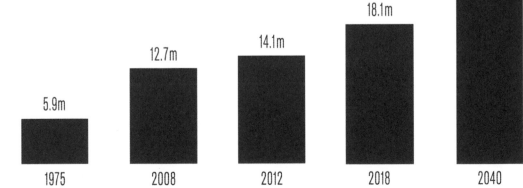

Year	Cases
1975	5.9m
2008	12.7m
2012	14.1m
2018	18.1m
2040	29.4m

Childhood-cancer survival rates

Observed in cases diagnosed with lymphoid leukemia

2018

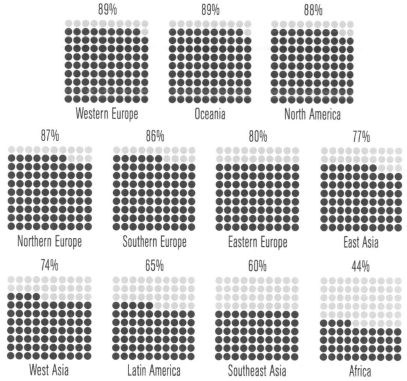

Environmental factors

Contributing to development of cancer

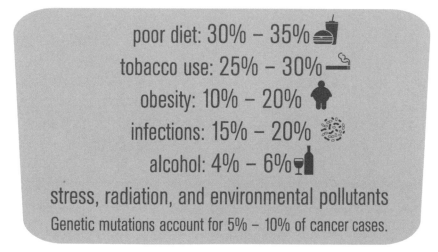

Cancer in men

Most common type

2018

- bladder
- colorectum
- Kaposi's sarcoma
- lip, mouth
- liver
- lung
- oesophagus
- prostate
- stomach
- no data

SOLOMON ISLANDS

NEW ZEALAND

JAPAN

NEW GUINEA

AUSTRALIA

PHILIPPINES

I N D O N E S I A

MALAYSIA

SINGAPORE

BRUNEI

NORTH KOREA

SOUTH KOREA

JAPAN

VIETNAM

C H I N A

YEMEN

MYANMAR

BANGLADESH

BHUTAN

SRI LANKA

INDIA

MALDIVES

MONGOLIA

KAZAKHSTAN

KYRGYZSTAN

TAJIKISTAN

TURKMENISTAN

AFGHANISTAN

PAKISTAN

IRAN

KUWAIT

BAHRAIN

SAUDI ARABIA

OMAN

ERITREA

DJIBOUTI

ETHIOPIA

SOMALIA

COMOROS

MAURITIUS

RÉUNION

MADAGASCAR

MOZAMBIQUE

R U S S I A

GEORGIA

ARMENIA

AZERBAIJAN

TURKEY

UGANDA

KENYA

TANZANIA

MALAWI

ZAMBIA

ZIMBABWE

BOTSWANA

SOUTH AFRICA

SWAZILAND

NAMIBIA

ANGOLA

DR CONGO

RWANDA

BURUNDI

CONGO

GABON

SÃO TOMÉ & PRÍNCIPE

CAMEROON

C.A.R.

SUDAN

CHAD

EGYPT

LIBYA

NIGER

NIGERIA

MALI

ALGERIA

MOROCCO

MAURITANIA

SENEGAL

CAPE VERDE

GAMBIA

GUINEA-BISSAU

SIERRA LEONE

LIBERIA

CÔTE D'IVOIRE

DENMARK

GERMANY

FRANCE

SPAIN

PORTUGAL

IRELAND

MALTA

BRAZIL

PARAGUAY

URUGUAY

ARGENTINA

CHILE

BOLIVIA

PERU

ECUADOR

COLOMBIA

VENEZUELA

GUYANA

SURINAME

TRINIDAD & TOBAGO

BARBADOS

ST LUCIA

PUERTO RICO (USA)

DOMINICAN REP.

JAMAICA

BAHAMAS

CUBA

BELIZE

HONDURAS

GUATEMALA

EL SALVADOR

NICARAGUA

COSTA RICA

PANAMA

MEXICO

USA

CANADA

150

Cancer in women

Most common type

2018

- breast
- cervix
- liver
- thyroid
- no data

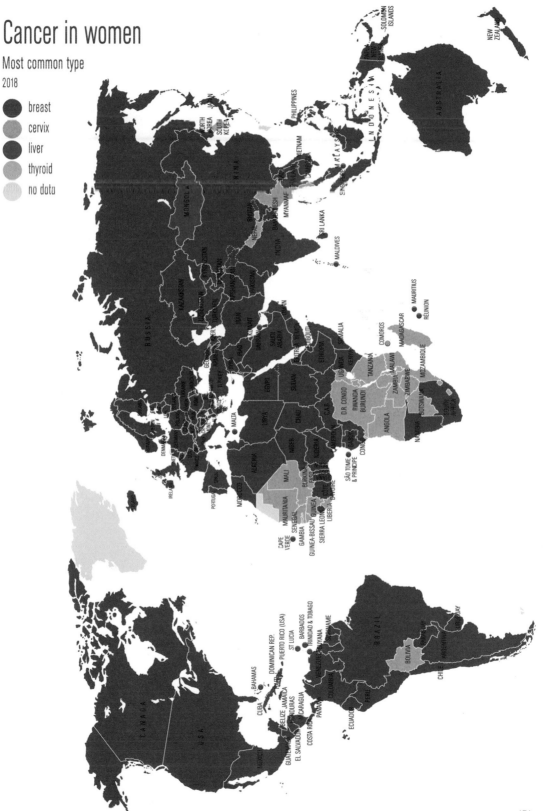

HIV/AIDS

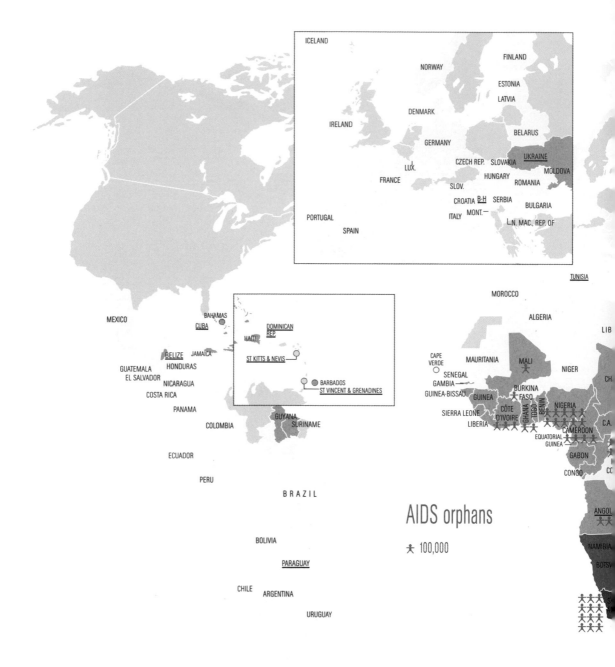

ICELAND

NORWAY

FINLAND

ESTONIA

LATVIA

DENMARK

IRELAND

GERMANY

BELARUS

CZECH REP. SLOVAKIA

UKRAINE

LUX.

MOLDOVA

FRANCE

HUNGARY

ROMANIA

SLOV.

CROATIA B-H SERBIA

BULGARIA

PORTUGAL

ITALY MONT.

N. MAC., REP. OF

SPAIN

TUNISIA

MOROCCO

ALGERIA

LIB

MEXICO

BAHAMAS

CUBA

DOMINICAN REP.

CAPE VERDE

MAURITANIA

MALI

NIGER

HAITI

SENEGAL

CH.

BELIZE JAMAICA

ST KITTS & NEVIS

GAMBIA

BURKINA FASO

GUATEMALA

HONDURAS

GUINEA-BISSAU

NIGERIA

EL SALVADOR

NICARAGUA

BARBADOS

GUINEA

CÔTE D'IVOIRE

GHANA

TOGO

BENIN

COSTA RICA

ST VINCENT & GRENADINES

SIERRA LEONE

C.A.

PANAMA

LIBERIA

CAMEROON

EQUATORIAL GUINEA

COLOMBIA

GUYANA

SURINAME

GABON

CO

ECUADOR

CONGO

PERU

B R A Z I L

AIDS orphans

PARAGUAY

ANGOL

BOLIVIA

👤 100,000

NAMIBIA

BOTS

CHILE ARGENTINA

URUGUAY

Impact of HIV/AIDS

Percentage of people
age 15–49 living with HIV

2018

20.0% – 28.0%	1.0% – 9.9%
10.0% – 19.9%	less than 1.0%

no data

RUSSIA

KAZAKHSTAN

MONGOLIA

UZBEKISTAN

GEORGIA

KYRGYZSTAN

JAPAN

MARSHALL ISLANDS

AZER. TURKMEN.

TAJIKISTAN

PALAU

LEBANON SYRIA

ISRAEL IRAQ IRAN

AFGHANISTAN

TUVALU

JORDAN

KUWAIT PAKISTAN

NEPAL BHUTAN

SAMOA

BAHRAIN QATAR

U.A.E.

SAUDI
ARABIA BANGLADESH

EGYPT OMAN MYANMAR LAOS

THAILAND PHILIPPINES

SUDAN ERITREA YEMEN VIETNAM

DJIBOUTI CAMBODIA

TONGA

SOUTH
SUDAN ETHIOPIA SRI LANKA BRUNEI

SOMALIA MALDIVES MALAYSIA

UGANDA SINGAPORE

KENYA

RWANDA

BURUNDI

TANZANIA INDONESIA

COMOROS

ZAMBIA MALAWI PAPUA
NEW
GUINEA SOLOMON
ISLANDS

MADAGASCAR

ZIMBABWE MAURITIUS

MOZAMBIQUE

SWAZILAND AUSTRALIA

LESOTHO

Barring the door

OMAN country imposing restrictions on entry, stay,
or residence of people living with HIV

2018

NEW ZEALAND

HIV/AIDS treatment

HIV/AIDS has claimed around 32 million lives over nearly four decades. In 2018, there were nearly 40 million people living with HIV.

A cure for HIV infection has not been found, but anti-retroviral therapy (ART) drugs enable people to live a healthy and productive life. ART can also stop transmission of HIV from mother to unborn child and has prevented more than 1.6 million children from becoming infected. The drugs are, however, by no means universally available.

Neither denying the problem nor trying to bar the door to people living with HIV/AIDS (as 44 countries still do) has worked as a preventive strategy. But, thanks to treatment and education, the numbers of new infections and deaths are declining. So, the epidemic can be stopped – but only if more resources are provided to fight it.

HIV/AIDS over time

Among adults and children
1990–2018

—— number newly infected with HIV
—— number of deaths

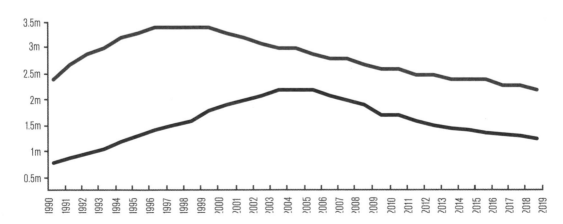

Anti-retroviral therapy (ART)

People receiving ART as
percentage of adults and children
living with HIV

2018

 number of adults and children living with HIV/AIDS

● percentage receiving ART

1.7m

38%

Eastern Europe and Central Asia

0.2m

◉ 32%

Middle East and North Africa

5m

51%

Western and Central Africa

2.2m

79%

Western and Central Europe and North America

5.9m

54%

Asia and the Pacific

2.2m

62%

Latin American and Caribbean

20.6m

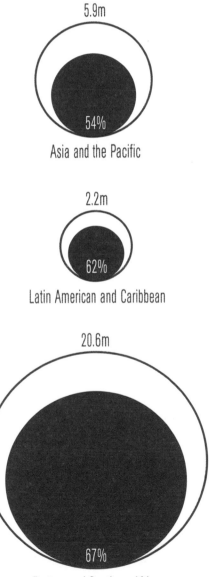

67%

Eastern and Southern Africa

Mental health

Worldwide, around one person in 10 is estimated to be living with a mental health disorder at any time. In all, around one in four people will be affected by mental or neurological disorders at some point in their lives.

The majority who suffer from poor mental health experience anxiety and depression; women are more likely to be affected than men. Growing numbers of children and adolescents have mental health problems of some degree; about half of mental disorders begin before the age of 14.

People with mental disorders are at greater risk of catching and passing on communicable diseases, and of suicide. About 800,000 people take their own lives each year. Suicide is the third leading cause of death among young people.

In many countries, mental disorder is a taboo subject, more shaming to a family than other diseases or abnormal behaviours. Stigma leads to this large and highly visible health issue being under-resourced and to the human rights of psychiatric patients being routinely abused in most countries. Average global spending on mental health is less than $2 per person per year; in high-income countries, where there remain criticisms and complaints that provision for this aspect of health is not adequate, the level of spending per person is 4,000 times the level in low-income countries.

Mental health disorders

Number of people worldwide estimated to have disorder
2017

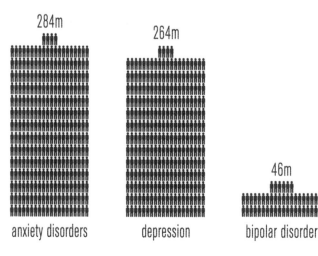

284m
anxiety disorders

264m
depression

46m
bipolar disorder

20m
schizophrenia

16m
eating disorders

Spending on mental health

Median government expenditure in US$ on
mental health per capita

2016

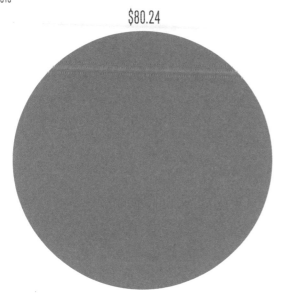

$80.24

High-income countries

$2.62

Upper-middle
income
countries

$1.05

Lower-
middleincome
countries

$0.02

Low-income
countries

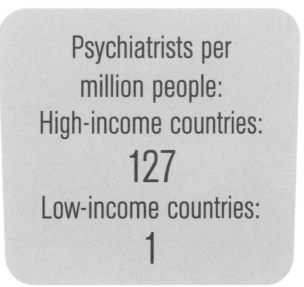

Psychiatrists per
million people:
High-income countries:
127
Low-income countries:
1

Suicide by men

Number of suicides
per million men
2016

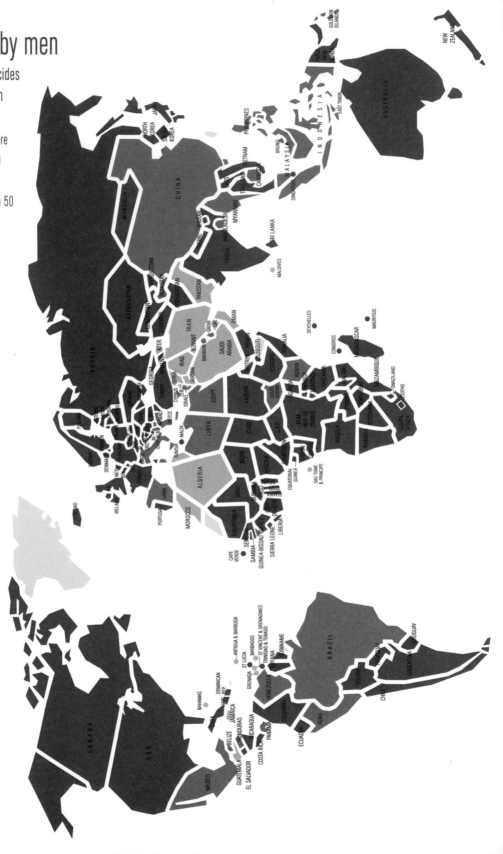

- 250 or more
- 100 – 249
- 50 – 99
- fewer than 50
- no data

SOLOMON ISLANDS
NEW ZEALAND
PAPUA NEW GUINEA
AUSTRALIA
EAST TIMOR
PHILIPPINES
INDONESIA
BRUNEI
VIETNAM
MALAYSIA
CAMBODIA
THAILAND
SINGAPORE
JAPAN
NORTH KOREA
SOUTH KOREA
CHINA
MONGOLIA
NEPAL
BHUTAN
BANGLADESH
MYANMAR
LAOS
INDIA
SRI LANKA
MALDIVES
PAKISTAN
AFGHANISTAN
KYRGYZSTAN
TAJIKISTAN
TURKMENISTAN
UZBEKISTAN
KAZAKHSTAN
RUSSIA
IRAN
OMAN
QATAR
UAE
KUWAIT
BAHRAIN
SAUDI ARABIA
YEMEN
IRAQ
SYRIA
JORDAN
ISRAEL
LEB
CYPRUS
GEORGIA
ARMENIA AZER.
TURKEY
GREECE
MALTA
TUNISIA
EGYPT
LIBYA
ALGERIA
MOROCCO
PORTUGAL
SPAIN
IRELAND
ICELAND
NORWAY
FINLAND
DENMARK
SWEDEN
GERMANY
NETH.
FRANCE
SEYCHELLES
MADAGASCAR
COMOROS
MAURITIUS
ERITREA
DJIBOUTI
ETHIOPIA
SOMALIA
SUDAN
SOUTH SUDAN
KENYA
UGANDA
TANZANIA
MALAWI
MOZAMBIQUE
SWAZILAND
LESOTHO
SOUTH AFRICA
NAMIBIA
BOTSWANA
ZIMBABWE
ZAMBIA
ANGOLA
DEM. REP. OF CONGO
CONGO
GABON
CHAD
NIGER
NIGERIA
C.A.R.
CAMEROON
EQUATORIAL GUINEA
SAO TOME & PRINCIPE
BENIN
TOGO
GHANA
BURKINA FASO
MALI
CÔTE D'IVOIRE
LIBERIA
SIERRA LEONE
GUINEA
GUINEA-BISSAU
GAMBIA
SENEGAL
MAURITANIA
CAPE VERDE

CANADA
USA
MEXICO
GUATEMALA
BELIZE
EL SALVADOR
HONDURAS
NICARAGUA
COSTA RICA
PANAMA
JAMAICA
HAITI
DOMINICAN REP.
BAHAMAS
CUBA
ANTIGUA & BARBUDA
ST LUCIA
BARBADOS
ST VINCENT & GRENADINES
GRENADA
TRINIDAD & TOBAGO
GUYANA
SURINAME
VENEZUELA
COLOMBIA
ECUADOR
PERU
BRAZIL
BOLIVIA
PARAGUAY
URUGUAY
ARGENTINA
CHILE

158

Suicide by women

Number of suicides
per million women
2016

- 250 – 499
- 100 – 249
- 50 – 99
- fewer than 50
- no data

159

Water and sanitation

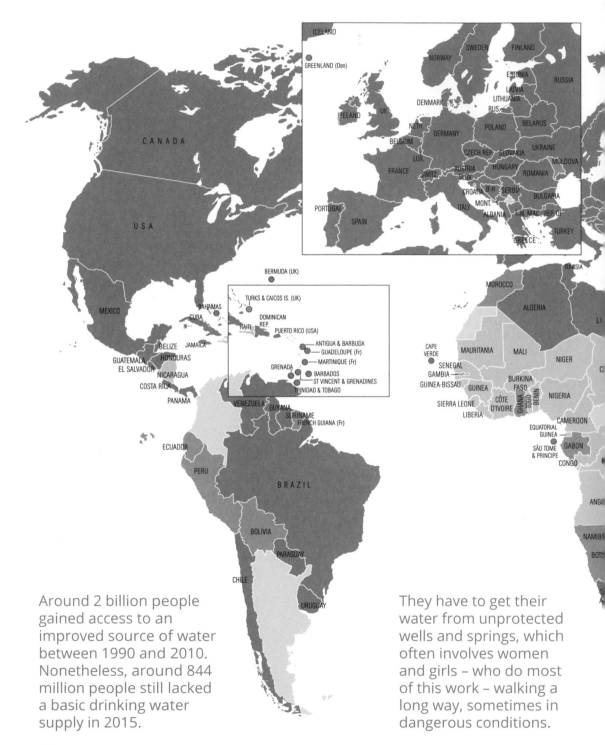

Around 2 billion people gained access to an improved source of water between 1990 and 2010. Nonetheless, around 844 million people still lacked a basic drinking water supply in 2015.

They have to get their water from unprotected wells and springs, which often involves women and girls – who do most of this work – walking a long way, sometimes in dangerous conditions.

Drinking water

Percentage of population with easy access to
an improved water source

2017

less than 75%

75% – 84%

85% – 94%

95% or more

no data

RUSSIA

KAZAKHSTAN

MONGOLIA

GEORGIA
ARMENIA   AZER.
UZBEKISTAN   KYRGYZSTAN
TURKMEN.
TAJIKISTAN

NORTH
KOREA   JAPAN
SOUTH
KOREA

US   LEB.
SYRIA
IRAEL
IRAQ   IRAN
JORDAN
PALESTINE

AFGHANISTAN

CHINA

KUWAIT
BAHRAIN   QATAR
UAE
SAUDI
ARABIA   OMAN

PAKISTAN

NEPAL   BHUTAN
BANGLADESH
INDIA   MYANMAR

YPT

YEMEN

DJIBOUTI

SUDAN

SOUTH
SUDAN   ETHIOPIA

UGANDA
KENYA

RWANDA
BURUNDI
TANZANIA

SEYCHELLES

COMOROS
MAYOTTE (Fr)

BIA   MALAWI

MADAGASCAR

BABWE

MAURITIUS
RÉUNION (Fr)

MOZAMBIQUE

SWAZILAND

LESOTHO

SOMALIA

MALDIVES

SRI LANKA

LAOS
THAILAND
CAMBODIA   VIETNAM

PHILIPPINES

BRUNEI
MALAYSIA
SINGAPORE

INDONESIA

TIMOR-LESTE

PAPUA
NEW
GUINEA   SOLOMON
ISLANDS

AUSTRALIA

NEW
ZEALAND

GUAM (USA)
MICRONESIA, FED. ST. OF
MARSHALL ISLANDS
PALAU
NAURU
KIRIBATI
TUVALU
TOKELAU

SAMOA

VANUATU
FIJI
COOK IS. (NZ)
NIUE (NZ)
TONGA
NEW CALEDONIA (Fr)

Women and girls are responsible in 8 out of 10 households where water has to be collected from outside the home

Sanitation

Percentage of population with access to basic sanitation facilities

2017

● less than 25%	● 50% – 74%	● 99% or more
● 25% – 49%	● 75% – 99%	● no data

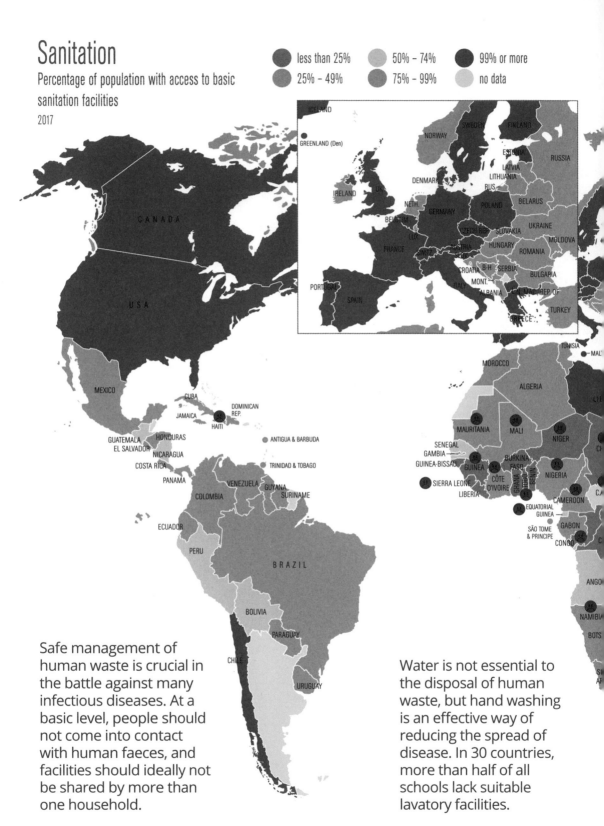

Safe management of human waste is crucial in the battle against many infectious diseases. At a basic level, people should not come into contact with human faeces, and facilities should ideally not be shared by more than one household.

Water is not essential to the disposal of human waste, but hand washing is an effective way of reducing the spread of disease. In 30 countries, more than half of all schools lack suitable lavatory facilities.

Unsafe schools

50% or more of schools have no drinking water, sanitation, or hand-washing facilities

2016

In 24 countries, more than **20%** of people **have to defecate in the open,** which poses great health risks to the community

RUSSIA

KAZAKHSTAN

MONGOLIA

GEORGIA
ARMENIA   AZER.   UZBEKISTAN   KYRGYZSTAN

NORTH KOREA

JAPAN

MARSHALL ISLANDS

TURKMEN.   TAJIKISTAN

SOUTH KOREA

RUS.
LEB.
ISRAEL   SYRIA
PALESTINE   JORDAN   IRAQ   IRAN   AFGHANISTAN

CHINA

KIRIBATI
TUVALU

KUWAIT
BAHRAIN   QATAR   PAKISTAN   NEPAL   BHUTAN

AMERICAN SAMOA (USA)

EGYPT   U.A.E.
SAUDI ARABIA   OMAN

INDIA   BANGLADESH
MYANMAR   LAOS

HONG KONG SAR (CHINA)

VANUATU

SUDAN   YEMEN

THAILAND   VIETNAM

PHILIPPINES

DJIBOUTI   CAMBODIA

TONGA

SOUTH SUDAN   ETHIOPIA

SRI LANKA

UGANDA   SOMALIA

MALDIVES

KENYA

MALAYSIA

RWANDA
BURUNDI

SINGAPORE

TANZANIA

COMOROS

INDONESIA

PAPUA NEW GUINEA

SOLOMON ISLANDS

MBIA   MALAWI

MADAGASCAR

TIMOR-LESTE

MBABWE
MOZAMBIQUE

AUSTRALIA

SWAZILAND
LESOTHO

NEW ZEALAND

163

Living with disease

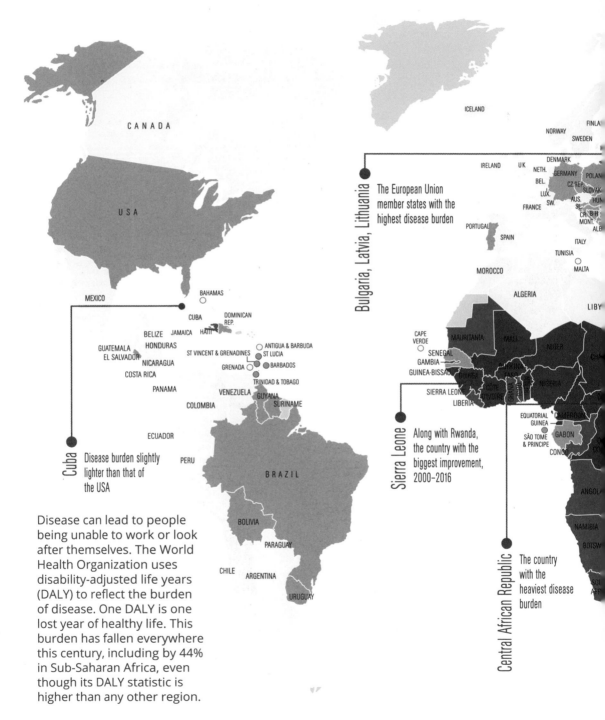

CANADA

ICELAND

NORWAY   FINLA
SWEDEN

IRELAND   UK   DENMARK
NETH.   GERMANY   POLAN
BEL.   CZ.REP.   SLOVAK
LUX.   AUS.   HUN
FRANCE   SW.   SL.   CR. B-H
CR.   MONT.
SPAIN   ITALY   ALB

PORTUGAL

TUNISIA
MOROCCO   MALTA

USA

MEXICO

BAHAMAS

CUBA   DOMINICAN
REP.

BELIZE   JAMAICA   HAITI

GUATEMALA   HONDURAS   ANTIGUA & BARBUDA
EL SALVADOR   NICARAGUA   ST VINCENT & GRENADINES   ST LUCIA
COSTA RICA   GRENADA   BARBADOS

PANAMA   TRINIDAD & TOBAGO
VENEZUELA   GUYANA
COLOMBIA   SURINAME

ECUADOR

PERU

BRAZIL

BOLIVIA

PARAGUAY

CHILE   ARGENTINA

URUGUAY

ALGERIA   LIBY

CAPE
VERDE   MAURITANIA   MALI   NIGER
SENEGAL   CHA
GAMBIA   BURKINA
GUINEA-BISSAU   GUINEA   FASO   NIGERIA
CÔTE   GHANA
SIERRA LEON   D'IVOIRE
LIBERIA

EQUATORIAL   CAMEROON
GUINEA
SÃO TOME   GABON
& PRINCIPE   CONGO

ANGOLA

NAMIBIA

BOTSW

Bulgaria, Latvia, Lithuania

The European Union
member states with the
highest disease burden

Cuba

Disease burden slightly
lighter than that of
the USA

Sierra Leone

Along with Rwanda,
the country with the
biggest improvement,
2000–2016

Central African Republic

The country
with the
heaviest disease
burden

Disease can lead to people
being unable to work or look
after themselves. The World
Health Organization uses
disability-adjusted life years
(DALY) to reflect the burden
of disease. One DALY is one
lost year of healthy life. This
burden has fallen everywhere
this century, including by 44%
in Sub-Saharan Africa, even
though its DALY statistic is
higher than any other region.

National disease burden

DALYs per 100 people

2016

60 – 91
45 – 59
30 – 44
15 – 29

A DALY (disability-adjusted life year) measures the number of years lost due to ill-health, disability, or early death.

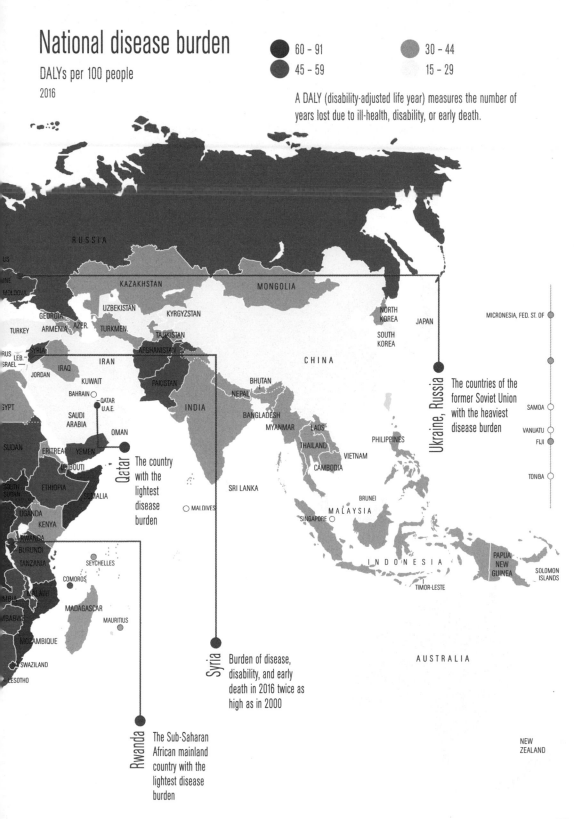

RUSSIA

US

INE

MOLDOVA.

KAZAKHSTAN

MONGOLIA

UZBEKISTAN

KYRGYZSTAN

GEORGIA

ARMENIA   AZER.

TURKEY

TURKMEN.

TAJIKISTAN

AFGHANISTAN

NORTH
KOREA

SOUTH
KOREA

JAPAN

MICRONESIA, FED. ST. OF

CYPRUS   LEB.—
ISRAEL —

SYRIA

IRAN

CHINA

JORDAN

IRAQ

KUWAIT

BAHRAIN

BHUTAN

NEPAL

Ukraine, Russia

The countries of the former Soviet Union with the heaviest disease burden

SAMOA

GYPT

QATAR
U.A.E.

SAUDI
ARABIA

PAKISTAN

INDIA

VANUATU

FIJI

OMAN

BANGLADESH

MYANMAR

LAOS

Qatar

The country with the lightest disease burden

SUDAN

ERITREA   YEMEN

THAILAND

PHILIPPINES

VIETNAM

TONGA

DJIBOUTI

CAMBODIA

SOUTH
SUDAN

ETHIOPIA

SOMALIA

SRI LANKA

BRUNEI

UGANDA

KENYA

MALDIVES

MALAYSIA

SINGAPORE

RWANDA

BURUNDI

TANZANIA

SEYCHELLES

INDONESIA

PAPUA
NEW
GUINEA

SOLOMON
ISLANDS

COMOROS

MBIA   ALAWI

TIMOR-LESTE

MBABWE

MADAGASCAR

MAURITIUS

MOZAMBIQUE

AUSTRALIA

SWAZILAND

LESOTHO

Syria

Burden of disease, disability, and early death in 2016 twice as high as in 2000

Rwanda

The Sub-Saharan African mainland country with the lightest disease burden

NEW
ZEALAND

Health of the planet

Humanity has made a serious mess of our relationship with nature. The past 200 years have generated extraordinary progress, as more people live longer lives than ever before; and for many those longer lives are better than our forebears enjoyed. But that success is working against us.

The extent of human activity is extraordinary: 75 per cent of land surface has been significantly altered and we have had a major effect on 66 per cent of ocean area. Over 85 per cent of wetlands have been lost. With this, our species puts others at risk; the current decline in biodiversity is historically unprecedented.

Soaring economic output has pumped billions of tonnes of carbon dioxide and other greenhouse gases into the atmosphere; the laws of physics say that will increase average global temperatures with consequent changes in climate – and that is what is happening.

We have also pumped out noxious substances, creating a global crisis of air pollution that is exacerbated by the warming atmosphere. Our increasing output has generated enormous amounts of waste, often not disposed of responsibly, and we can see the consequences with our own eyes. And we are using (and wasting) more water than we can afford to: half the world's population will face water scarcity in the coming decade.

These things we know but we do not yet know how these environmental issues interact. Nature is essential for our existence and for a decent quality of life yet we have treated it with ignorant, clumsy disdain. We have tried to conquer nature while never ceasing to rely on it.

Awareness of our environmental predicament is rising. Action is being taken on different fronts: bans on plastic bags; state-funded incentives for low-carbon infrastructure; protecting sea and land areas from industrial intrusion; funding ecological restoration. These actions need to go further, faster. And they need to be knitted together by international cooperation.

The difficulty is that the most far-reaching and beneficial measures require deep changes in how our economy works and in our attitudes to consumption and waste. Many will oppose changes they see as weakening their privileges. Yet they too are part of nature; their well-being is also at stake. The tools are there. What is needed now is the intelligence and will to pick them up and use them.

Beyond the bounds

In this age of more, most, and never before, humanity is getting to the limit of the planet's hospitality to us. Our impact on the natural environment increases as the global population grows, and as industry and agriculture grow with it, along with consumption and extraction of natural resources.

Because it is unprecedented, the full consequences of humanity's impact on the environment are unknown. It is not clear how far we can go before the consequences get very serious. And compared to how much is already known about climate change, biodiversity loss, and other issues, not much at all is known about the interaction between the impacts.

A multinational group of scientists devised the concept of planetary boundaries to quantify how close we are to danger. The boundaries have not all been calculated and not every scientist agrees with the concept, the definitions, or the calculations. But the idea brings the key issues into sharp relief. Inside the boundaries, humanity is operating more or less safely. If we cross them, we don't know what will unfold. According to these scientists, we have crossed five boundaries, and in two cases have moved into the high-risk zone. There is time to ensure we do not cross more.

novel entities
not yet quantified

atmospheric aerosol loading
not yet quantified

Boundary dimensions

	Measured by:	Boundary calculated as:
Biosphere integrity	Functional diversity	Not yet assessed
	Genetic diversity	Extinction rate of fewer than 10 extinctions per million species years
Climate change	Carbon dioxide in atmosphere	350 parts per million
Ocean acidification	Aragonite depletion in ocean	Reduction to not less than 80% of pre-industrial level
Stratospheric ozone depletion	Concentration of ozone in stratosphere	No more than 5% reduction from pre-industrial level
Biogeochemical flows	Phosphorus flow into oceans	11 million tonnes per year
	Nitrogen removed from atmosphere	62 million tonnes per year
Freshwater use	Maximum amount used	4,000 cubic kilometres per year
Land-system change	Area of forested land as % of original forest cover	75% of land surface
Atmospheric aerosol loading	Particles in the atmosphere	Not yet calculated
Novel entities		Not yet calculated

Planetary boundaries

Assessment of the extent to which safe operating levels have
been reached or transgressed on selected impacts

2015

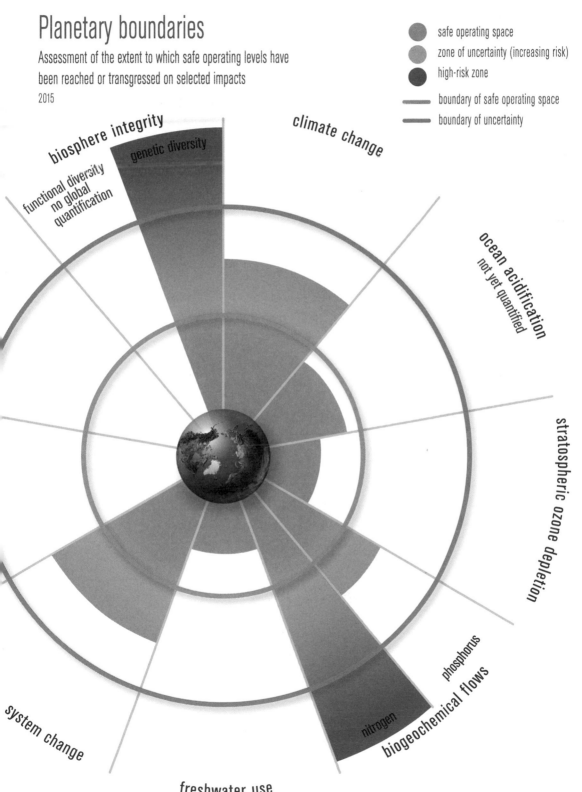

safe operating space

zone of uncertainty (increasing risk)

high-risk zone

boundary of safe operating space

boundary of uncertainty

biosphere integrity

genetic diversity

functional diversity
no global
quantification

climate change

ocean acidification
not yet quantified

stratospheric ozone depletion

phosphorus

nitrogen

biogeochemical flows

system change

freshwater use

Biodiversity loss

Threatened mammals, birds, and amphibians

Number of species threatened
2019

- ● 100 or more
- ● 50 – 99
- ● 25 – 49
- ● 10 – 24
- ● fewer than 10
- ● no data

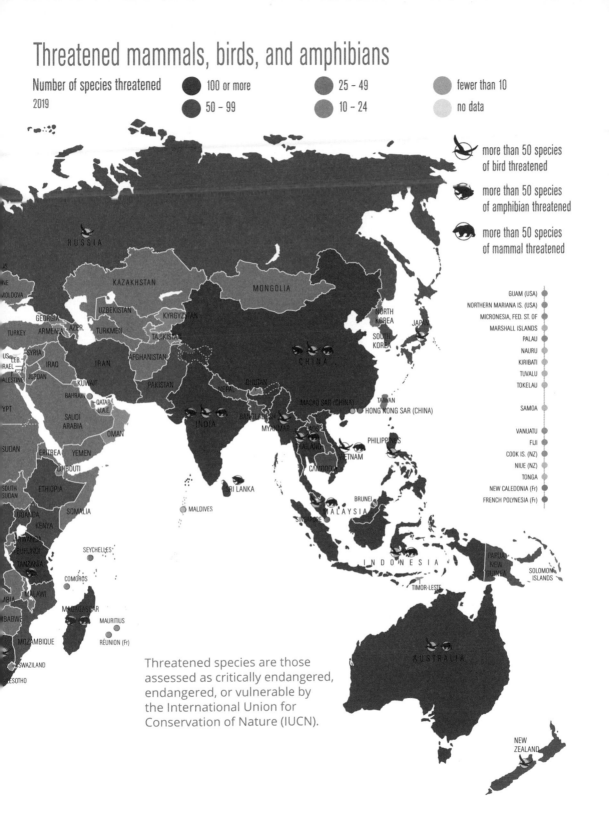

🐦 more than 50 species of bird threatened

🐸 more than 50 species of amphibian threatened

🐾 more than 50 species of mammal threatened

RUSSIA

KAZAKHSTAN

MONGOLIA

UZBEKISTAN

KYRGYZSTAN

TURKMEN.

TAJIKISTAN

GEORGIA
ARMENIA AZER.
TURKEY

US
RAEL
ALESTINE
SYRIA
IRAQ
JORDAN
KUWAIT
IRAN
AFGHANISTAN
PAKISTAN
NEPAL
BHUTAN

BAHRAIN
QATAR
U.A.E.
SAUDI
ARABIA
OMAN
YEMEN

INDIA
BANGLADESH
MYANMAR
LAO

SUDAN
ERITREA
DJIBOUTI
ETHIOPIA

SOUTH
SUDAN
SOMALIA
UGANDA
KENYA
RWANDA
BURUNDI
TANZANIA

NORTH
KOREA
SOUTH
KOREA
JAPAN

CHINA

MACAO SAR (CHINA)
TAIWAN
HONG KONG SAR (CHINA)

THAILAND
VIETNAM
CAMBODIA

PHILIPPINES

SRI LANKA

MALDIVES

SINGAPORE

BRUNEI
MALAYSIA

INDONESIA

PAPUA
NEW
GUINEA

SOLOMON
ISLANDS

TIMOR-LESTE

SEYCHELLES

COMOROS

MADAGASCAR
MAURITIUS
RÉUNION (Fr)

MALAWI
ZAMBIA
ZIMBABWE
MOZAMBIQUE
SWAZILAND
LESOTHO

AUSTRALIA

NEW
ZEALAND

GUAM (USA)
NORTHERN MARIANA IS. (USA)
MICRONESIA, FED. ST. OF
MARSHALL ISLANDS
PALAU
NAURU
KIRIBATI
TUVALU
TOKELAU

SAMOA

VANUATU
FIJI
COOK IS. (NZ)
NIUE (NZ)
TONGA
NEW CALEDONIA (Fr)
FRENCH POLYNESIA (Fr)

Threatened species are those assessed as critically endangered, endangered, or vulnerable by the International Union for Conservation of Nature (IUCN).

Biodiversity

Biodiversity is the variety between and within species and the different ecosystems in which they (and we) live. Human actions currently threaten more species with global extinction than ever before, and biodiversity is declining faster than at any time in human history.

Not all species have been identified and counted but estimates are that around 1 million species face extinction within decades, unless action is taken to reduce the pace of biodiversity loss. In fact, without countermeasures, the rate of species extinction will accelerate; it is already at least some tens and maybe several hundreds of times higher than the average rate over the past 10 million years.

This loss creates problems for human well-being. Biodiversity is important economically, socially, and medically. An estimated 4 billion people rely primarily on natural medicines for health care. About 70% of drugs used to treat cancer are either natural or are synthetic products that were inspired by natural products. More than 75% of our food crops rely on pollination by insects, birds, and mammals. This includes fruit and vegetables and important cash crops such as coffee, cocoa, and almonds.

Based on satellite data, it has been estimated that there are more trees on Earth than stars in the Milky Way: 3 trillion, or 400 for every living person. But there are fewer now than there used to be. Forests have shrunk by about 20% since 1900 – a loss of 3.9 million square miles (10 million km^2).

Forests matter. More than 2 billion people worldwide rely on burning wood to meet their energy needs. The whole world relies on forests to absorb carbon as part of the planet's natural balance that makes human life possible.

The rate of loss of the world's forests has slowed since 2000; it is 80% less than in the 20th century. But the process is uneven. New planting of temperate and boreal forest in China, USA, and Russia is outweighed by the destruction of highly biodiverse rainforest in Brazil, Indonesia, and the Congo, despite projects regenerating small areas of tropical and subtropical forests.

Unfortunately, for biodiversity, newly planted trees are a poor substitute for mature trees. Better than relying on replacement would be to end the destruction of existing forest land.

Threatened species

Threatened species as percentage of those evaluated by IUCN

2019

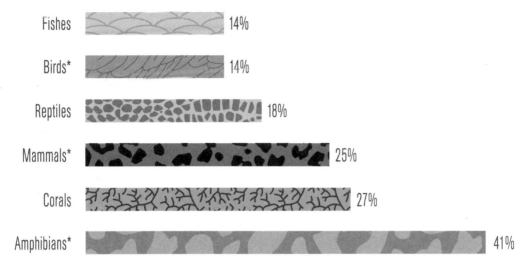

Fishes 14%

Birds* 14%

Reptiles 18%

Mammals* 25%

Corals 27%

Amphibians* 41%

*80% or more of species within group have been evaluated

Forest lost and gained

Top ten most forested countries

2000–2015

square kilometres

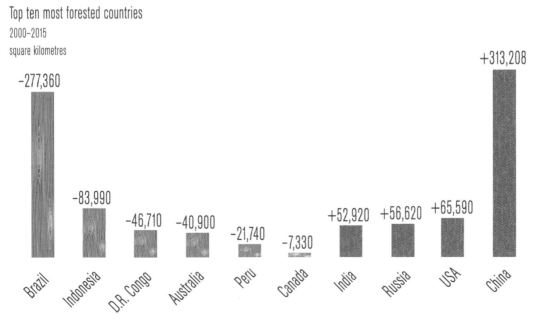

−277,360 Brazil

−83,990 Indonesia

−46,710 D.R. Congo

−40,900 Australia

−21,740 Peru

−7,330 Canada

+52,920 India

+56,620 Russia

+65,590 USA

+313,208 China

Protected areas

Terrestrial protected areas (designated reserves of 1,000 hectares or larger) as percentage of total land area

2018

- 30% or more
- 20% – 29%
- 10% – 19%
- less than 10%

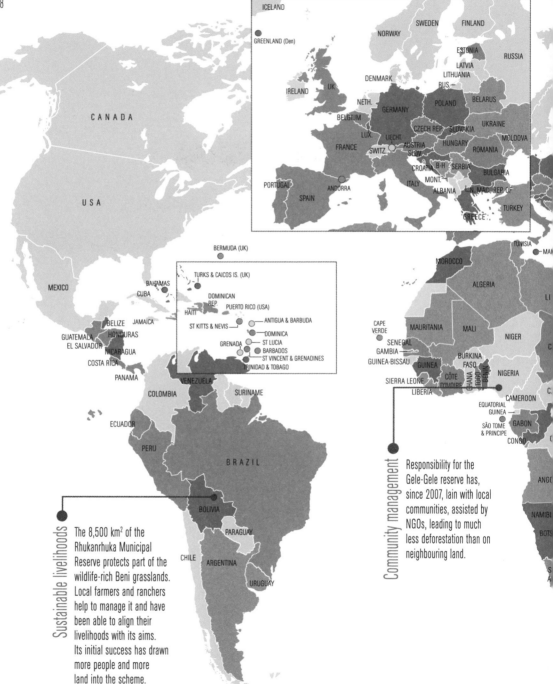

Sustainable livelihoods

The 8,500 km² of the Rhukanrhuka Municipal Reserve protects part of the wildlife-rich Beni grasslands. Local farmers and ranchers help to manage it and have been able to align their livelihoods with its aims. Its initial success has drawn more people and more land into the scheme.

Community management

Responsibility for the Gele-Gele reserve has, since 2007, lain with local communities, assisted by NGOs, leading to much less deforestation than on neighbouring land.

RUSSIA

KAZAKHSTAN

MONGOLIA

UZBEKISTAN

KYRGYZSTAN

GEORGIA

ARMENIA   AZER.   TURKMEN.   TAJIKISTAN

NORTH
KOREA

JAPAN

SOUTH
KOREA

RUS.   LEB.   SYRIA

ISRAEL   IRAQ   IRAN   AFGHANISTAN

CHINA

PALESTINE   JORDAN

KUWAIT   PAKISTAN

GYPT   BAHRAIN   QATAR
U.A.E.

NEPAL   BHUTAN

HONG KONG SAR (CHINA)

SAUDI
ARABIA   OMAN

BANGLADESH

SUDAN   ERITREA   YEMEN   INDIA   MYANMAR   LAOS

DJIBOUTI   THAILAND   PHILIPPINES

SOUTH
SUDAN   ETHIOPIA   VIETNAM

CAMBODIA

UGANDA   SOMALIA   SRI LANKA

KENYA   MALDIVES   BRUNEI

MALAYSIA

RWANDA   SINGAPORE

BURUNDI

TANZANIA   SEYCHELLES   INDONESIA

COMOROS   PAPUA
NEW
GUINEA   SOLOMON
ISLANDS

MBIA   MALAWI

MADAGASCAR   TIMOR-LESTE

BABWE   MAURITIUS

MOZAMBIQUE   AUSTRALIA

SWAZILAND

LESOTHO

GUAM (USA)

MICRONESIA, FED. ST. OF

MARSHALL ISLANDS

PALAU

KIRIBATI

TUVALU

SAMOA

VANUATU

FIJI

TONGA

NEW CALEDONIA (Fr)

NEW
ZEALAND

Preservation and public awareness

The Ethiopian wolf, Africa's most endangered carnivore, has benefited from the preservation of its habitat and a reduction in hunting.

Benefits of forest protection

Mainly due to increased forest cover and protection, the population of the endangered Rodrigues fruit bat has recovered from only 70 – 100 individuals in the 1970s to more than 25,000 today.

Water resources

The world as a whole has plenty of fresh water but, like every natural resource, it is distributed unevenly. And, like most natural resources, people are using it at an ever increasing rate. It features in personal use, food production, construction of roads and buildings, and industrial processes, including the manufacture of electronic components.

Freshwater is an unpredictable resource, but is vital for healthy soil and vegetation. When more water is withdrawn than nature resupplies that has an impact on all aspects of the environment: soil, vegetation, the survival of plant and animal species. Countries using more than 25% of their renewable supply are considered by the UN to be water stressed, and those using more than 70% to be seriously stressed.

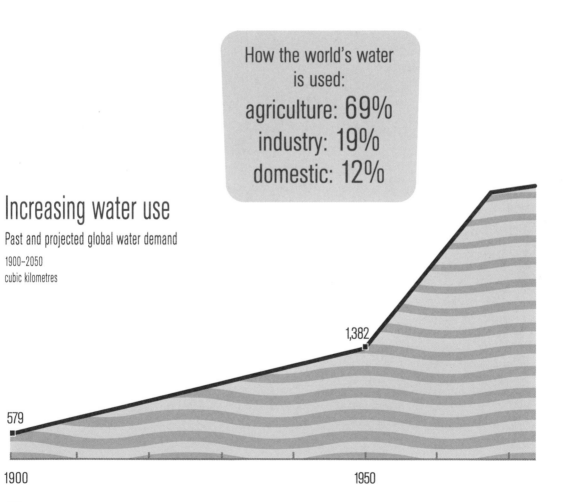

How the world's water is used:

agriculture: **69%**

industry: **19%**

domestic: **12%**

Increasing water use

Past and projected global water demand

1900–2050
cubic kilometres

1,382

579

1900

1950

Whether a country has a sufficient, renewable supply of fresh water seems to have little impact on the way of life of its richest inhabitants. Many countries use more water than falls on their territory as rain, flows through it in rivers, or is stored in lakes. In some parts of the world – notably North Africa – water held for millennia in natural underground aquifers is being relentlessly drained. In the Middle East, meagre natural water supplies are supplemented by expensive, energy-consuming desalination plants that have negative effects on the local environment.

Many developed countries compensate for a lack of water by importing food and other goods from countries where water is more plentiful. Others take it a step further. Northern India and areas of China are under severe water stress, which is likely to worsen, and Indian and Chinese investors have purchased large areas of arable land in countries such as Ethiopia, where water supplies are more plentiful.

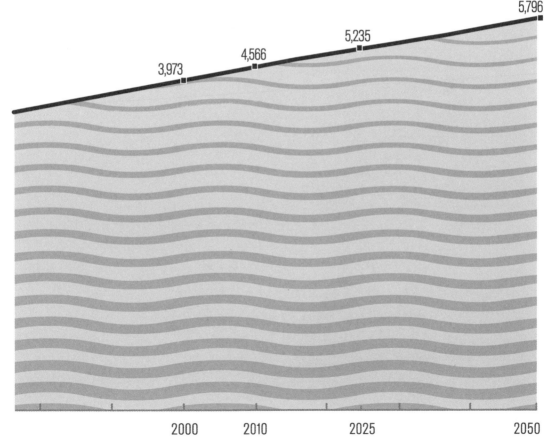

3,973

4,566

5,235

5,796

2000   2010   2025   2050

Water used

Water withdrawn annually per capita for domestic,
industrial, and environmental use

latest available data
2002–2017
cubic metres

- 1,000 – 5,739
- 500 – 999
- 100 – 499
- less than 100
- no data

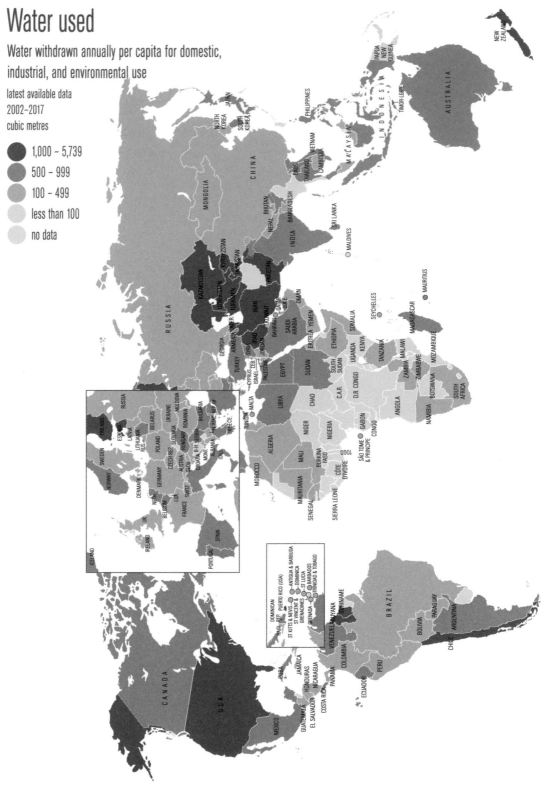

Water stress

Freshwater withdrawal as a percentage
of available resources

latest available data
2002–2017

- 70% or more
  serious water stress
- 25% – 69%
  water stress
- 24% or less
- no data

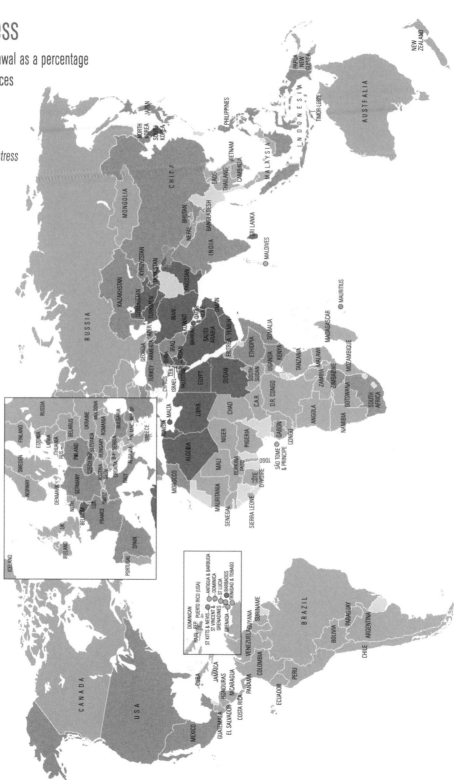

Waste

Waste is one of the world's biggest challenges and, so far, failures. National and local regulations have reduced the use of plastic bags in some countries, but more than half of all waste goes into landfills, often badly managed, and vast areas of ocean are a soup of tiny pieces of plastic.

Disposable plastic bag use in England's main supermarkets fell by more than 90% in 2015–2018 after the introduction of a 5p charge.

England

Ireland A levy on plastic bags reduced usage from 328 per person in 2002 to around 20 per person in 2003. The levy can be raised to maintain its efficacy.

Chile A law banning single-use plastic bags was passed in August 2018 – the first such ban in South America. Businesses were given until August 2020 to comply.

CANADA

USA

MEXICO

JAMAICA
BELIZE
GUATEMALA   HONDURAS   HAITI

COSTA RICA
PANAMA

ANTIGUA & BARBUDA
ST VINCENT & GRENADINES

COLOMBIA

ECUADOR

GUYANA

BRAZIL

CHILE   ARGENTINA

URUGUAY

IRELAND

PORTUGAL

MOROCCO

CAPE VERDE   MAURITANIA

SENEGAL
GAMBIA
GUINEA-BISSAU

CÔTE D'IVOIRE

Plastic waste

Regulations (including ban, levy, or law)
on plastic bags and Styrofoam products
as of 2018

Regulations introduced:

- national
- national regulations announced
- local

area where circulating ocean currents cause plastic waste to collect

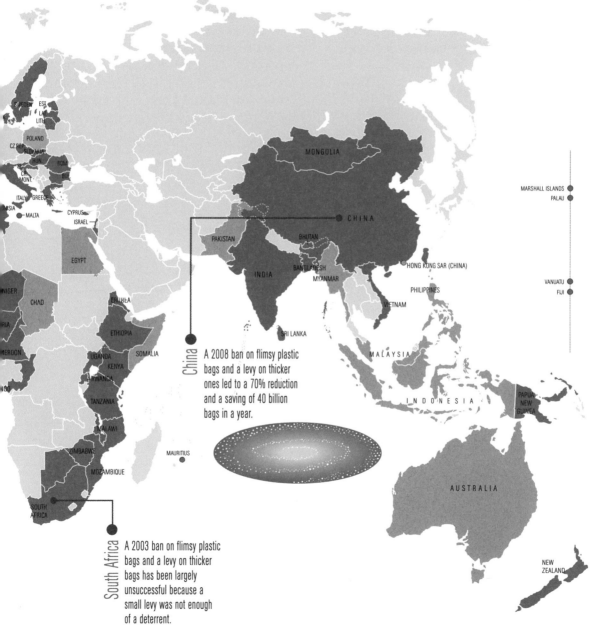

MARSHALL ISLANDS
PALAU

MONGOLIA

CHINA

PAKISTAN
BHUTAN
INDIA
BANGLADESH
MYANMAR
HONG KONG SAR (CHINA)

PHILIPPINES

VIETNAM
SRI LANKA

VANUATU
FIJI

MALAYSIA

INDONESIA

PAPUA NEW GUINEA

SWEDEN EST
LAT
LITH
POLAND
CZ.REP
SLOVAKIA
HUN. ROM
CR
MONT.
ITALY GREECE
NISIA
MALTA
CYPRUS
ISRAEL

EGYPT

NIGER
CHAD
ERITREA
RIA
ETHIOPIA
MEROON
UGANDA
SOMALIA
KENYA
RWANDA
NGO
TANZANIA
MALAWI
ZIMBABWE
MOZAMBIQUE
MAURITIUS

SOUTH AFRICA

AUSTRALIA

NEW ZEALAND

China

A 2008 ban on flimsy plastic bags and a levy on thicker ones led to a 70% reduction and a saving of 40 billion bags in a year.

South Africa

A 2003 ban on flimsy plastic bags and a levy on thicker bags has been largely unsuccessful because a small levy was not enough of a deterrent.

Waste production

Each year, the world produces about 2 billion tonnes of regular, non-hazardous waste – and this is likely to grow by 70% by 2050 unless urgent action is taken. The USA generates disproportionate amounts: Americans account for only 4% of the world's population, yet generate 12% of its waste.

Only about 16% of global waste is recycled. The US rate of recycling is twice the world average at 35% but well behind the most efficient recycler – Germany – which hits 68%.

It has been estimated that since 1950, the world has produced 8.3 billion tonnes of plastic. Far too much plastic waste has been mishandled and become part of the environment. Most kinds of plastic take from 400 to 1,000 years to degrade. Microplastics – tiny particles of the material – are everywhere, including in our bodies. Their full health and environmental effects are not yet fully known.

By 2050
almost all seabirds
will have
ingested plastic

Plastic world

Global plastic production
million tonnes
1950–2018

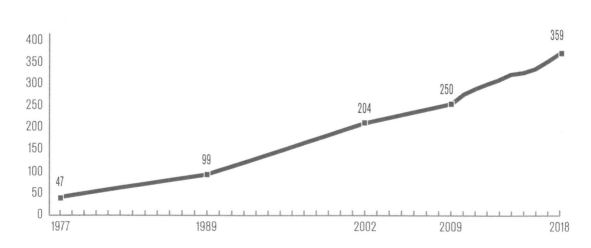

Beach trash

Number of most common items of debris picked up by volunteers
worldwide as Part of Ocean Conservancy clean-up
1985–2018

73m

29m

24m

20m

17m

Plastic bags and
Styrofoam containers
can take up to

1,000 years

to decompose

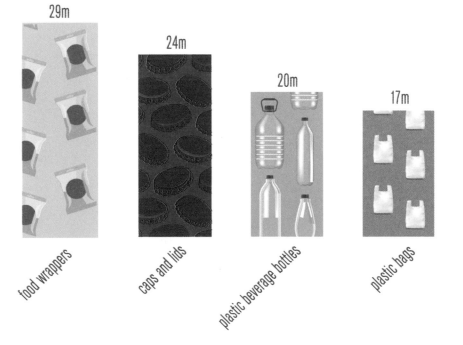

cigarettes and filters

food wrappers

caps and lids

plastic beverage bottles

plastic bags

Oceans

About 40% of sharks and rays in European waters are threatened with extinction.

Coral reefs
Coral reefs cover only 0.1% of the ocean floor but are home to about 25% of marine fish species. The total area of reefs has halved in the past 150 years, increasing pressure on both the animals and people relying on them for nutrition, income, and protection from floods and hurricanes.

Seagrass
The area of seagrass has declined by about 30% in the last 100 years. It stabilizes the seabed, provides habitat for marine species, and stores vast amounts of carbon.

Mangroves
Important for coastal protection from erosion and storms, as habitat for marine life, and as a CO_2 sink, mangroves have declined by about 30% in the past century.

North Atlantic right whales
Only 300–350 North Atlantic right whales are known to be alive.

Ocean dead zones
Industrial effluent and climate change has led to at least 500 "dead zones" with very low oxygen levels in coastal waters – a tenfold increase since 1950. Most sea creatures cannot survive in these conditions, but some microbes can. They produce a greenhouse gas that is 300 times more potent than CO_2.

As of February 2020, 8% of global oceans were classed as protected areas

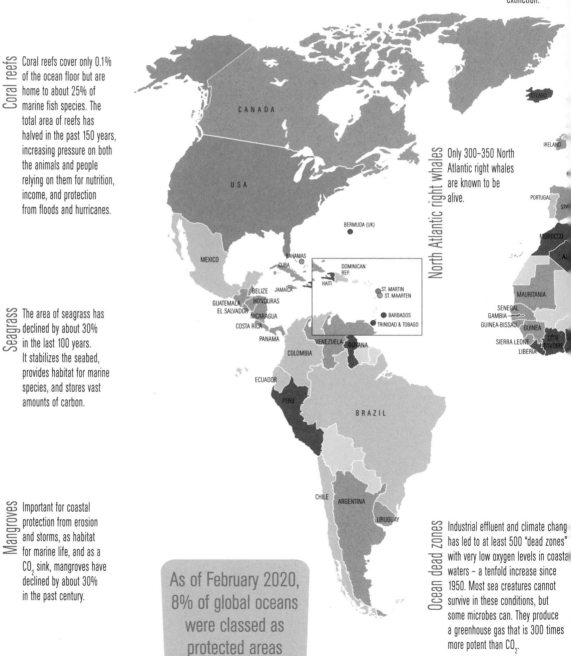

CANADA

USA

MEXICO

BERMUDA (UK)

BAHAMAS
CUBA
HAITI
DOMINICAN REP.
JAMAICA
BELIZE
GUATEMALA
EL SALVADOR
HONDURAS
NICARAGUA
COSTA RICA
PANAMA

ST. MARTIN
ST. MAARTEN
BARBADOS
TRINIDAD & TOBAGO

VENEZUELA
GUYANA
COLOMBIA
ECUADOR
PERU
BRAZIL
CHILE
ARGENTINA
URUGUAY

ICELAND
IRELAND
PORTUGAL
SPAIN
MOROCCO
AL...
MAURITANIA
SENEGAL
GAMBIA
GUINEA-BISSAU
GUINEA
SIERRA LEONE
LIBERIA
CÔTE D'IVOIRE

Marine protection

Marine protected area as percentage of
country's territorial waters

2018

83% or more	11% – 30%
31% – 50%	1% – 10%
local	no access to marine waters, or no data

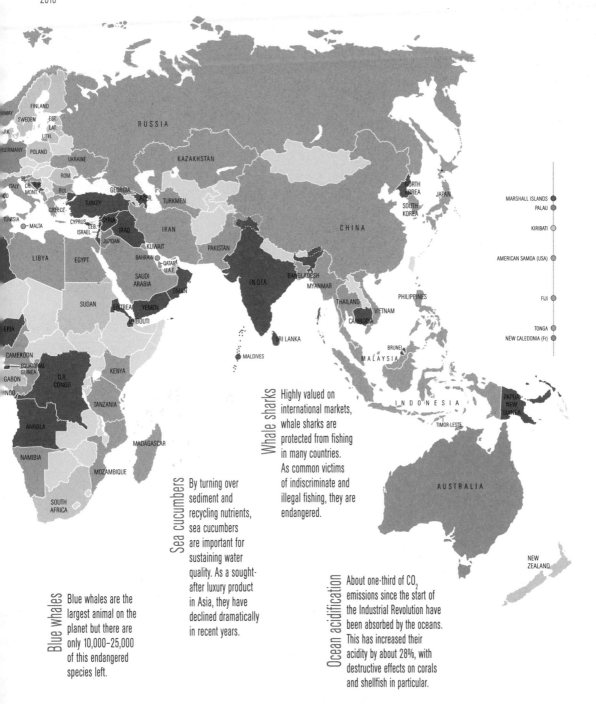

Blue whales
Blue whales are the largest animal on the planet but there are only 10,000–25,000 of this endangered species left.

Sea cucumbers
By turning over sediment and recycling nutrients, sea cucumbers are important for sustaining water quality. As a sought-after luxury product in Asia, they have declined dramatically in recent years.

Whale sharks
Highly valued on international markets, whale sharks are protected from fishing in many countries. As common victims of indiscriminate and illegal fishing, they are endangered.

Ocean acidification
About one-third of CO_2 emissions since the start of the Industrial Revolution have been absorbed by the oceans. This has increased their acidity by about 28%, with destructive effects on corals and shellfish in particular.

Energy

Everything that runs, runs on energy. As countries get richer they use more energy until a point comes when their economic base shifts from natural resources and industry to information and the service sectors.

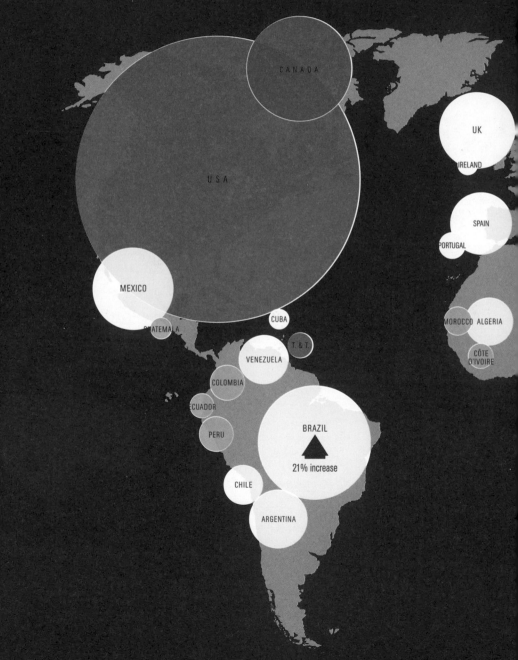

Energy use

2015 or latest available data

Total used per year

◯ = 10 million kg of oil equivalent

Use per capita

kg of oil equivalent

● 5,000 or more

● 3,000 – 4,999

○ 1,000 – 2,999

● fewer than 1,000

△ ▽ % change in per capita energy use 2009–2014

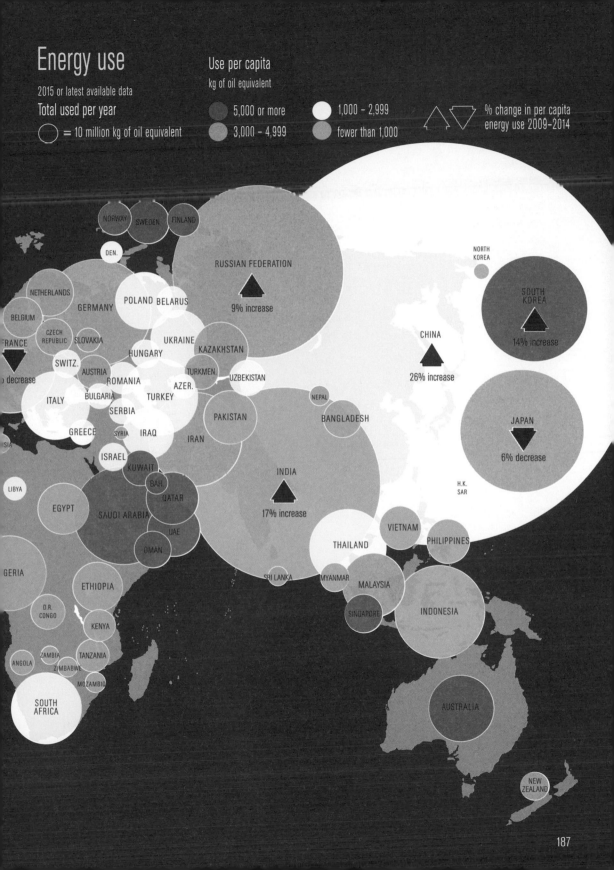

NORWAY SWEDEN FINLAND

DEN.

NETHERLANDS

GERMANY POLAND BELARUS

BELGIUM

FRANCE

CZECH REPUBLIC SLOVAKIA

SWITZ.

AUSTRIA

HUNGARY

UKRAINE

KAZAKHSTAN

ITALY BULGARIA ROMANIA TURKMEN.

AZER.

UZBEKISTAN

SERBIA

GREECE

SYRIA IRAQ

ISRAEL

KUWAIT

BAH.

QATAR

SAUDI ARABIA

UAE

OMAN

LIBYA

EGYPT

GERIA

ETHIOPIA

D.R. CONGO

KENYA

ZAMBIA TANZANIA

ZIMBABWE

ANGOLA

MOZAMBIQ.

SOUTH AFRICA

TURKEY

IRAN

PAKISTAN

NEPAL

BANGLADESH

INDIA

17% increase

SRI LANKA

RUSSIAN FEDERATION

9% increase

CHINA

26% increase

NORTH KOREA

SOUTH KOREA

14% increase

JAPAN

6% decrease

H.K. SAR

VIETNAM PHILIPPINES

THAILAND

MYANMAR MALAYSIA

SINGAPORE

INDONESIA

AUSTRALIA

NEW ZEALAND

o decrease

187

A changing climate

Continued increase in the average global temperature could trigger the irreversible and catastrophic destabilization of the Greenland ice sheet later this century, intensifying a sea-level rise predicted to put about 400 million people at risk of flooding. As the height of the surface ice decreases it is exposed to warmer temperatures at lower altitudes, leading to increased melting.

Arctic sea ice
Melting of the Arctic sea ice over recent decades has reduced its extent and thickness. Heat from the sun is absorbed by the expanded area of open water, possibly creating a feedback loop leading to increased ice melt.

CANADA
2.1%

USA
24%

World's oceans
Absorbing and storing about 40% of CO_2 emissions, the world's oceans are crucial for the global climate. As sea temperatures rise, absorption declines.

Central America & Caribbean
1.6%

SOUTH AMERICA
2.7%

Global emissions of carbon dioxide (CO_2) since 1750 amount to 1.5 trillion tonnes.

Eighty per cent of that total – 1.2 trillion tonnes – has been emitted since 1950, as the use of oil and coal increased sharply in the 1950s and thereafter.

CO_2 makes up 75% of greenhouses gases (GHG). Methane (17%) and nitrous oxide (7%) are the other main GHGs, caused by intensive agriculture. These gases together are warming the atmosphere, with consequences that are unfolding and will intensify.

Amazon rainforest
Continuing deforestation will push the Amazon rainforest to a tipping point whereby it loses its ability to renew itself and turns into a source rather than a sink of CO_2. This is expected to occur sometime between 2030 and 2100.

Past emissions and future consequences

Share of total CO_2 emissions from fossil fuels and cement

1950–2014

■ 1% = 12,030 million tonnes CO_2

Permafrost Areas of permafrost in the northern hemisphere are thawing, releasing stored greenhouse gases into the atmosphere. This increases global warming, which further accelerates the thawing process.

EUROPE
23%

RUSSIA &
CENTRAL ASIA
10%

rest of
EAST ASIA
1.6%

CHINA
14%

JAPAN
4.4%

MIDDLE EAST & NORTH AFRICA
4.8%

SOUTH-EAST ASIA
2.2%

AFRICA
1.9%

SOUTH ASIA
3.5%

3.3%
Other
countries,
plus international
aviation and
shipping

OCEANIA
1.3%

West and East Antarctic ice sheet The break-up of the West Antarctic ice sheet, a process already begun, could add about 3 m to sea level over the next centuries. Similar processes in the East Antarctic could add an additional 3 – 4 m to sea level.

Impact of increasing emissions

Greenhouse gases continue to build up in the atmosphere. Their impact has already been felt. The world is warmer by an average of 1°C compared to pre-industrial times. That seemingly small change is actually a big difference. Scientists have described the likely effects for at least four decades. These are now unfolding.

In many parts of the world, weather patterns are changing and extreme weather events – prolonged droughts, frequent floods and storms – have become the new norm. Scientific scenarios forecast mostly negative effects on biodiversity and the functioning of ecosystems. Even if global warming is limited to an average of 1.5°C to 2°C, the consequences will be serious.

CO_2 in the atmosphere

Global tropospheric concentration of CO_2
1750–2020
parts per million

◼ ice-core measurements   ▬ atmospheric readings

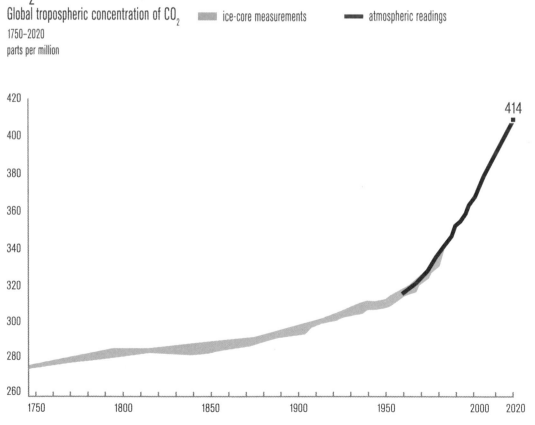

Human cost of natural disasters

As a result of geophysical, meteorological, hydrological, climatological, and extraterrestrial disasters
(excluding biological disasters such as insect infestation and diseases)

Total number of people affected:

● 1990–1999   ● 2000–2009   ● 2010–2019

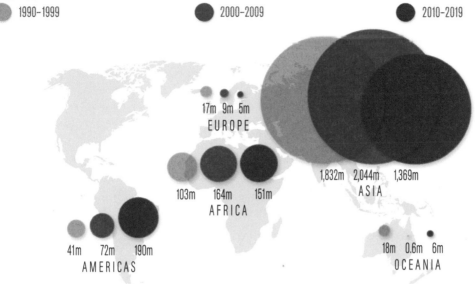

EUROPE
17m   9m   5m

ASIA
1,832m   2,044m   1,369m

AFRICA
103m   164m   151m

AMERICAS
41m   72m   190m

OCEANIA
18m   0.6m   6m

Financial cost of natural disasters

Worldwide
US$

Losses from natural disasters in **2010–2019** nearly double that of previous period.

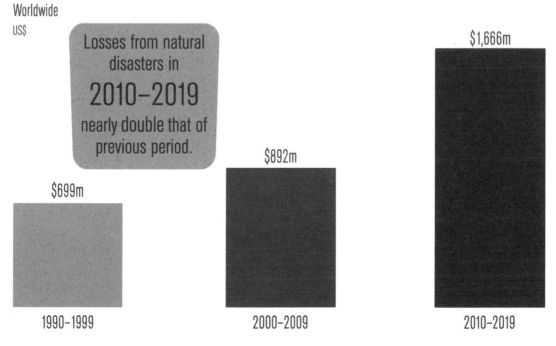

$699m
1990–1999

$892m
2000–2009

$1,666m
2010–2019

Agreement to change

The 2015 Paris Agreement on climate change established the intention to keep global warming "well below 2°C above pre-industrial levels" and to try to keep it below a 1.5°C rise.

Almost all governments are parties to the Agreement. The USA announced in 2017 that it would withdraw, the only state to do so thus far.

In 2018, the International Governmental Panel on Climate Change (IPCC) set out a timetable of interim targets for reducing greenhouse gas emissions (GHGs).

It also set out the transformations different sectors of the economy will need to make in order to meet these targets.

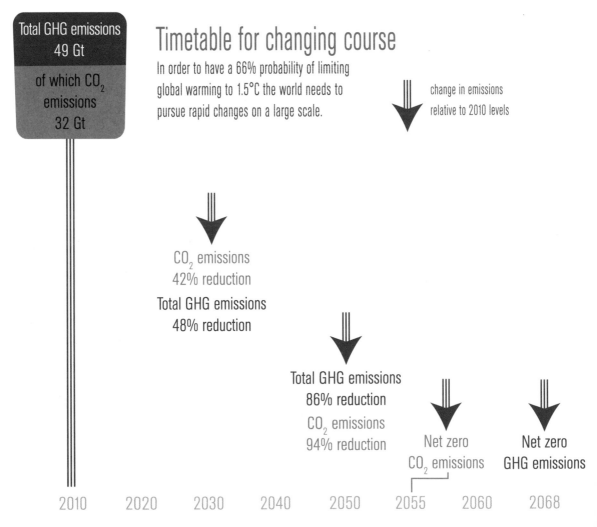

Total GHG emissions
49 Gt

of which CO_2 emissions
32 Gt

Timetable for changing course

In order to have a 66% probability of limiting global warming to 1.5°C the world needs to pursue rapid changes on a large scale.

change in emissions relative to 2010 levels

CO_2 emissions
42% reduction

Total GHG emissions
48% reduction

Total GHG emissions
86% reduction

CO_2 emissions
94% reduction

Net zero
CO_2 emissions

Net zero
GHG emissions

2010   2020   2030   2040   2050   2055   2060   2068

Sectoral changes

Considered necessary by IPCC to achieve 1.5°C goal

Sector	GHG-emitting technologies	Renewables
Energy	Coal as primary energy source: reduce by 75% Oil as primary energy source: reduce by 60%	Non-biomass renewables: increase by 570% Energy-related investment: US$830 billion more a year
Power	Coal-fired power: reduce by 70% by 2030 reduce by 100% by 2050	Renewables as share of electricity generation increase by 75%+
Transport	Oil consumption: reduce by 25% – 75% through electrification, greater use of public transport, bicycles and walking	Low-emission final energy: increase to 35% – 65% share in transport
Industry	CO_2 emissions: reduce by 65% – 90% through increased efficiency, electrification, substitution of carbon-intensive products, and use of carbon capture and storage methods	
Building	Electricity as share of energy used in buildings: reduce by 55% – 75%	Energy use intensity of buildings: improve through modernization, behavioural change, and increased efficiency of heating/ventilation-systems.
Land-use	Reforms: reduction to net zero land-use emissions by 2025–2040 and negative emissions by 2050 reduction in non-CO_2 emissions in agricultural sector reduction in food waste reduction in meat consumption	Means to reach these goals: increase in re/afforestation increase in restoration and conservation of natural ecosystems improvement in management of resources increased use of bioenergy, carbon capture, and storage mechanisms

A greening world

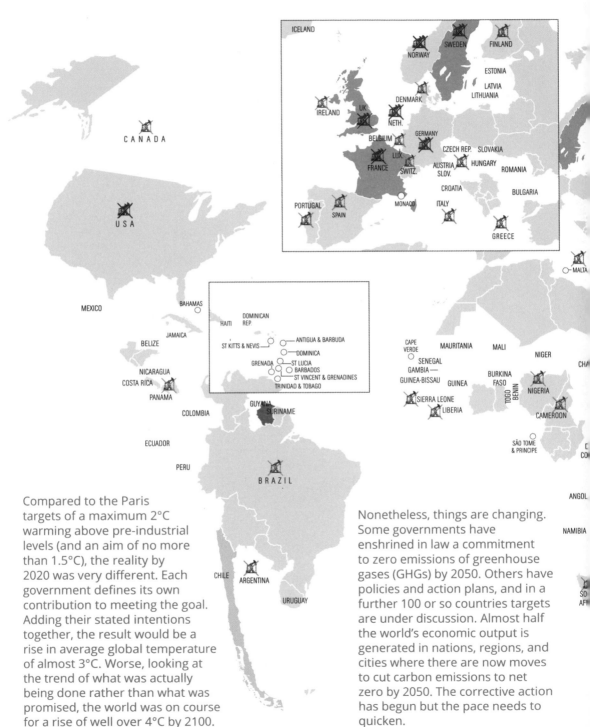

Compared to the Paris targets of a maximum 2°C warming above pre-industrial levels (and an aim of no more than 1.5°C), the reality by 2020 was very different. Each government defines its own contribution to meeting the goal. Adding their stated intentions together, the result would be a rise in average global temperature of almost 3°C. Worse, looking at the trend of what was actually being done rather than what was promised, the world was on course for a rise of well over 4°C by 2100.

Nonetheless, things are changing. Some governments have enshrined in law a commitment to zero emissions of greenhouse gases (GHGs) by 2050. Others have policies and action plans, and in a further 100 or so countries targets are under discussion. Almost half the world's economic output is generated in nations, regions, and cities where there are now moves to cut carbon emissions to net zero by 2050. The corrective action has begun but the pace needs to quicken.

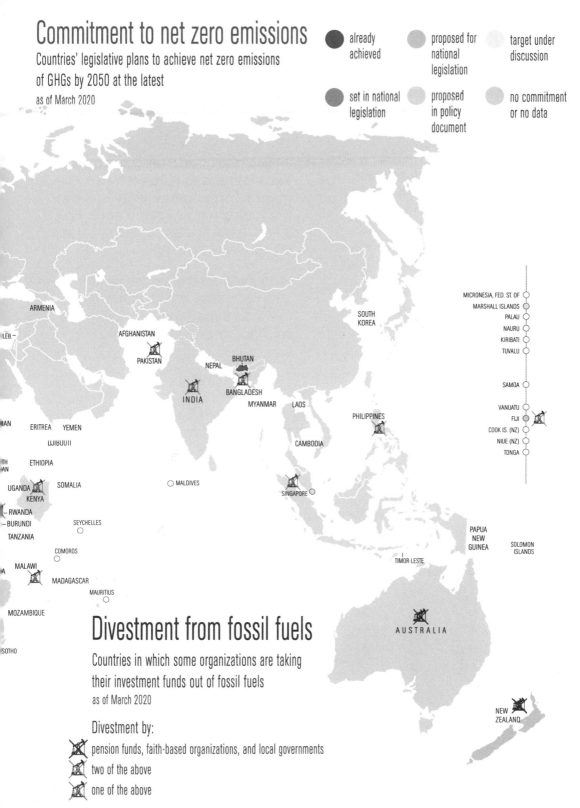

Commitment to net zero emissions

Countries' legislative plans to achieve net zero emissions
of GHGs by 2050 at the latest

as of March 2020

- already achieved
- set in national legislation
- proposed for national legislation
- proposed in policy document
- target under discussion
- no commitment or no data

Divestment from fossil fuels

Countries in which some organizations are taking
their investment funds out of fossil fuels

as of March 2020

Divestment by:

- pension funds, faith-based organizations, and local governments
- two of the above
- one of the above

MICRONESIA, FED. ST. OF
MARSHALL ISLANDS
PALAU
NAURU
KIRIBATI
TUVALU

SAMOA

VANUATU
FIJI
COOK IS. (NZ)
NIUE (NZ)
TONGA

ARMENIA

LEB.-

AFGHANISTAN

PAKISTAN

NEPAL

BHUTAN

BANGLADESH

INDIA

MYANMAR

LAOS

SOUTH KOREA

PHILIPPINES

CAMBODIA

MALDIVES

SINGAPORE

TIMOR-LESTE

PAPUA NEW GUINEA

SOLOMON ISLANDS

AUSTRALIA

NEW ZEALAND

AN

ERITREA   YEMEN

DJIBOUTI

ETHIOPIA

SOMALIA

UGANDA

KENYA

RWANDA

BURUNDI

TANZANIA

SEYCHELLES

COMOROS

MALAWI

MADAGASCAR

MAURITIUS

MOZAMBIQUE

SOTHO

TH
AN

195

Finding alternatives

The climate-change risks of continuing to emit carbon from fossil fuels have led to interest and investment in alternatives.

Because each has benefits and drawbacks, the lobbies for and against have cogent arguments. Nuclear power can look good from a climate perspective, less so when viewed through the lens of hazardous waste.

Biofuels seem environmentally responsible, but producing them takes so much energy it is not clear how big the gain is, and they also take land out of food production. The wind, waves, tide, and sun are all sources of unending energy. Technologies to convert these natural forces into energy and heat are improving at a rapid pace, and solar, in particular, is seeing a huge increase in capacity.

Whatever differences these energy sources make, the key alternative in the end may well turn out to be simply using less.

Growth in renewables

Average annual growth rate of renewables capacity and biofuels production

2009–2018
2011–2018*
2013–2018**

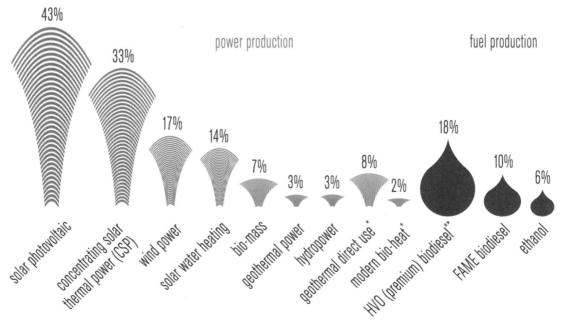

power production   fuel production

43% solar photovoltaic
33% concentrating solar thermal power (CSP)
17% wind power
14% solar water heating
7% bio-mass
3% geothermal power
3% hydropower
8% geothermal direct use *
2% modern bio-heat *
18% HVO (premium) biodiesel **
10% FAME biodiesel
6% ethanol

Green initiatives

Trees and plants absorb carbon dioxide, and 11% of global emissions of greenhouse gases (GHGs) are caused by the destruction of forests. Much work has been done over recent decades to try and reduce deforestation, most recently through schemes that provide local people with economic incentives and opportunities linked to the protection or restoration of forested areas.

In the Sahel region of Africa, a scheme was launched in 2007 to restore degraded lands that are being encroached on by the desert. The aim is that by 2030 a Great Green Wall, consisting of 100 million hectares of restored land, will stretch 5,000 miles (8,000 km) across the continent. As well as bringing environmental benefits, it will improve the economy and food security of the communities in the region, and provide millions of jobs for the people living along it.

The Great Green Wall

as of March 2020

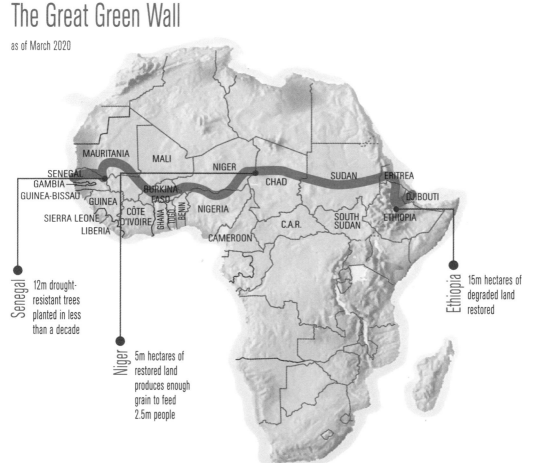

Senegal 12m drought-resistant trees planted in less than a decade

Niger 5m hectares of restored land produces enough grain to feed 2.5m people

Ethiopia 15m hectares of degraded land restored

Sources

WHO WE ARE

United Nations Department of Economic and Social Affairs (DESA), Population Division. World Population Prospects 2019. Retr'd 17 June 2019, population.un.org/wpp

King R. The atlas of human migration. London: Earthscan, 2010.

14–17 States of the world

Sovereignty

Heath-Brown N. The statesman's yearbook – The politics, cultures and economies of the world. London: Palgrave Macmillan; 2019.

CIA. The World Factbook. Retr'd 17 June 2019, www.cia.gov

State formation

Encyclopedia Britannica. Retr'd 1 Oct 2019, www.britannica.com

BBC. BBC Country Profiles. Retr'd 27 Sept 2019, www.bbc.com

Heath-Brown N. op cit.

CIA. The World Factbook. Retr'd 17 June 2019, www.cia.gov

18–19 Population

World Demographics. Retr'd 17 June 2019, www.worldometers

People in the world

UN DESA, Population Division. World Population Prospects 2019. Retr'd 17 June 2019, population.un.org/wpp

Changing population

UN DESA, Population Division. The world at six billion. Author; 1999.

UN DESA; 2019, op cit.

20–21 Life expectancy

Life expectancy at birth

WHO. Global Health Observatory Data Repository. Life expectancy and healthy life expectancy. Retr'd 17 June 2019, www.who.int

CIA. The World Factbook. Retr'd 17 June 2019, www.cia.gov

Living longer

Riley JC. Estimates of regional and global life expectancy, 1800–2001. Population and Development Review. 2005;31(3):537-543.

WHO, op cit.

22–23 Women and men

Women in the world

World Bank. World Development Indicators. Retr'd 19 June 2019, www.data.worldbank.org

CIA. The World Factbook: Sex ratio. Retr'd 17 June 2019, www.cia.gov

Baby boys and girls

World Bank, op cit.

China Statistical Yearbook 2018. Beijing: China Statistics Press; 2019. stats.gov.cn

24–27 Ethnicity and diversity

Ethnic, national, and racial minorities

Minority Rights Group. World directory of minorities and indigenous peoples. 2019. Retr'd 31 July 2019, www.minorityrights.org

CIA. The World Factbook. Retr'd 31 July 2019, www.cia.gov

Migrants

United Nations Department of Economic and Social Affairs (DESA), Population Division. Trends in international migrant stock: The 2017 revision.

China Statistical Yearbook 2018. Beijing: China Statistics Press; 2019. stats.gov.cn

The language of government

CIA. op cit.

Holmes O, Balousha, H. One more racist law: Reactions as Israel axes Arabic as official language. The Guardian, 19 July 2018. www.theguardian.com

28–31 Religious beliefs

Believers

CIA. The World Factbook. Retr'd 19 June 2019, www.cia.gov

Hackett C et al. Global Christianity: A report on the size and distribution of the world's Christian population. Washington, DC: Pew Research Centre; 2011.

Miller T. Mapping the global Muslim population: A report on the size and distribution of the world's Muslim population. Washington, DC: Pew Research Center; 2009.

PEW Research Center. PEW-Templeton Global Religious Futures Project. Retr'd 20 June 2019, www.globalreligiousfutures.org

Kosovo: Mughal AG. Muslims in Kosovo: A socio-economic and demographic profile: Is the Muslim population exploding? Balkan Social Science Review. 2015;6:155-201.

Oman: Who are the Ibadis?

The Economist. 18 Dec 2018. www.economist.com

World faiths

Grim, BJ, et al. Yearbook of international religious demography 2018. Brill; 2018.

Hackett, op cit.

Miller, op cit.

Non-believers

Hackett, op cit.

32–35 Literacy and education

Adult illiteracy

UNESCO Institute for Statistics. Literacy rate, adult total. Retr'd 20 June 2019, www.data.uis.unesco.org

Primary education • Secondary education • Tertiary education

World Bank. World Development Indicators. Retr'd 19 June 2019, www.data.worldbank.org

36–39 Urbanization

UN DESA. 68% of the world population projected to live in urban areas by 2050, says UN. 16 May 2018. Retr'd 12 Dec 2019, www.un.org

Urban population

UN DESA, Population Division. World Population Prospects 2019. Retr'd 19 June 2019, population.un.org

World Bank. World Development Indicators 2019. Retr'd 19 June 2019, www.data.worldbank.org

Global urban population • Ten largest cities • City scale

UN DESA. World Urbanization Prospects 2018. New York: United Nations, 2018, population.un.org. Retr'd 26 May 2020.

WEALTH AND POVERTY

42–43 Income

Gross National Income • Economic growth

World Bank. World Development Indicators. Retr'd 19 June 2019, www.data.worldbank.org

44–47 Inequality

Distribution of wealth

World Bank. World Development Indicators. Retr'd 19 June 2019, www.data.worldbank.org

Gender pay gap

International Labour Organization. Global wage report 2018/19: What lies behind gender pay gaps? Geneva: ILO; 2018.

World poverty

CIA. The World Factbook. Retr'd 23 Oct 2019, www.cia.gov

World Bank, op cit.

The hands of a few

Kroll L. Billionaires – The richest people in the world: Mapping the world's richest. 2019. Retr'd 25 June 2019, www.forbes.com

Bouncing back

Kroll L, Miller M, Serafin T. The world's billionaires. Forbes; 2009.

Kroll, op cit.

48–49 Quality of Life

Relative human development • Wealth for wellbeing?

United Nations Development Programme (UNDP). Human Development Indices and Indicators – 2018 Statistical Update. New York: Author; 2018.

50–51 Transnationals

Corporate wealth exceeds country wealth

Fortune. Global 500. Retr'd 28 June 2019, www.fortune.com

World Bank. World Development Indicators. Retr'd 23 July 2019, www.data.worldbank.org

Winners and losers

Dehua C. Fortune Global 500 rankings sees China closing gap on US. Retr'd July 23 2019, www.gbtimes.com

Global 500, 2017.

Global 500, 2018.

52–53 Banks

Comparative wealth • Weighed in the balance

Fortune. Global 500. Retr'd 28 June 2019, www.fortune.com

World Bank. World Development Indicators. Retr'd 23 July 2019, www.data.worldbank.org

54–59 Corruption

Rate of corruption

Transparency International. Corruption Perceptions Index 2018. Retr'd 28 June 2019, www.transparency.org

Shadow economy

Schneider LMF. Shadow economies around the world: What did we learn over the last 20 years? IMF Working Paper. Washington, DC: International Monetary Fund (IMF); 2018.

Panama and Paradise Papers

Bullough O. Moneyland. London: Profile; 2018.

Obermaier F, Wormer V, Jaschensky W. About the Panama Papers. Retr'd 20 Sept 2019, www.panamapapers.sueddeutsche.de

Obermayer B, Obermaier F. The Panama Papers. London: Oneworld; 2016.

Offshore financial services

International Consortium of Investigative Journalists (ICIJ). Explore the Panama Papers key figures. 2017. Retr'd 20 Sept 2019, www.icij.org

Panama and Paradise • power players

ICIJ. The power players. Retr'd 20 Sept 2019, www.icij.org

Panama Papers • effects of leak

Shabbir, LGN. Gauging the global impacts of the Panama Papers three years later. Reuters Institute for the Study of Journalism; 2019.

60–61 Debt

Global debt edged up in 2018, debt ratio little changed: IIF. Reuters. Business News. 2 Apr 2019. www.reuters.com

Government debt

International Monetary Fund (IMF). General government gross debt (Percentage of GDP). Retr'd 1 July 2019, www.imf.org

Household debt

IMF. Private debt, loans and debt securities (percent of GDP). 2019. Retr'd 1 July 2019, www.imf.org

Total household debt

Samuelson RJ. With booming global debt we're entering unexplored territory. The Washington Post. 16 Jan 2019.

62–63 How the money's made

Which sector dominates a country's economy?

The World Bank. World Development Indicators: Structure of output. Retr'd 24 July 2019, www.wdi.worldbank.org

Tourism dependency

World Travel & Tourism Council. Total contribution to GDP. Retr'd 2 July 2019, www.wttc.org

RIGHTS AND RESPECT

65–69 Political systems

Current political systems

Freedom House. Freedom in the world 2018 – Country reports. Retr'd 17 July 2019, www.freedomhouse.org

Heath-Brown N. The statesman's yearbook – The politics, cultures and economies of the world. London: Palgrave Macmillan; 2019.

Congo, Dem Rep: Doss A, Ibrahim M. Congo's Election: A defeat for democracy, a disaster for the people. 9 Feb 2019. Retr'd 18 July 2019, www.theguardian.com

Libya: BBC News. Libya country profile. Retr'd 18 July 2019, www.bbc.com

Mauritania: Thomas-Johnson A. Mauritanian authorities brutally crack down on post-election protests, videos show. 2019. Retr'd 22 July 2019, www.middleeasteye.net

South Sudan: UN News. South Sudan's peace process precarious, but progress is being made, Security Council hears. 2019. Retr'd 24 Oct 2019, www.news.un.org

Living politics

UN DESA, Population Division. World Population Prospects 2019, Online Edition.

Transition to and from democracy

Heath-Brown N. The statesman's yearbook – The politics, cultures and economies of the world. London: Palgrave Macmillan; 2019.

Albania and Colombia: CIA. The World Factbook. Retr'd 16 July 2019, www.cia.gov

Algeria, Bhutan, Chad, Republic of Congo, Denmark, Egypt, El Salvador, Japan, Kyrgyzstan, Lebanon, Mozambique, South Sudan, Tonga, Tunisia, United Kingdom: BBC News. Country Profiles. www.bbc.co.uk

Cameroon, Dominica, Liberia, Libya, Moldova, Tanzania: Encyclopedia Britannica. Country profiles. Retr'd 27 Nov 2019, www.britannica.com

New Zealand: Teara. The encyclopedia of New Zealand. teara.govt.nz

Trinidad & Tobago, Uganda: Freedom House. Freedom in the world 2018 – Country reports. www.freedomhouse.org

70–71 Religious rights
State attitude towards religion
Pew Research Center. Many countries favor specific religions, officially or unofficially. 3 Oct 2017.

US Department of State. 2018 Report on international religious freedom. www.state.gov

China: CIA. The World Factbook: China. Retr'd 23 Oct 2019, www.cia.gov

North Korea/Vietnam: United States Commission on International Religious Freedom (USCIRF). 2019 annual report. Washington, DC; 2019.

Samoa: Wyeth G. Samoa officially becomes a Christian state. 2017. www.thediplomat.com

Islamic law
CIA. The World Factbook: Legal System. Retr'd 23 Oct 2019, www.cia.gov

Hauser Global Law School Program, New York University School of Law, 2019. GlobaLex. Retr'd 23 Oct 2019, www.nyulawglobal.org

Heath-Brown N. The statesman's yearbook – The politics, cultures and economies of the world. London: Palgrave Macmillan; 2019.

US Department of State. 2018 Report on International Religious Freedom, 2019. Retr'd 23 Oct 2019, www.state.gov

72–77 Human rights
Extreme abuses of human rights
Amnesty International. Amnesty International report 2017/18 – The state of the world's human rights. 2018.

Human Rights Watch. World report 2019 – Events of 2018 USA. 2019.

US Department of State. 2018 Country reports on human rights practices. 2019.

Judicial killings
Amnesty International, op cit.

Death Penalty Information Center. Retr'd 21 Oct 2019, www.deathpenaltyinfo.org

Sex trafficking
United Nations Office on Drugs and Crime (UNODC). Global report on trafficking in persons 2018: Country profiles. Vienna; 2018.

Cambodia: US Department of State. 2017, p.25.

France: US Department of State. Trafficking in persons report 2016, p.12.

Honduras to USA, Romania to Germany: US Department of State. Trafficking in persons report 2019, p.13.

Nigeria to Italy: US Department of State. Trafficking in persons report 2018, op. cit. p.8.

Syria to Lebanon: US Department of State. Trafficking in persons report 2017, p.4.

USA: US Department of State. op cit, 2018, p.10.

Child abuse
Swarens T. How many people are victims of sex trafficking? IndyStar. 14 Dec 2019. eu.indystar.com

78–81 Children's rights
Unregistered children
UNICEF Global Databases. Birth registration. Retr'd 16 Oct 2019, www.data.unicef.org

Children at work • Children at risk
International Labour Organization (ILO). Methodology: Global estimates of child labour, 2012–2016. Geneva: Author; 2017, pp.96–98.

Children not in school
The World Bank. Education statistics. Retr'd 15 Nov 2019, www.databank.worldbank.org

82–85 Women's rights
Equal rights • Change in gender inequality
United Nations Development Programme (UNDP). Human Development Reports Data (1990–2017): Gender Inequality Index (GII). Retr'd 7 July 2019, www.hdr.undp.org

Women in parliament
UNDP. Human Development Reports Data (1990–2017): Share of seats in parliament (% held by women). Retr'd 7 July 2019, www.hdr.undp.org

Powerful women
Wikipedia. List of elected and appointed female heads of state and government. Retr'd 25 Nov 2019, www.wikipedia.org

86–89 LGBTQ rights
Legal status
Mendos LR. State-sponsored homophobia 2019. Geneva: International Lesbian, Gay, Bisexual, Trans and Intersex-Association; 2019.

Greenland, Taiwan: Pew Research Center (PEW). Same-sex marriage around the world. Retr'd 12 Nov 2019, www.pewforum.org

The right to adopt
Mendos, op cit.

The right to serve
Polchar J, Sweijs T, Marten P, Galdiga JH. LGBT Military Index 2014. The Hague: The Hague Centre for Strategic Studies; 2014.

90–91 Minorities
Peoples under threat
Minority Rights Group. Peoples under threat 2019. Retr'd 24 Oct 2019, www.peoplesunderthreat.org

92–93 Freedom
Freedom in the world • Changing times
Freedom House. Freedom in the World Countries. Retr'd 17 July 2019, www.freedomhouse.org

WAR AND PEACE

96–99 Wars this century
At war
Raleigh C, Linke A, Hegre H, Karlsen J. Introducing ACLED-Armed Conflict Location and Event Data. Journal of Peace Research. 2010;47(5):651-660. Retr'd 2 Nov 2019, www.acleddata.com

Chad: Pujol-Mazzini A. Suicide bomber kills five in Chad, including soldier. 12 Oct 2019. Retr'd 18 Nov 2019, www.reuters.com

Israel: Morris L, Eglash R, Balousha H. Death toll rises as Gaza militants fire hundreds of rockets into Israel, which responds with airstrikes. Washington Post, 5 May 2019. www.washingtonpost.com

Kenya: Bomb kills Kenyan police near Somali border. The Guardian, 13 Oct 2019. www.theguardian.com

Kenya: Torchia C. Death toll in Nairobi attack climbs to 21, plus 5 attackers. 2019. Retr'd 18 Nov 2019, www.apnews.com

Mozambique: Helms E. Regional overview: Africa. 27 Oct – 2 Nov 2019. The Armed Conflict Location & Event Data Project (ACLED).

Nigeria: BBC News. Dozens of mourners killed by Boko Haram at a funeral in north Nigeria. 28 July 2019. www.bbc.com

Rwanda: Helms E, Karacalti A. Regional overview: Africa. 6 – 12 Oct 2019. The Armed Conflict Location & Event Data Project (ACLED).

Uganda: Nantulya P. Ever-adaptive allied democratic forces insurgency. 2019. Retr'd 18 Nov 2019, www.africacenter.org

Rising tensions

Gleditsch NP et al. Armed Conflict 1946–2001: A new dataset. Journal of Peace Research. 2002;39(5):615-637.

Pettersson T, Högbladh S, Öberg M. Organized Violence, 1989–2018 and peace agreements. Journal of Peace Research. 2019;56(4).

Pettersson T. UCDP/PRIO Armed Conflict Dataset Codebook v 19.1.

Uppsala Conflict Data Program (UCDP) www.ucdp.uu.se

Uppsala Conflict Data Program (UCDP) www.ucdp.uu.se

Fighting outside borders

Aspa JMR, Rufanges JC. Democratic Republic of Congo: A review of 20 years of war. Centre Delàs d'Estudis per la Pau/Escola de Cultura de Pau; 2016.

Gleditsch et al, 2002, op cit.

Pettersson et al, 2019, op cit.

Pettersson, 2019, op cit.

100–103 Warlords, ganglords, and militias

Non-state armed forces

Aboudi, S. In Yemen chaos, Islamic State grows to rival al Qaeda. Reuters, 30 June 2015. www.reuters.com

Al Jazeera. Saudi-UAE coalition cut deals with al-Qaeda in Yemen. Al Jazeera, 6 Aug 2018. www.aljazeera.com

Allister EM. Gunmen kill 13 in Senegal's Casamance region: Army. Reuters, 6 Jan 2018 www.reuters.com

BBC News. IS caliphate defeated but jihadist group remains a threat. BBC News, 23 Mar 2019. www.bbc.com

Behera A, Sharma SK. Militant groups in South Asia. Institute for Defence Studies and Analyses. New Delhi: Pentagon Press; 2014.

Bhaumik S. Myanmar has a new insurgency to worry about. This Week in Asia, 1 Sept 2017. www.scmp.com

Blanford N, Spyer J. Israel raises alarm over advances by Hizbullah and Iran. Jane's Military & Security Assessments Intelligence Centre; 2017.

Brady T. Threat level remains severe after merger of terror groups.

Irish Independent, 14 Sept 2012. www.independent.ie

Browning N, Sharafedin B. In Iran, Islamic State seeks to fan militancy among minorities. Reuters, 15 Aug 2017. www.reuters.com

Casey N. Colombia's peace deal promised a new era. So why are these rebels rearming? The New York Times, 17 May 2019. www.nytimes.com

Center for Strategic and International Studies. Backgrounder. Islamic State Khorasan (IS-K). 2018.

Chang I-W, Haiyun Ma J. For them, Afghanistan is safer than China. Foreign Policy, 1 Nov 2018. www.foreignpolicy.com

Congo Research Group, New York University's Center on International Cooperation & Human Rights Watch (2019). KIVU Security Tracker: Armed groups. Retr'd 20 Nov 2019, www.kivusecurity.org

Cube C. The Taliban is gaining strength and territory in Afghanistan. NBC News, 30 Jan 2018. www.nbcnews.com

Dukhan, N. Splintered warfare: Alliances, affiliations, and agendas of armed factions and politico-military groups in the Central African Republic. Enough Project: 2017. enoughproject.org

Ebbighausen R. Southeast Asia in the crosshairs of Islamic State. 15 Oct 2019. www.dw.com

Heinrich M, Lewis A. Forces under Libya's Haftar say they're close to taking final eastern holdout. Reuters (online), 14 June 2018. www.af.reuters.com

Immigration and Refugee Board of Canada (2016). Brazil: First Command of the Capital (Primeiro Comando da Capital, PCC), including activities, targets, group structure and areas of operation; state protection for victims and witnesses of PCC crimes (2012 – Mar 2016). Ottawa.

Immigration and Refugee Board of Canada (2019). Brazil: The Red Command (Comando Vermelho, CV) criminal organization, including activities, areas of operation, membership, structure, networks, political connections, and resources; state protection available for victims of crimes committed by the Red Command (2017–Mar 2019). Ottawa.

International Crisis Group. Q&A: Boko Haram in Cameroon: Interview with Hans de Marie Heungoup.

2016. Retr'd 25 Nov 2019, www.crisisgroup.org

Jason Warner J, Hulme C. The Islamic State in Africa: Estimating fighter numbers in cells across the continent. CTC Sentinel. 2018;11(7):21-27.

Knights M. The JRTN Movement and Iraq's next insurgency. CTC Sentinel. 2011;4(7):1-6.

Lister C. Al Qaeda is starting to swallow the Syrian opposition. Foreign Policy, 15 Mar 2017. www.foreignpolicy.com

Martin P, Piccolino G, Speight J. Rebel networks' deep roots cause concerns for Côte d'Ivoire transition. Global Observatory, International Peace Institute; 2017. Retr'd 25 Nov 2019, www.theglobalobservatory.org

Morris L. Is China backing Indian insurgents? The Diplomat. 22 Mar 2011. www.thediplomat.com

Nayak D K. Naxal violence: The Peoples' Liberation Front of India (PLFI) in Jharkhand. Institute of Peace and Conflict Studies (IPCS); 29 Mar 2013. www.ipcs.org

Neuhof F. Iran's forgotten Kurds step up the struggle. The National, 16 Apr 2016. www.thenational.ae.

Pack J. Kingdom of militias: Libya's second war of post-Qadhafi succession, Italian Institute for International Political Studies (ISPI); 2019.

Reuters. Search for PJAK in 2019.

Sánchez MIC. Paramilitarism and state-terrorism in mexico as a case study of shrinking functions of the neoliberal state. Perspectives on Global Development and Technology. 2014;13:176-196.

Shih, G. AP Exclusive: Uighurs fighting in Syria take aim at China. AP News, 27 Dec 2017. www.apnews.com

South Asia Terrorism Portal (SATP), Institute of Conflict Management (ICM). India - Terrorists, Insurgents and extremist groups. 2017. Retr'd 21 Nov 2019, www.satp.org

Stanford University, Center for International Security and Cooperation (CISAC), SU. Mapping militants. 2018. www.cisac.fsi.stanford.edu

The Economic Times. Government bans militant outfit NSCN(K) for five years. 14 July 2018. www.economictimes.indiatimes.com

United Nations Security Council (2018). Final report of the Group of Experts on the Democratic Republic of the Congo S/2018/531.

United Nations Security Council (2018). Jemmah Anshorut Tauhid (JAT). Update as of 17 July 2018. www.un.org

Uppsala University, Department of Peace and Conflict Research, Uppsala Conflict Data Program. Retr'd 21 Nov 2019, www.ucdp.uu.se

US Department of Defense, US Department of State, US Agency for International Development (2019). Operation Freedom's Sentinel. Lead Inspector General Report to the United States Congress, 1 Jan 2019 – 31 Mar 2019.

Armed conflict

Pettersson T, Högbladh S, Öberg M. Organized violence, 1989-2018 and peace agreements. Journal of Peace Research. 2019;56(4).

Pettersson T. UCDP Non-state conflict codebook v 19.1. Uppsala Conflict Data Program, Department of Peace and Conflict Research Uppsala University; 2019.

Sundberg R, Eck K, Kreutz J. Introducing the UCDP Non-State Conflict Dataset. Journal of Peace Research, 2012;49(2):351-362.

Children at war

Nations General Assembly Security Council (2019). Children and armed conflict: Report of the Secretary-General A/73/907-S/2019/509.

104–07 Military muscle

Military spending • Top military spenders

Stockholm International Peace Research Institute (SIPRI). SIPRI Military Expenditure Database. Stockholm 2020.

Armed forces top ten

International comparisons of defence expenditure and military personnel. The Military Balance. 2020;120(1): 529-534.

108–111 Mass destruction

Declining stockpiles • Nuclear warhead stockpiles

Natural Resources Defense Council. Global nuclear stockpiles, 1945-2006. Bulletin of the Atomic Scientists. 2006;62(4):64-66.

Stockholm International Peace Research Institute (SIPRI). SIPRI yearbook. Oxford, UK: Oxford University Press. 2000–2019.

Nuclear accidents

atomicarchive.com (2015). Broken arrows: Nuclear weapons accidents. www.atomicarchive.com

Edwards A, Gregory S. The hidden cost of deterrence: Nuclear weapons accidents 1950–88. Bulletin of Peace Proposals 1989;20(1):3-26.

Hansen C. The swords of Armageddon. v2. vol VII. The development of US nuclear weapons (CD-ROM version), Chukelea Publications; 2007.

Petersen B. The atomic bomb that faded into South Carolina history. Military Times. 31 Mar 2018. www.militarytimes.com

US Department of Defense. Narrative summaries of accidents involving US nuclear weapons 1950–1980.

Chemical weapons in Syria

Sanders-Zakre A. Timeline of Syrian chemical weapons activity, 2012–2019. Arms Control Association; 2019. Retr'd 25 Nov 2019, www.armscontrol.org

Chemical attacks in Syria

Lütkefend T, Schneider T. Nowhere to hide. The logic of chemical weapons use in Syria. Global Public Policy Institute (GPPi); 2019.

112–115 Casualties of War

Death toll this century • Regional toll • Type of conflict

Iraq Body Count. Documented civilian deaths from violence from 2003–2019. Retr'd 2 Dec 2019, www.iraqbodycount.org

Raleigh C, Linke A, Hegre A, Karlsen J. Introducing ACLED-Armed Conflict Location and Event Data. Journal of Peace Research. 2010;47(5):651-660.

Ralph S, Melander E. Introducing the UCDP georeferenced event dataset. Journal of Peace Research. 2013;50(4):523-532.

Syrian Observatory for Human Rights. More than 570 thousand people were killed on the Syrian territory within 8 years of revolution demanding freedom, democracy, justice, and equality. Retr'd 2 Dec 2019, www.syriahr.com.

United Nations Office for the Coordination of Humanitarian Affairs Occupied Palestinian Territory (OCHA oPt) (2019). Data on casualties. Retr'd 2 Dec 2019, www.ochaopt.org

116–117 Terrorism

Incidents

National Consortium for the Study of Terrorism and Responses to Terrorism (START), University of Maryland. Global Terrorism Database (GTD). 2019.

118–121 Refugees

Where refugees come from

United Nations High Commissioner for Refugees (UNHCR). Global trends: Forced displacement in 2018. Table 2. 2019.

Palestinian territories: Communication Division, United Nations Relief and Works Agency for Palestine Refugees in the Near East (UNRWA) Headquarters. UNRWA in figures 2019. Jerusalem. 2019.

Dispersal of major refugee populations • Where refugees go to

United Nations High Commissioner for Refugees (UNHCR) Global trends: Forced displacement in 2018. Table 1. 2019.

Internally displaced people

International displacement monitoring center (iDMC). 2018 internal displacement figures by country. Retr'd 5 Dec 2019, www.internal-displacement.org

Stateless people

United Nations High Commissioner for Refugees (UNHCR) Global trends: Forced displacement in 2018. Table 7, Excel annex. 2019. www.unhcr.org

122–127 Keeping the peace

Peace agreements since 1990

Bell C et al. PA-X Peace Agreements Database and Dataset, Version 2. 2019.

Cost of violence ...and what it could be spent on

de Coninck H et al. Strengthening and implementing the global response. In: Masson-Delmotte, P et al, editors. Global warming of 1.5°C. 2019.

Institute for Economics & Peace (IEP). Global Peace Index 2019: Measuring peace in a complex world. Sydney: IEP; 2019.

International Federation of Red Cross and Red Crescent Societies (IFRC). The cost of doing nothing: The humanitarian price of climate change and how it can be avoided. Geneva: IFRC; 2019.

Ritchie H, Roser M. Natural disasters: Global damage costs from natural disasters. All natural disasters. Retr'd 20 Dec 2019, www.ourworldindata.org

United Nations Conference on Trade and Development (UNCTAD). Promoting investment in the sustainable development goals. Investment Advisory Series A, number 8. Geneva: UNCTAD; 2018.

UN peacekeeping missions

United Nations Peacekeeping. Where we operate. Retr'd 20 Dec 2019, www.peacekeeping.un.org

Peacekeeping missions

Stockholm International Peace Research Institute (SIPRI). SIPRI yearbook 2019: Armaments, disarmament and international security. Oxford: Oxford University Press; 2019.

United Nations Peacekeeping, op cit.

Forces for peace

United Nations Peacekeeping. Peacekeeping operations Fact Sheet. 30 Sept 2019.

Contributing to peace

United Nations Peacekeeping, op cit. Retr'd 9 Dec 2019

128–131 The new front line

Cyber warfare

Center for Strategic & International Studies (CSIS). Significant cyber incidents since 2006. Retr'd Nov 2019, www.csis.org

Sanger DE. The perfect weapon. War, sabotage, and fear in the cyber age. New York: Crown Publishing Group; 2018.

Kaplan F. Dark territory. The secret history of cyber war. New York: Simon & Schuster; 2017.

Associated Press. China victim of 500,000 cyber-attacks in 2010, says security agency. Guardian, 9 Aug 2011. www.theguardian.com

Beaumont P. Stuxnet worm heralds new era of global cyberwar. Guardian, 30 Sept 2010. www.theguardian.com

Saul J. Global shipping feels fallout from Maersk cyberattack. Reuters, 29 June 2017. www.reuters.com.

Weatherford M. Lessons to be learned from a $10 billion cyberattack. Retr'd from www.whitehawk.com

3D printing

Daase C et al. WMD capabilities enabled by additive manufacturing.

NDS Report 1908. Monterey, CA: Jupiter; 2019.

Bauer S, Brockmann K. 3D printing and missile technology controls. SIPRI Background Paper. Stockholm: Stockholm International Peace Research Institute; Nov 2017. www.sipri.org

Brockmann K. 3D-printable guns and why export controls on technical data matter. SIPRI Commentary/WritePeace blog, 1 Aug 2018. www.sipri.org

Brockmann K. Advances in 3D printing technology: Increasing biological weapon proliferation risks? SIPRI Commentary/WritePeace blog, 29 July 2019. www.sipri.org

Petch M. W3D Printing Community Responds to Covid-19 and Coronavirus Resources. 3D Printing Industry. Retr'd 9 April 2020, from www.3dprintingindustry.com

Artificial intelligence and the arms race

Peldán Carlsson M. Autonomous weapon systems and the impact on strategic stability. Presentation at Rio Seminar on Autonomous Weapon Systems. Rio de Janeiro, Naval War College. 20 Feb 2020. www.funag.gov.br

THE HEALTH OF THE PEOPLE

134–135 Pandemics

Neuman S. Global lockdowns resulting in "horrifying surge" in domestic violence, UN warns. NPR 6 April 2020. www.npr.org

Graham-Harrison E, Giuffrida A, Smith H, Ford L. Lockdowns around the world bring rise in domestic violence. 28 Mar 2020. www.theguardian.com

US Department of Health & Human Services, Centers for Disease Control and Prevention, National Center for Emerging and Zoonotic Infectious Diseases (NCEZID) (2017). "Zoonotic Diseases". Retr'd 4 June 2020, from www.cdc.gov.

The age of epidemics and pandemics

WHO. Summary table of SARS cases by country, 1 November 2002–7 August 2003. www.who.int

WHO. WHO MERS global summary and assessment of risk. August 2018. www.who.int

WHO Regional Office for the Eastern Mediterranean: Monthly MERS Situation updates July 2019 – January 2020. www.wmro.who.int

WHO. Ebola data and statistics. Summary data, as of 11 May 2016. www.apps.who.int

WHO Regional Office for Africa. Ebola Virus Disease Democratic Republic of the Congo. External Situation Report94. 26 May 2020. www.apps.who.int

Centers for Disease Control and Prevention, National Center for Immunization and Respiratory Diseases (NCIRD). 2009 H1N1 Pandemic (H1N1pdm09 virus). Retr'd 8 June 2020 from www.cdc.gov

Rogers S. Full list of swine flu cases, country by country. The Guardian, 28 October 2009. www.theguardian.com

Covid-19 • Covid-19 confirmed cases

WHO. WHO Coronavirus Disease (COVID-19) Dashboard. Retr'd 22 June 2020 from covid19.who.int

136–139 Malnutrition

Undernourished people

World Bank. World Development Indicators: Prevalence of undernourishment (% of population). Retr'd 16 Oct 2019, www.data.worldbank.org

Feeding America: Hunger in America. Retr'd 3 Jan 2020, www.feedingamerica.org

The Trussell Trust. End of year stats. Retr'd 3 Jan 2020, www.trusselltrust.org

Dramatic rise in Germans relying on food banks. 19 Sept 2019. www.dw.com

Undernourishment

Micronutrient deficiencies: Vitamin A deficiency. Retr'd 3 Jan 2020, www.who.int/nutrition/topics/vad/en/

Growing hunger

FAO, IFAD, UNICEF, WFP, WHO. The state of food security and nutrition in the world 2019. Safeguarding against economic slowdowns and downturns. Rome: FAO. Table 1. 2019.

Food shortages

FAO. Crop prospects and food situation. Quarterly Global Report no. 3, Rome: FAO. Sept 2019.

140–143 Obesity

Overweight adults

WHO. Global Health Observatory data repository: Prevalence of overweight among adults. Estimates by country. Retr'd 25 Oct 2019, www.apps.who.int

Impact of obesity
WHO. Obesity and overweight. Key facts. Retr'd 8 Jan 2020, www.who.int

Overweight as cause of death
Institute for Health Metrics and Evaluation (IHME). GBD compare data visualization. Retr'd 30 Oct 2019, www.vizhub.healthdata.org

America's growing obesity problem
Centres for Disease Control and Prevention (CDC). Adult obesity prevalence maps. Retr'd 6 Jan 2020, www.cdc.gov/obesity/data/prevalence-maps.html

144–147 Smoking

Tobacco smokers
WHO. WHO global report on trends in prevalence of tobacco smoking 2000–2025, Table A1.5. Geneva: Author; 2018.

Cigarettes smoked • Smoke-free legislation
American Lung Association. Smokefree air laws. Retr'd 6 Jan 2020, www.lung.org

Drope J et al. The tobacco atlas. Retr'd 30 Oct 2019, www.tobaccoatlas.org

Tobacco-related deaths
Shafey, O, Eriksen M, Ross H, Mackay J. The tobacco atlas, 3rd ed. Atlanta, GA: American Cancer Society; 2009.

148–151 Cancer

World Cancer Research Fund. American Institute for Cancer Research. Comparing more and less developed countries. Retr'd 6 Jan 2020, www.wcrf.org/dietandcancer/cancer-trends/comparing-more-and-less-developed-countries

WHO. Cancer. Key facts. Retr'd 6 Jan 2020, www.who.int

Cancer on the increase
International Agency for Research on Cancer (IARC). World cancer report 2014. Stewart BW, Wild CP, editors. Lyon: Author; 2014.

IARC. World Cancer Report 2008. Boyle P, Levin B, editors. Lyon: Author; 2008.

Jemal A, Torre L, Soerjomataram I, Bray F (eds). The cancer atlas. 3rd ed. Atlanta, GA: American Cancer Society; 2019. www.cancer.org/canceratlas

Childhood-cancer survival rates
Jemal A, op cit.

Environmental factors
Anand P et al. Cancer is a preventable disease that requires major lifestyle changes. Pharmaceutical Research. 2008;25(9):2097–2116.

Cancer in men • Cancer in women
IARC. GLOBOCAN 2018: Top cancer per country, estimated age-standardized incidence rates (World) in 2018, females/males, all ages. Retr'd 28 Oct 2019, www.gco.iarc.fr

152–155 HIV/AIDS

Impact of HIV/AIDS

HIV/AIDS over time
UNAIDS. HIV estimates with uncertainty bounds 1990–2018. 2019. Retr'd 18 Dec 2019, www.unaids.org

AIDS orphans
The World Bank. Health nutrition and population statistics. Retr'd 18 Dec 2019, www.databank.worldbank.org

Barring the door
UNAIDS 2019. AIDSinfo: Epidemic transition metrics – Laws and policies scorecard. Retr'd 4 Nov 2019, www.aidsinfo.unaids.org

Anti-Retroviral Therapy (ART)
UNAIDS. HIV treatment data and estimates 2010-2018.

Text
WHO. Global Health Observatory (GHO) data. HIV/AIDS. Retr'd 7 Jan 2020.

UNAIDS. HIV infections among children falling. 13 May 2019.

156–159 Mental health

Ritchie H, Roser M. Mental Health. Our world in data. Apr 2018. ourworldindata.org/mental-health

WHO. Fact sheet. Adolescent mental health. 23 Oct 2019.

WHO. Fact sheet. Suicide. 2 Sept 2019.

Mental health disorders
Ritchie, op cit.

Spending on mental health • Psychiatrists
WHO. Mental health atlas 2017. Geneva: WHO; 2018.

Suicide by men • Suicide by women
WHO. Global Health Observatory (GHO) data: Age-standardized suicide rates (per 100 000 population), 2016. www.who.int. Retr'd 29 Oct 2019.

160–163 Water and sanitation

WHO, UNICEF. Millennium Development Goal drinking water target met. 6 Mar 2012. www.who.int

WHO, UNICEF. Progress on drinking water, sanitation and hygiene, 2017 update and SDG baselines. 2017.

Drinking water
UNICEF. UNICEF data: Cross-sector indicators. Proportion of population using improved drinking water sources. Retr'd 20 Dec 2019, www.data.unicef.org

Women and girls...
WHO, UNICEF; 2017 op cit.

Sanitation

In 24 countries...
WHO, UNICEF. Estimates on the use of sanitation (2000–17). Joint Monitoring Programme for Sanitation. 2019. www.data.unicef.org

Unsafe schools
WHO, UNICEF. Drinking water, sanitation and hygiene in schools: Global baseline report. 2018. www.data.unicef.org

164–165 Living with disease

WHO. Global Health Observatory (GHO) data. Disability-adjusted life years (DALYs).

National disease burden
Global Health Estimates 2016: Disease burden by cause, age, sex, by country and by region, 2000–16. Geneva, WHO; 2018.

HEALTH OF THE PLANET

Diaz S, Settele J, Brondizio E et al. Summary for policymakers of the global assessment report on biodiversity and ecosystem services of the Intergovernmental Science-Policy Platform on Biodiversity and Ecosystem Services. IPBES: 2019. ipbes.net/global-assessment

168–169 Beyond the bounds

Steffen W et al. Planetary boundaries: Guiding human development on a changing planet. Science 2015;347(6223).

Planetary boundaries
Lokrantz J/Azote based on Steffen et al. 2015 www.stockholmresilience.org/research/planetary-boundaries.html

170–175 Biodiversity Loss

Crowther T, Glick H, Covey K et al.

Mapping tree density at a global scale. Nature 2015;525:201–05.

Khokhar T, Tabary ME. Five forest figures for the International Day of Forests. 21 Mar 2016.

Threatened mammals, birds, and amphibians

IUCN. Table 5: Threatened species in each country (totals by taxonomic group). 2019.

Threatened species

IUCN. Table1a: Number of species evaluated in relation to the overall number of described species, and numbers of threatened species by major groups of organisms. 2019.

Forest lost and gained

FAO. Global forest resources assessment 2015. Desk reference. Second edition. Author: 2015.

Protected areas

World Database on Protected Areas. World Development Indicators: Terrestrial protected areas (% of total land area). The World Bank: 2019. Retr'd 18 Dec 2019, www.data.worldbank.org

Sustainable livelihoods

Rainforest Trust. Conservation in Latin America: Year in review. 27 Dec 2019. www.rainforesttrust.org/conservation-in-latin-america-year-in-review/

Community management

Sunday O. A tale of two Nigerian reserves underscores importance of community. 9 Apr 2020. Mongabay. news.mongabay.com/2020/04/a-tale-of-two-nigerian-reserves-underscores-importance-of-community/

Benefits of forest protection • Preservation and public awareness

12 conservation success stories – in pictures. The Guardian. 22 May 2018. www.theguardian.com

176–179 Water resources

UN. Sustainable Development Goal 6. Synthesis report 2018 on water and sanitation. United Nations: New York; 2018.

Increasing water use

Shiklomanov I. World water resources at the beginning of the 21st century. The dynamics. Table 7. webworld.unesco.org

Burek P et al. Water futures and solutions. Fast track initiative – Final report. ADA Project Number 2725-00/2014). Table 4-10. Laxenburg: IIASA; 2016.

How water is used • Water used • Water stress

FAO. AQUASTAT main database. Retr'd 4 June 2019, www.fao.org

180–183 Waste

McGrath M. US top of the garbage pile in global waste crisis. BBC: 3 July 2019. www.bbc.com/news/science-environment-48838699

World Bank. Trends in solid waste management. datatopics.worldbank.org

Holden E. US produces far more waste and recycles far less of it than other developed countries. Guardian: 3 July 2019.

Cagle S. Humans have made 8.3bn tons of plastic since 1950. Guardian: 24 June 2019. www.theguardian.com

EPA's Report on the Environment (ROE). www.epa.gov/roe

Plastic waste

Belize: Ambergris Today Online (2019). Belize's Single-Use Plastic ban starts today!. Ambergris Today Online. Retr'd 8 Feb 2020, www.ambergistoday.com

Chile: BBC News. Chile bans plastic bags for businesses. BBC News online. 3 Aug 2018. Retr'd 8 Feb 2020, www.bbc.com

China: UNEP, 2018. p.53.

Cyprus: Cyprus introduces plastic bag law. Gold News: 2 July 2018. www.goldnews.com.cy

DR Congo: Soi C. The deadly cost of DR Congo's pollution. Reuters: 2 Oct 2018. www.Aljazeera.com

East African Legislative Assembly: Karuhanga, 2017.

England: Woodcock A. Plastic bag usage in supermarkets down 90 per cent since introduction of 5p charge in 2015. 31 July 2019. www.independent.co.uk

EU and Hong Kong: Single-use plastics. A roadmap for sustainability. Nairobi (Kenya): UNEP: 2018.

France: France to phase out single-use plastics starting Jan 1. France 24: 31 Dec 2019. www.france24.com

Jamaica: Ministry of Economic Growth and Job Creation Jamaica. Statement: Reduction of plastic waste. 2019. www.megjc.gov.jm

Lithuania: Supermarkets in Lithuania to face fines for free plastic bags. Lithuanian Radio and Television: 28 Jan 2020. www.lrt.lt.

New Zealand: Ministry for the Environment, New Zealand. Single-use plastic shopping bags are banned in New Zealand. 2019. www.mfe.govt.nz.

Nigeria: Reps adopt bill banning use of plastic bags, prescribe N500,000 fine. Channels Television. 21 May 2019. www.channelstv.com

Slovenia: No more free plastic bags in Slovenian stores. The Slovenia Times, 2 Jan 2019. www.sloveniatimes.com

Tanzania: Tanzania bans plastic bags to clean up environment. Deutsche Welle: 1 June 2019. www.dw.com

UNEP. Single-use plastics. A roadmap for sustainability. Nairobi (Kenya): UNEP; 2018.

Uruguay: Plastic bags banned in Uruguay, but no hope for larger waste bill. Bloomberg Environment: 29 Jan 2019. www.new.bloombergenvironment.com

What is the great pacific garbage patch? Retr'd 29 Dec 2019, www.theoceancleanup.com

Waste production

World Bank. Global waste to grow by 70 percent by 2050 unless urgent action is taken. Press release: 20 Sept 2018. worldbank.org

Plastic world

PlasticsEurope (2013). Plastics - the Facts 2013, 2015, 2017, 2019. All Retr'd 29 Dec 2019, www.plasticseurope.org

Beach trash

Ocean Conservancy. Annual reports, 2011–2019. oceanconservancy.org

184–185 Oceans

Marine protection

The World Bank. World Development Indicators: Marine protected areas (% of territorial waters). Retr'd 29 Dec 2019, www.data.worldbank.org

Coral reefs

Heron et al. Impacts of climate change on world heritage coral reefs : A first global scientific assessment. Paris: UNESCO World Heritage Centre, 1-2. 2017.

International Union for Conservation of Nature (IUCN) Issue brief: Coral reefs and climate change. 2017. www.iucn.org

Spalding, MD, Brumbaugh RD, Landis E. Atlas of ocean wealth. Arlington, VA: The Nature Conservancy; 2016.

Three examples of reefs: Wikipedia. List of reefs. Retr'd 8 Feb 2020, www.en.wikipedia.org

Seagrass

WWF and ZSL; 2015. op cit.

Mangroves

Bindoff et al. Changing ocean, marine ecosystems, and dependent communities In: IPCC special report on the ocean and cryosphere in a changing climate. 2019. p. 495.

Baxter JM, Laffoley D (eds) Explaining ocean warming. Causes, scale, effects and consequences. Gland: IUCN; 2016. pp. 136-138.

North Atlantic right whales • Blue whales • Whale sharks

WWF. Fact sheets on species. Retr'd 4 Feb 2020, www.worldwildlife.org

Sharks, rays

WWF and ZSL; 2015. op cit.

Neslen A. 40% of Europe's sharks and rays face extinction, says IUCN. The Guardian. 3 June 2015. www.theguardian.com

Ocean dead zones

Carrington D. Oceans suffocating as huge dead zones quadruple since 1950, scientists warn. The Guardian. 4 January 2018. www.theguardian.com

Sea cucumbers

de Greef K. Sea cucumbers are being eaten to death. National Geographic. 14 Nov 2014. www.nationalgeographic.com

World Wildlife Fund International (WWF) & Zoological Society of London (ZSL). Living blue planet report. Species, habitats and human well-being. Gland: WWF and London: ZSL: 2015.

Ocean acidification

Borunda A. Ocean acidification, explained. National Geographic. 7 August 2019. www.nationalgeographic.com

8% of oceans...

UNEP-WCMC and IUCN. Marine protected planet, UNEP-WCMC and IUCN. 2019. www.protectedplanet.net

186–187 Energy

Energy use • Change in energy use

World Bank. World Development Indicators 2019. Retr'd 4 Feb 2020, www.data.worldbank.org

188–191 A changing climate

Past emissions and future consequences • Arctic sea ice

Potsdam Institute for Climate Impact Research. Tipping elements – the Achilles heels of the earth system. Retr'd 25 Jan 2020, www.pik-potsdam.de

Kashiwase H et al. Evidence for ice-ocean albedo feedback in the Arctic Ocean shifting to a seasonal ice zone. Sci Rep. 2017;7:8170. doi.org/10.1038/s41598-017-08467-z

Greenland ice sheet

IPCC. Summary for Policymakers. In: Global Warming of 1.5°C. IPCC; 2018. B.2.2.

West and East Antarctic ice sheets

Potsdam Institute for Climate Impact Research. op cit.

Lenton TM et al. Climate tipping points – too risky to bet against. Nature. 27 Nov 2019. www.nature.com

World's oceans

Potsdam Institute for Climate Impact Research. op cit.

Permafrost

IPCC, op cit. Table 3.7.

Amazon rainforest

Gatehouse G. Deforested parts of Amazon 'emitting more CO2 than they absorb'. BBC News. 11 Feb 2020. www.bbc.com

CO_2 in atmosphere

Tans P. NOAA/ESRL (www.esrl.noaa.gov/gmd/ccgg/trends/), Keeling R, Scripps Institution of Oceanography (scrippsco2.ucsd.edu/). Accessed Mar 2020 from: Global Monitoring Laboratory. Mauna Loa CO_2 records.

Human cost of natural disasters • Financial cost of natural disasters

Centre for Research on the Epidemiology of Disasters (CRED) (2020). EM-DAT. The International Disaster Database. Data as of 30 Jan 2020. www.emdat.be

Text

United Nations (UN). Paris Agreement. 2015. sustainabledevelopment.un.org

Timetable for changing course • Sectoral changes

Schaeffer M et al. Insights from the IPCC Special Report on 1.5°C for preparation of long-term strategies. Berlin (Germany): Climate Analytics gGmbH; 2019.

IPCC. Summary for Policymakers. In: Global Warming of 1.5°C. IPCC; 2018.

194–197 A greening world

Energy & Climate Intelligence Unit. www.eciu.net

ITV. World sees growing move towards net zero emissions goals – analysis. 18 Feb 2020. www.itv.com

Commitment to net zero emissions

Climate Analytics & New Climate Institute. Climate Action Tracker: Countries. Retr'd 7 Mar 2020, www.climateactiontracker.org

Energy & Climate Intelligence Unit. Net zero tracker. Retr'd 8 Mar 2020, www.eciu.net

Divestment from fossil fuels

350.org. 1000+ divestment commitments. Overview. Retr'd 16 Mar 2020, www.gofossilfree.org

Growth in Renewables

REN21. Renewables Global Status Report. Paris: REN21 Secretariat. 2009–2019.

The Great Green Wall

United Nations Convention to Combat Desertification (2020). Partner countries. Retr'd 16 Mar 2020, www.greatgreenwall.org

Baker A, Toubab M. Can a 4,815-mile wall of trees help curb climate change in Africa? Time. 12 Sept 2019. www.time.com

United Nations Convention to Combat Desertification. The Great Green Wall Initiative. Retr'd 8 Mar 2020, www.unccd.int

Index